PowerShell for Office 365

Automate Office 365 administrative tasks

Martin Machado
Prashant G Bhoyar

BIRMINGHAM - MUMBAI

PowerShell for Office 365

First published: July 2017

Production reference: 1250717

Published by Packt Publishing Ltd.
Livery Place
35 Livery Street
Birmingham
B3 2PB, UK.

ISBN 978-1-78712-799-9

www.packtpub.com

Credits

Authors
Martin Machado
Prashant G Bhoyar

Reviewer
Steve Parankewich

Acquisition Editor
Rahul Nair

Content Development Editor
Sweeny Dias

Technical Editor
Khushbu Sutar

Production Coordinator
Aparna Bhagat

Copy Editors
Stuti Srivastava
Madhusudan Uchil

Project Coordinator
Virginia Dias

Proofreader
Safis Editing

Indexer
Aishwarya Gangawane

Graphics
Kirk D'Penha

About the Authors

Martin Machado is an MCSD with over 15 years, experience in designing and implementing systems. He moved into consulting as a way to satisfy his curiosity and interest in diverse IT scenarios and applications very early in his career. He started as an Oracle developer and quickly moved into systems integration with Microsoft technologies. He has a passion for designing complex systems and intricate migrations.

Martin currently works for Microsoft as a Senior Consultant in the Modern Applications Division. He has extensive experience helping customers of all sizes and currently spends most of his time designing solutions that take advantage of Azure and Office 365. When he is not working, Martin enjoys the company of his wife, Raquel, and son, David. He also spends time with his soldering gun, creating custom keyboards and other tinkering projects. Martin is originally from Uruguay but currently lives in the Washington DC metro area.

I would like to thank the Packt Publishing team for their professionalism, and my colleagues who helped make this happen.

Special thanks to my wife, Raquel and son, David, for their support throughout the writing process. My hope is that one day David will read this book and be inspired to follow his dreams.

Prashant G Bhoyar is a Microsoft Office Server and Services MVP and a Microsoft Certified Professional. He is a trusted advisor and subject matter expert and specializes in the development and post-implementation adoption of complex custom solutions in Office 365, Azure, and SharePoint. He has supported many commercial and government agencies and non-profit organizations in the Washington D.C. metropolitan area. He serves on the leadership committee for the DC Metro Office 365 User Group, the SharePoint Saturday Baltimore event, and the SharePoint Saturday Washington DC event. He actively speaks at technical conferences across the United States of America.

Prashant is a recipient of the Antarctic Service Medal of the United States of America for his outstanding service in Antarctica. He currently works as a Senior Consultant at WithumSmith+Brown, PC, and hails from the Washington DC metro area. When not working, Prashant likes to explore new places with his wife, Mayuri.

I would like to take this opportunity to express my gratitude and thank the following people for their support and encouragement:

The editorial team at Packt Publishing, especially Rahul Nair, Sweeny Dias, and Khushbu Sutar, and the technical reviewers for making sure that the project gets completed on time and with quality content.

My parents and the rest of my family for their encouragement and support. Without their guidance, I would not have been where I am right now.

Above all, my beloved and supportive wife, Mayuri Lahane, for standing by me throughout my career and through the process of writing this book. Without her constant encouragement, this book would not have been possible; for more than often, we had to sacrifice our personal time to focus on this book.

Martin Machado, a former colleague, good friend, and the co-author of this book for his encouragement and constant support. We made it happen.

All my colleagues at WithumSmith+Brown, PC for their encouragement and constant support.

Last but not least, the Office 365 community for being such a great community and constantly encouraging and helping people by sharing knowledge.

About the Reviewer

Steve Parankewich is a professional systems analyst, architect, and engineer. With over 20 years experience Steve has always had a passion for automation. He is currently a PowerShell evangelist and leads the Boston PowerShell user group, organizing monthly meetups with fellow IT professionals. Steve currently focuses on implementation and migration to both Office 365 and Azure. You can reach Steve, or read additional PowerShell-based articles that he has written, on the powershellblogger website.

Customer Feedback

Thanks for purchasing this Packt book. At Packt, quality is at the heart of our editorial process. To help us improve, please leave us an honest review on this book's Amazon page at `https://www.amazon.com/dp/1787127990`.

If you'd like to join our team of regular reviewers, you can e-mail us at `customerreviews@packtpub.com`. We award our regular reviewers with free eBooks and videos in exchange for their valuable feedback. Help us be relentless in improving our products!

Table of Contents

Preface

PowerShell for Office 365 is a powerful tool that is used to perform common administrative tasks. However, there is much more that it can do. PowerShell for Office 365 helps automate repetitive and complex administrative tasks, which can greatly increase the speed and efficiency of your business. This book will walk you through all the aspects of PowerShell for Office 365 and enable you to get greater control over it and extract more from Office 365.

This step-by-step guide focuses on teaching the fundamentals of working with PowerShell for Office 365. It covers practical usage examples such as managing user accounts, licensing, and administering common Office 365 services. You will be able to leverage the processes laid out in the book so that you can move forward and explore other less common administrative tasks or functions.

What this book covers

`Chapter 1`, *PowerShell Fundamentals*, covers the basics of working with PowerShell. We will cover topics from command structures, to logical syntax.

`Chapter 2`, *Managing Office 365 with PowerShell*, explains the various PowerShell packages and permissions required to manage Office 365 through PowerShell.

`Chapter 3`, *Azure AD and Licensing Management*, gives an overview on how to use basic PowerShell skills discussed in previous chapter to create, manage, and remove Office 365 accounts and licenses. This chapter also addresses group management.

`Chapter 4`, *Managing SharePoint Online using PowerShell*, focuses on tips and tricks working with SharePoint Online with PowerShell.

`Chapter 5`, *Managing Exchange Online using PowerShell*, focuses on tips and tricks working with Exchange Online using PowerShell with practical examples.

`Chapter 6`, *Script Automation*, explains taking a script and turning it into an automated process. This can be useful for repetitive tasks such as license and account management.

`Chapter 7`, *Patterns and Practices PowerShell*, explores Office 365 PnP PowerShell to manage artifacts in SharePoint Online.

`Chapter 8`, *OneDrive For Business*, explains OneDrive, which is another key component for the digital workplace. Individuals can safely keep/sync content on the cloud, making it available anywhere while businesses can manage and retain content securely. In this chapter, we go over common provisioning and management scenarios.

`Chapter 9`, *PowerShell Core*, ends this book by covering how to use PowerShell on other platforms. It also explains how to use Office 365 APIs through remoting.

What you need for this book

A basic understanding of PowerShell.

Who this book is for

The book is aimed at sys admins administering office 365 tasks and looking forward to automating manual tasks. They need not have knowledge of PowerShell; however, a basic understanding of PowerShell would be advantageous.

Conventions

In this book, you will find a number of text styles that distinguish between different kinds of information. Here are some examples of these styles and an explanation of their meaning. Code words in text, database table names, folder names, filenames, file extensions, pathnames, dummy URLs, user input, and Twitter handles are shown as follows: "The `Get-Credential` cmdlet does not tell us whether the username and password are correct or not."

A block of code is set as follows:

```
$i=0
do
{

   $var = $set[$i]

}
while ($i -ge $Set.Count)
```

When we wish to draw your attention to a particular part of a code block, the relevant lines or items are set in bold:

```
$i=0
do
{

   $var = $set[$i]

}
while ($i -ge $Set.Count)
```

Any command-line input or output is written as follows:

```
Get-MsolUser -UserPrincipalName "valid Office 365 work or school user name"
```

New terms and **important words** are shown in bold. Words that you see on the screen, for example, in menus or dialog boxes, appear in the text like this: "When creating the account, make sure you check the **Password never expires** setting."

Warnings or important notes appear like this.

Tips and tricks appear like this.

Reader feedback

Feedback from our readers is always welcome. Let us know what you think about this book-what you liked or disliked. Reader feedback is important for us as it helps us develop titles that you will really get the most out of. To send us general feedback, simply e-mail `feedback@packtpub.com`, and mention the book's title in the subject of your message. If there is a topic that you have expertise in and you are interested in either writing or contributing to a book, see our author guide at `www.packtpub.com/authors`.

Customer support

Now that you are the proud owner of a Packt book, we have a number of things to help you to get the most from your purchase.

Downloading the example code

You can download the example code files for this book from your account at `http://www.packtpub.com`. If you purchased this book elsewhere, you can visit `http://www.packtpub.com/support`, and register to have the files e-mailed directly to you. You can download the code files by following these steps:

1. Log in or register to our website using your e-mail address and password.
2. Hover the mouse pointer on the **SUPPORT** tab at the top.
3. Click on **Code Downloads & Errata**.
4. Enter the name of the book in the **Search** box.
5. Select the book for which you're looking to download the code files.
6. Choose from the drop-down menu where you purchased this book from.
7. Click on **Code Download**.

Once the file is downloaded, please make sure that you unzip or extract the folder using the latest version of:

- WinRAR / 7-Zip for Windows
- Zipeg / iZip / UnRarX for Mac
- 7-Zip / PeaZip for Linux

The code bundle for the book is also hosted on GitHub at `https://github.com/PacktPublishing/PowerShell-for-Office-365`. We also have other code bundles from our rich catalog of books and videos available at `https://github.com/PacktPublishing/`. Check them out!

Downloading the color images of this book

We also provide you with a PDF file that has color images of the screenshots/diagrams used in this book. The color images will help you better understand the changes in the output. You can download this file from `https://www.packtpub.com/sites/default/files/downloads/PowerShellforOffice365_ColorImages.pdf`.

Errata

Although we have taken every care to ensure the accuracy of our content, mistakes do happen. If you find a mistake in one of our books-maybe a mistake in the text or the code-we would be grateful if you could report this to us. By doing so, you can save other readers from frustration and help us improve subsequent versions of this book. If you find any errata, please report them by visiting `http://www.packtpub.com/submit-errata`, selecting your book, clicking on the **Errata Submission Form** link, and entering the details of your errata. Once your errata are verified, your submission will be accepted and the errata will be uploaded to our website or added to any list of existing errata under the Errata section of that title. To view the previously submitted errata, go to `https://www.packtpub.com/books/content/support`, and enter the name of the book in the search field. The required information will appear under the **Errata** section.

Piracy

Piracy of copyrighted material on the Internet is an ongoing problem across all media. At Packt, we take the protection of our copyright and licenses very seriously. If you come across any illegal copies of our works in any form on the Internet, please provide us with the location address or website name immediately so that we can pursue a remedy. Please contact us at `copyright@packtpub.com` with a link to the suspected pirated material. We appreciate your help in protecting our authors and our ability to bring you valuable content.

Questions

If you have a problem with any aspect of this book, you can contact us at `questions@packtpub.com`, and we will do our best to address the problem.

1
PowerShell Fundamentals

PowerShell is a command-line environment that is designed for system administrators. It helps you manage and automate administrative tasks on the Windows operating system. With the trend of DevOps, developers are also getting on board with PowerShell.

Microsoft first introduced PowerShell in 2006. 10 years later, in 2016, Microsoft announced that they have made PowerShell open source and cross-platform with support for Windows, macOS X, CentOS, and Ubuntu. The source code is available on GitHub.

Office 365 is a subscription-based SAS offering from Microsoft. To manage Office 365, we have the following options:

- **Office 365 admin center**: We can use this web-based administration center provided by Microsoft to manage users, licenses, support tickets, billing and subscription, and other services such as Exchange, SharePoint, and Skype for Business that are part of our Office 365 subscription. To sign up for Office 365, we need to use Office 365 admin center. During this signing up process, we select the unique name for our tenant and the global admin account:

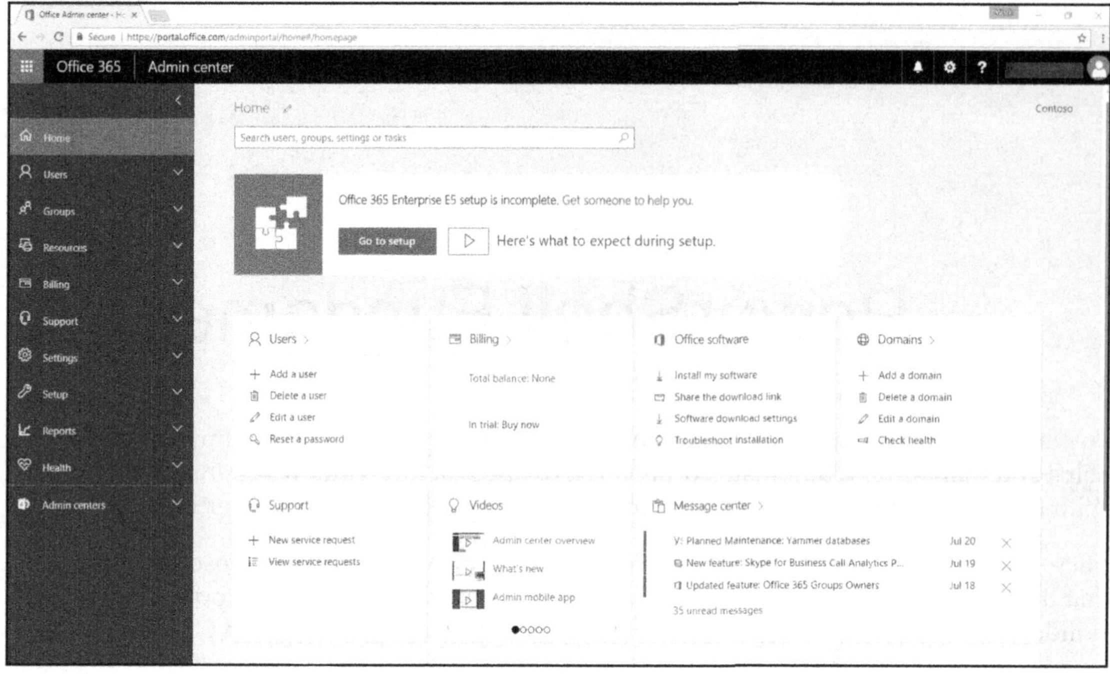

- **Office 365 Admin app**: This app allows us to manage Office 365 with limited functionality. We can reset user passwords, manage support tickets, and so on. It is not a full management tool. However, it helps you to be connected to your subscription when you are away from your computer:

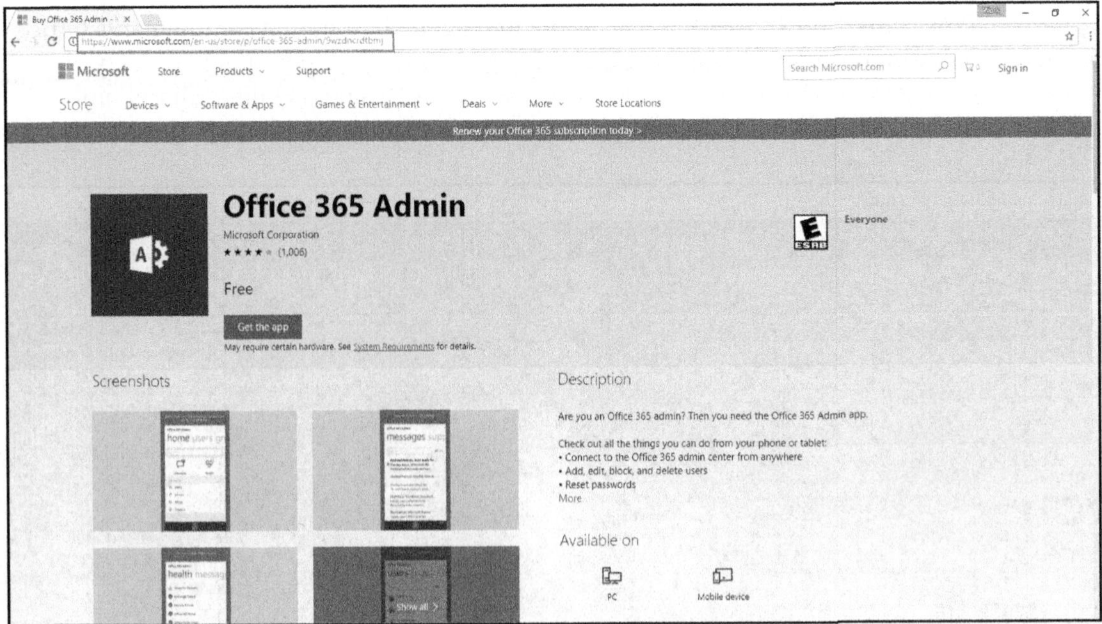

- **Office 365 management API**: The APIs are designed for developers to create custom apps to manage Office 365: `https://msdn.microsoft.com/en-us/office-365/office-365-managment-apis-overview`. ISVs use these APIs to create products to manage Office 365. These APIs are out of the scope of this book.

- **PowerShell for Office 365**: This is the management tool that complements Office 365 admin center. We can use Office 365 PowerShell automation to quickly manage Office 365 users and licenses, Skype for Business Online, SharePoint Online, and Microsoft Exchange Online, and create reports:

```
Administrator: Windows PowerShell
Cmdlet          Remove-MsolUser                                          1.1.130.0  MSOnlineExtended
Cmdlet          Reset-MsolStrongAuthenticationMethodByUpn                1.1.130.0  MSOnline
Cmdlet          Reset-MsolStrongAuthenticationMethodByUpn                1.1.130.0  MSOnlineExtended
Cmdlet          Restore-MsolUser                                         1.1.130.0  MSOnline
Cmdlet          Restore-MsolUser                                         1.1.130.0  MSOnlineExtended
Cmdlet          Set-MsolADFSContext                                      1.1.130.0  MSOnline
Cmdlet          Set-MsolAdministrativeUnit                               1.1.130.0  MSOnline
Cmdlet          Set-MsolAdministrativeUnit                               1.1.130.0  MSOnlineExtended
Cmdlet          Set-MsolCompanyContactInformation                        1.1.130.0  MSOnline
Cmdlet          Set-MsolCompanyContactInformation                        1.1.130.0  MSOnlineExtended
Cmdlet          Set-MsolCompanySecurityComplianceContactInforma...       1.1.130.0  MSOnline
Cmdlet          Set-MsolCompanySecurityComplianceContactInforma...       1.1.130.0  MSOnlineExtended
Cmdlet          Set-MsolCompanySettings                                  1.1.130.0  MSOnline
Cmdlet          Set-MsolCompanySettings                                  1.1.130.0  MSOnlineExtended
Cmdlet          Set-MsolDeviceRegistrationServicePolicy                  1.1.130.0  MSOnline
Cmdlet          Set-MsolDeviceRegistrationServicePolicy                  1.1.130.0  MSOnlineExtended
Cmdlet          Set-MsolDirSyncConfiguration                             1.1.130.0  MSOnline
Cmdlet          Set-MsolDirSyncConfiguration                             1.1.130.0  MSOnlineExtended
Cmdlet          Set-MsolDirSyncEnabled                                   1.1.130.0  MSOnline
Cmdlet          Set-MsolDirSyncEnabled                                   1.1.130.0  MSOnlineExtended
Cmdlet          Set-MsolDirSyncFeature                                   1.1.130.0  MSOnline
Cmdlet          Set-MsolDirSyncFeature                                   1.1.130.0  MSOnlineExtended
Cmdlet          Set-MsolDomain                                           1.1.130.0  MSOnline
Cmdlet          Set-MsolDomain                                           1.1.130.0  MSOnlineExtended
Cmdlet          Set-MsolDomainAuthentication                             1.1.130.0  MSOnline
Cmdlet          Set-MsolDomainAuthentication                             1.1.130.0  MSOnlineExtended
Cmdlet          Set-MsolDomainFederationSettings                         1.1.130.0  MSOnline
Cmdlet          Set-MsolDomainFederationSettings                         1.1.130.0  MSOnlineExtended
Cmdlet          Set-MsolGroup                                            1.1.130.0  MSOnline
Cmdlet          Set-MsolGroup                                            1.1.130.0  MSOnlineExtended
Cmdlet          Set-MsolPartnerInformation                               1.1.130.0  MSOnline
Cmdlet          Set-MsolPartnerInformation                               1.1.130.0  MSOnlineExtended
Cmdlet          Set-MsolPasswordPolicy                                   1.1.130.0  MSOnline
Cmdlet          Set-MsolPasswordPolicy                                   1.1.130.0  MSOnlineExtended
Cmdlet          Set-MsolServicePrincipal                                 1.1.130.0  MSOnline
Cmdlet          Set-MsolServicePrincipal                                 1.1.130.0  MSOnlineExtended
Cmdlet          Set-MsolSettings                                         1.1.130.0  MSOnline
Cmdlet          Set-MsolSettings                                         1.1.130.0  MSOnlineExtended
Cmdlet          Set-MsolUser                                             1.1.130.0  MSOnline
Cmdlet          Set-MsolUser                                             1.1.130.0  MSOnlineExtended
Cmdlet          Set-MsolUserLicense                                      1.1.130.0  MSOnline
Cmdlet          Set-MsolUserLicense                                      1.1.130.0  MSOnlineExtended
Cmdlet          Set-MsolUserPassword                                     1.1.130.0  MSOnline
Cmdlet          Set-MsolUserPassword                                     1.1.130.0  MSOnlineExtended
Cmdlet          Set-MsolUserPrincipalName                                1.1.130.0  MSOnline
Cmdlet          Set-MsolUserPrincipalName                                1.1.130.0  MSOnlineExtended
Cmdlet          Update-MsolFederatedDomain                               1.1.130.0  MSOnline

PS C:\WINDOWS\system32> _
```

In this chapter, we will discuss the following topics:

- Why do we need to learn PowerShell for Office 365?
- PowerShell is a cmdlet-based language with verb-noun syntax
- How to pass parameters to cmdlets and storing results as a variable
- How to get help with PowerShell?

- How PowerShell is an object-oriented language and how to work with objects?
- Using the if and where statements
- Using the for and while loops
- Creating your first script

Why do we need to learn PowerShell for Office 365?

Office 365 admin center is an out-of-the-box solution that is designed to handle the most common administrative tasks, such as creating new users and assigning licenses. There are situations where PowerShell for Office 365 helps us save time and effort. If you are a systems administrator, PowerShell is now a must-have skill. PowerShell for Office 365 helps you automate a lot of repetitive tasks and also work with advanced functions that are not available in Office 365 admin center:

- Office 365 PowerShell can reveal additional information that you cannot see with Office 365 admin center
- Office 365 has features that you can only configure using Office 365 PowerShell
- Office 365 PowerShell is great at performing bulk operations
- Office 365 PowerShell is great for filtering data
- Office 365 PowerShell allows us to automate repetitive tasks
- Office 365 PowerShell makes it easy to print or save data
- Office 365 PowerShell lets you manage operations across server products

I think using the Office 365 admin center is like using public transportation. We have to live with the options provided by Microsoft. If we need something custom, like in the case of transportation when we use taxis or personal vehicles, in Office 365, we can use PowerShell. We still have to write scripts in accordance with Microsoft's guidelines. However, we get far more flexibility and options as compared to Office 365 admin center.

Before we dive deep into PowerShell for Office 365, let's cover the basics of PowerShell in the next few sections.

PowerShell is a cmdlet based language with verb-noun syntax

The building blocks of PowerShell are called **cmdlets** (pronounced *command-lets*). Cmdlets allow us to get things done in PowerShell. A cmdlet is a lightweight command that is used in the Windows PowerShell environment. The Windows PowerShell runtime evokes these cmdlets within the context of automation scripts that are provided at the command line. We can put multiple cmdlets together into a set of commands to run all at once, or we can place them in a file with the extension `.ps1` to create a PowerShell script that we can run manually or using a scheduler. In Office 365, the following cmdlets are commonly used:

- `Get-MsolUser`
- `New-MsolUser`

In PowerShell, cmdlets follow a pattern with verb-noun syntax. For example, to manage users, the syntax is `<Verb>-MSOL<Noun>`.

Here, `MSOL` stands for Microsoft Online.

To manage SharePoint Online, the syntax is `<Verb>-SPO<Noun>`.

`SPO` is SharePoint Online.

The following is the list of the most commonly used verbs in PowerShell:

- `Get`
- `Set`
- `Add`
- `New`
- `Remove`
- `Connect`
- `Disconnect`

- `Test`
- `Enable`
- `Disable`
- `Invoke`
- `Start`
- `Stop`

How to pass parameters to cmdlets and storing results as a variable

A cmdlet is a lightweight command that is used in the Windows PowerShell environment. The Windows PowerShell runtime invokes these cmdlets within the context of automation scripts that are provided at the command line. The Windows PowerShell runtime also invokes them programmatically through Windows PowerShell APIs.

They basically accept input via parameters, perform the operation, and then output the results.

Cmdlets differ from commands in a command-shell environment in the following ways:

- Cmdlets are instances of .NET Framework classes; they are not standalone executables.
- Cmdlets can be created from as few as a dozen lines of code.
- Cmdlets do not generally do their own parsing, error presentation, or output formatting and these operations are normally handled by the Windows PowerShell runtime.
- Cmdlets process input objects from the pipeline rather than from streams of text, and typically deliver objects as output to the pipeline.
- Cmdlets are record-oriented because they process a single object at a time.

Parameters

Parameters are the input values that we pass to a cmdlet. For example, if we have to get the time zone, we can use the following cmdlet:

```
Get-TimeZone
```

This cmdlet gets the current time zone or a list of available time zones.

These are the parameters:

- `[-Id]`: Specifies, as a string array, the ID or IDs of the time zones that this cmdlet gets
- `[-ListAvailable]`: Indicates that this cmdlet gets all available time zones
- `[-Name]`: Specifies, as a string array, the name or names of the time zones that this cmdlet gets

We can use this command with or without these parameters:

```
Get-TimeZone
```

The following screenshot shows the output for the preceding command:

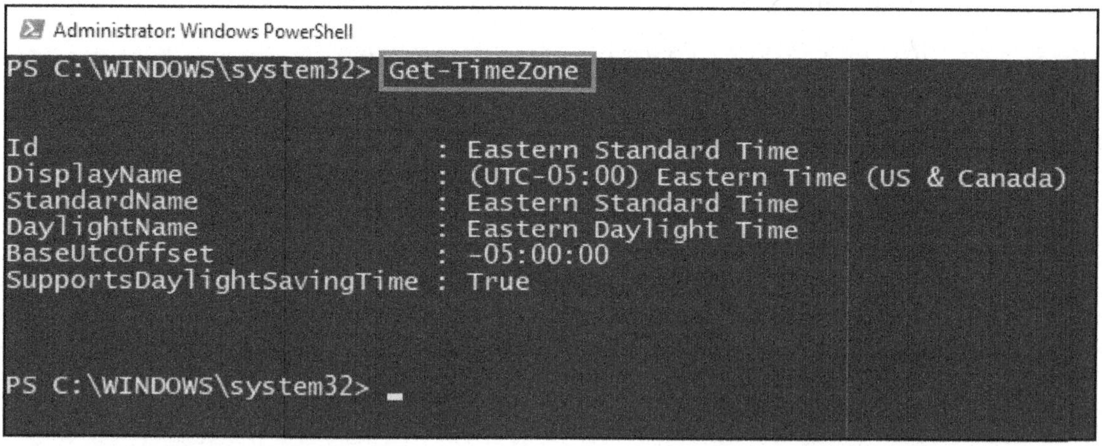

```
Administrator: Windows PowerShell
PS C:\WINDOWS\system32> Get-TimeZone

Id                         : Eastern Standard Time
DisplayName                : (UTC-05:00) Eastern Time (US & Canada)
StandardName               : Eastern Standard Time
DaylightName               : Eastern Daylight Time
BaseUtcOffset              : -05:00:00
SupportsDaylightSavingTime : True


PS C:\WINDOWS\system32> _
```

We can use this command with the `Name` parameter:

```
Get-TimeZone -Name "*pac*"
```

The following screenshot shows the output for the preceding command:

```
Administrator: Windows PowerShell
PS C:\WINDOWS\system32> Get-TimeZone -Name "*pac*"

Id                         : Pacific Standard Time (Mexico)
DisplayName                : (UTC-08:00) Baja California
StandardName               : Pacific Standard Time (Mexico)
DaylightName               : Pacific Daylight Time (Mexico)
BaseUtcOffset              : -08:00:00
SupportsDaylightSavingTime : True

Id                         : Pacific Standard Time
DisplayName                : (UTC-08:00) Pacific Time (US & Canada)
StandardName               : Pacific Standard Time
DaylightName               : Pacific Daylight Time
BaseUtcOffset              : -08:00:00
SupportsDaylightSavingTime : True

Id                         : SA Pacific Standard Time
DisplayName                : (UTC-05:00) Bogota, Lima, Quito, Rio Branco
StandardName               : SA Pacific Standard Time
DaylightName               : SA Pacific Daylight Time
BaseUtcOffset              : -05:00:00
SupportsDaylightSavingTime : False

Id                         : Pacific SA Standard Time
DisplayName                : (UTC-04:00) Santiago
StandardName               : Pacific SA Standard Time
DaylightName               : Pacific SA Daylight Time
BaseUtcOffset              : -04:00:00
SupportsDaylightSavingTime : True

Id                         : West Pacific Standard Time
DisplayName                : (UTC+10:00) Guam, Port Moresby
StandardName               : West Pacific Standard Time
DaylightName               : West Pacific Daylight Time
BaseUtcOffset              : 10:00:00
SupportsDaylightSavingTime : False

Id                         : Central Pacific Standard Time
DisplayName                : (UTC+11:00) Solomon Is., New Caledonia
StandardName               : Central Pacific Standard Time
DaylightName               : Central Pacific Daylight Time
BaseUtcOffset              : 11:00:00
SupportsDaylightSavingTime : False


PS C:\WINDOWS\system32> _
```

We can use this command with the `ListAvailable` parameter:

```
Get-TimeZone -ListAvailable
```

The following screenshot shows the output for the preceding command:

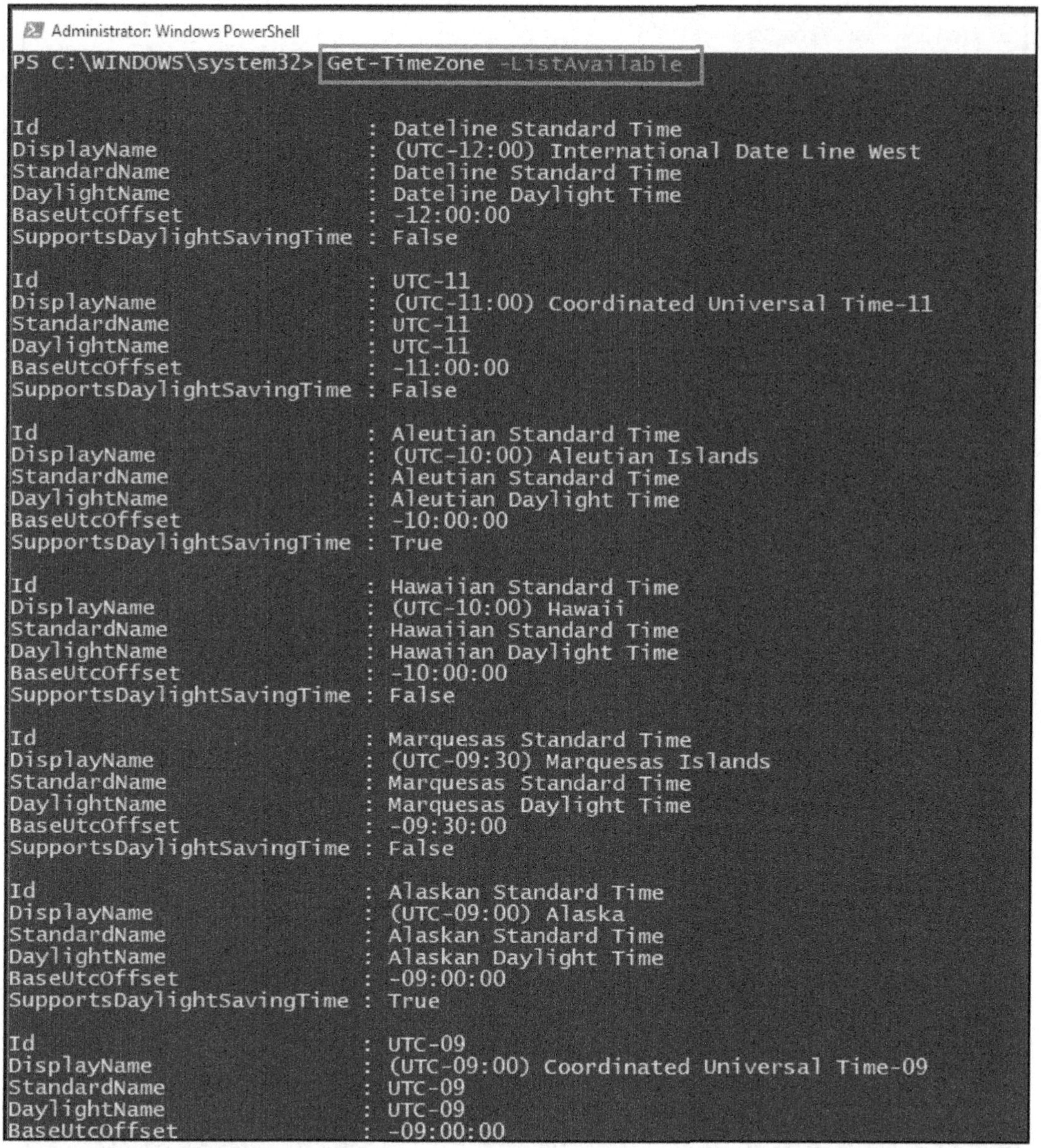

```
Administrator: Windows PowerShell
PS C:\WINDOWS\system32> Get-TimeZone -ListAvailable


Id                         : Dateline Standard Time
DisplayName                : (UTC-12:00) International Date Line West
StandardName               : Dateline Standard Time
DaylightName               : Dateline Daylight Time
BaseUtcOffset              : -12:00:00
SupportsDaylightSavingTime : False

Id                         : UTC-11
DisplayName                : (UTC-11:00) Coordinated Universal Time-11
StandardName               : UTC-11
DaylightName               : UTC-11
BaseUtcOffset              : -11:00:00
SupportsDaylightSavingTime : False

Id                         : Aleutian Standard Time
DisplayName                : (UTC-10:00) Aleutian Islands
StandardName               : Aleutian Standard Time
DaylightName               : Aleutian Daylight Time
BaseUtcOffset              : -10:00:00
SupportsDaylightSavingTime : True

Id                         : Hawaiian Standard Time
DisplayName                : (UTC-10:00) Hawaii
StandardName               : Hawaiian Standard Time
DaylightName               : Hawaiian Daylight Time
BaseUtcOffset              : -10:00:00
SupportsDaylightSavingTime : False

Id                         : Marquesas Standard Time
DisplayName                : (UTC-09:30) Marquesas Islands
StandardName               : Marquesas Standard Time
DaylightName               : Marquesas Daylight Time
BaseUtcOffset              : -09:30:00
SupportsDaylightSavingTime : False

Id                         : Alaskan Standard Time
DisplayName                : (UTC-09:00) Alaska
StandardName               : Alaskan Standard Time
DaylightName               : Alaskan Daylight Time
BaseUtcOffset              : -09:00:00
SupportsDaylightSavingTime : True

Id                         : UTC-09
DisplayName                : (UTC-09:00) Coordinated Universal Time-09
StandardName               : UTC-09
DaylightName               : UTC-09
BaseUtcOffset              : -09:00:00
```

In PowerShell, variables are always prefixed by the character `$` and can include any alphanumeric character or underscore in their names. We can store the output from a cmdlet in a variable and use it later on in other cmdlets or for other purposes in the script, such as writing to the host, using it for comparison, or creating another variable, such as this, for example:

```
$timeZone = Get-TimeZone
Write-Host "The current time zone is " $timeZone
```

The following screenshot shows the output for the preceding command:

```
Administrator: Windows PowerShell
PS C:\WINDOWS\system32> $timeZone = Get-TimeZone
PS C:\WINDOWS\system32> Write-Host "The current timezone is " $timeZone
The current timezone is  (UTC-05:00) Eastern Time (US & Canada)
PS C:\WINDOWS\system32> _
```

How to get help with PowerShell

PowerShell comes with a lot of in-built cmdlets, and with the addition of every new module, the list of available cmdlets increases. You can use your favorite search engine to get more information on a cmdlet. You can do this from the PowerShell window as well. The cmdlet to get the help is this:

```
Get-Help nameofcmdlet
```

Here's an, for example:

```
Get-Help Get-Service
```

The following screenshot shows the output for the preceding command:

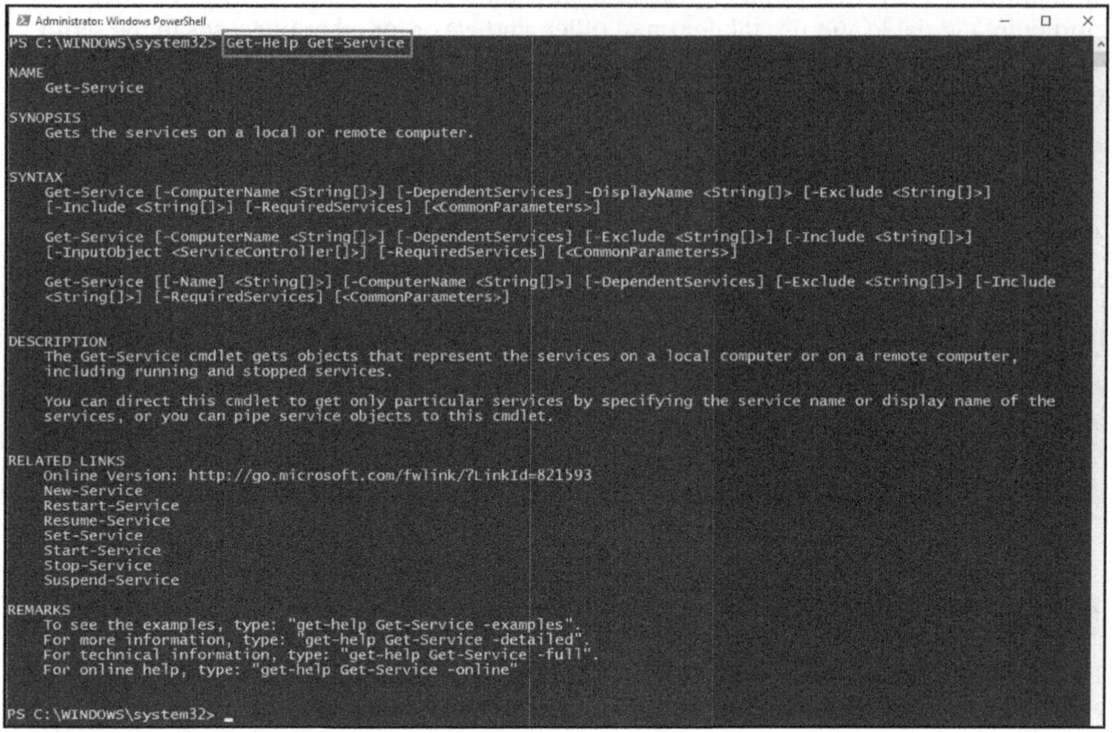

```
Administrator: Windows PowerShell
PS C:\WINDOWS\system32> Get-Help Get-Service

NAME
    Get-Service

SYNOPSIS
    Gets the services on a local or remote computer.


SYNTAX
    Get-Service [-ComputerName <String[]>] [-DependentServices] -DisplayName <String[]> [-Exclude <String[]>]
    [-Include <String[]>] [-RequiredServices] [<CommonParameters>]

    Get-Service [-ComputerName <String[]>] [-DependentServices] [-Exclude <String[]>] [-Include <String[]>]
    [-InputObject <ServiceController[]>] [-RequiredServices] [<CommonParameters>]

    Get-Service [[-Name] <String[]>] [-ComputerName <String[]>] [-DependentServices] [-Exclude <String[]>] [-Include
    <String[]>] [-RequiredServices] [<CommonParameters>]


DESCRIPTION
    The Get-Service cmdlet gets objects that represent the services on a local computer or on a remote computer,
    including running and stopped services.

    You can direct this cmdlet to get only particular services by specifying the service name or display name of the
    services, or you can pipe service objects to this cmdlet.


RELATED LINKS
    Online Version: http://go.microsoft.com/fwlink/?LinkId=821593
    New-Service
    Restart-Service
    Resume-Service
    Set-Service
    Start-Service
    Stop-Service
    Suspend-Service

REMARKS
    To see the examples, type: "get-help Get-Service -examples".
    For more information, type: "get-help Get-Service -detailed".
    For technical information, type: "get-help Get-Service -full".
    For online help, type: "get-help Get-Service -online"

PS C:\WINDOWS\system32> _
```

This is useful if we would like to get help but don't want to leave the Command Prompt.

If you would like to get help from the official online documentation, you can use the following cmdlet:

```
Get-Help Get-Service -online
```

This will open the online help manual of the cmdlet with your default browser:

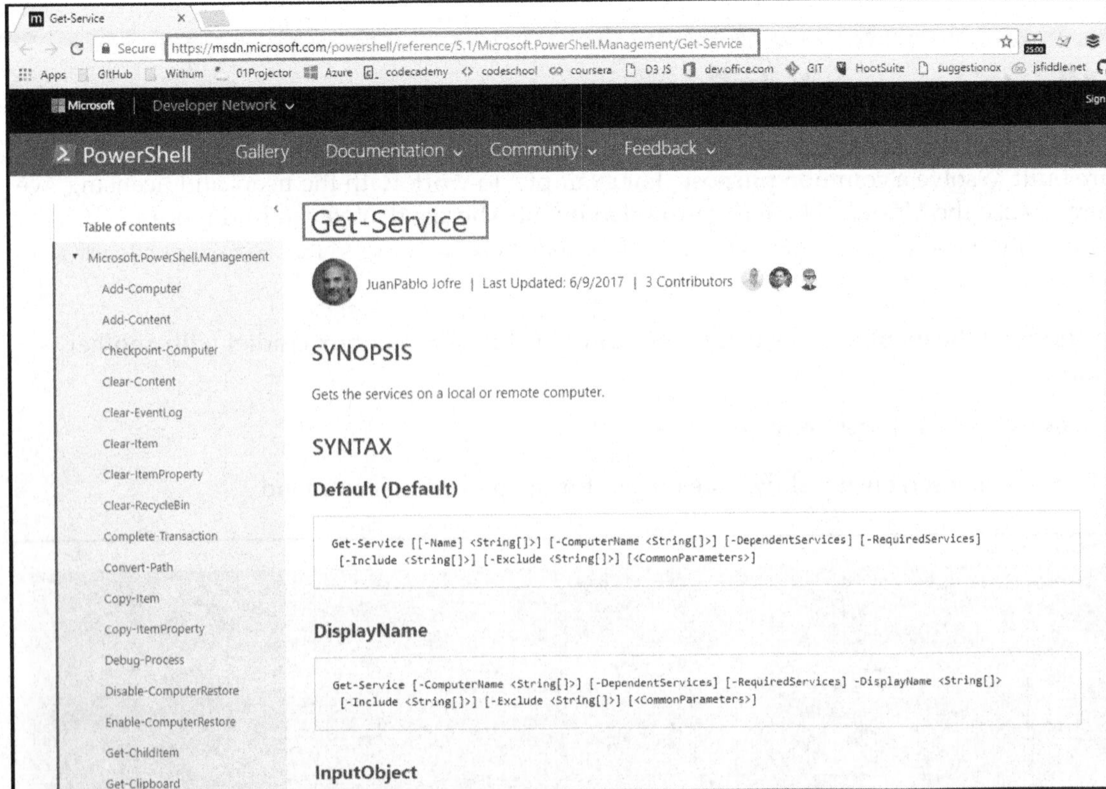

If you would like to quickly check whether there are any commands available for a particular service, you can use the following cmdlet:

```
Get-Command *Service*
```

This will give all the commands that contain the `Service` service in all the modules that are loaded:

What is a module?

A **module** is a combination of multiple PowerShell functionalities like scripts, cmdlets that are built to solve a common purpose. For example, to work with the users and licensing, we have to use the Module *MSOnline* provided by the Microsoft. You can find more information about the *Windows PowerShell module* here `https://msdn.microsoft.com/en-us/library/dd878324(v=vs.85).aspx`.

To find out the members of a cmdlet, we can pipe the `Get-Member` cmdlet with another cmdlet:

```
Get-Service | Get-Member
```

The following screenshot shows the output for the preceding command:

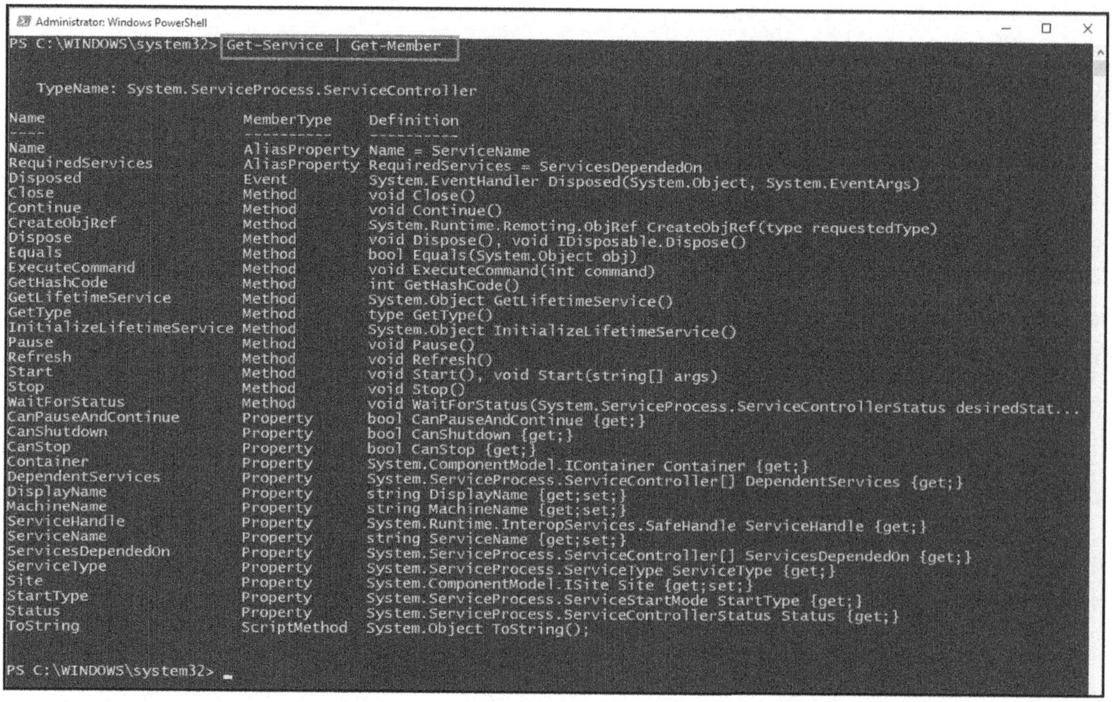

```
Administrator: Windows PowerShell
PS C:\WINDOWS\system32> Get-Service | Get-Member

   TypeName: System.ServiceProcess.ServiceController

Name                      MemberType    Definition
----                      ----------    ----------
Name                      AliasProperty Name = ServiceName
RequiredServices          AliasProperty RequiredServices = ServicesDependedOn
Disposed                  Event         System.EventHandler Disposed(System.Object, System.EventArgs)
Close                     Method        void Close()
Continue                  Method        void Continue()
CreateObjRef              Method        System.Runtime.Remoting.ObjRef CreateObjRef(type requestedType)
Dispose                   Method        void Dispose(), void IDisposable.Dispose()
Equals                    Method        bool Equals(System.Object obj)
ExecuteCommand            Method        void ExecuteCommand(int command)
GetHashCode               Method        int GetHashCode()
GetLifetimeService        Method        System.Object GetLifetimeService()
GetType                   Method        type GetType()
InitializeLifetimeService Method        System.Object InitializeLifetimeService()
Pause                     Method        void Pause()
Refresh                   Method        void Refresh()
Start                     Method        void Start(), void Start(string[] args)
Stop                      Method        void Stop()
WaitForStatus             Method        void WaitForStatus(System.ServiceProcess.ServiceControllerStatus desiredStat...
CanPauseAndContinue       Property      bool CanPauseAndContinue {get;}
CanShutdown               Property      bool CanShutdown {get;}
CanStop                   Property      bool CanStop {get;}
Container                 Property      System.ComponentModel.IContainer Container {get;}
DependentServices         Property      System.ServiceProcess.ServiceController[] DependentServices {get;}
DisplayName               Property      string DisplayName {get;set;}
MachineName               Property      string MachineName {get;set;}
ServiceHandle             Property      System.Runtime.InteropServices.SafeHandle ServiceHandle {get;}
ServiceName               Property      string ServiceName {get;set;}
ServicesDependedOn        Property      System.ServiceProcess.ServiceController[] ServicesDependedOn {get;}
ServiceType               Property      System.ServiceProcess.ServiceType ServiceType {get;}
Site                      Property      System.ComponentModel.ISite Site {get;set;}
StartType                 Property      System.ServiceProcess.ServiceStartMode StartType {get;}
Status                    Property      System.ServiceProcess.ServiceControllerStatus Status {get;}
ToString                  ScriptMethod  System.Object ToString();

PS C:\WINDOWS\system32> _
```

What is a pipe?

Using the pipe character (|), we can select the objects and then perform an action on them.

These three cmdlets--`Get-Command`, `Get-Help`, and `Get-Member`--are important to understand and use, especially when you are new to PowerShell. If you take a closer look, you will find the highlighted letters spell Microsoft compiled HTML help (`.chm`) files, which were the old-school help files available in Windows. We will use them throughout the book to get additional information on the commands we will use.

How PowerShell is an object-oriented language and how to work with objects

PowerShell works with objects, and these objects can have attributes and methods. An **attribute** is a property or a description. PowerShell is an object-oriented scripting language; however, moderately complex scripts are often written using a procedural/functional approach.

To get the members of any cmdlet, we can pipe the `Get-Member` cmdlet with any given cmdlet:

```
Get-TimeZone | Get-Member
```

The output of the preceding command is shown in the following screenshot:

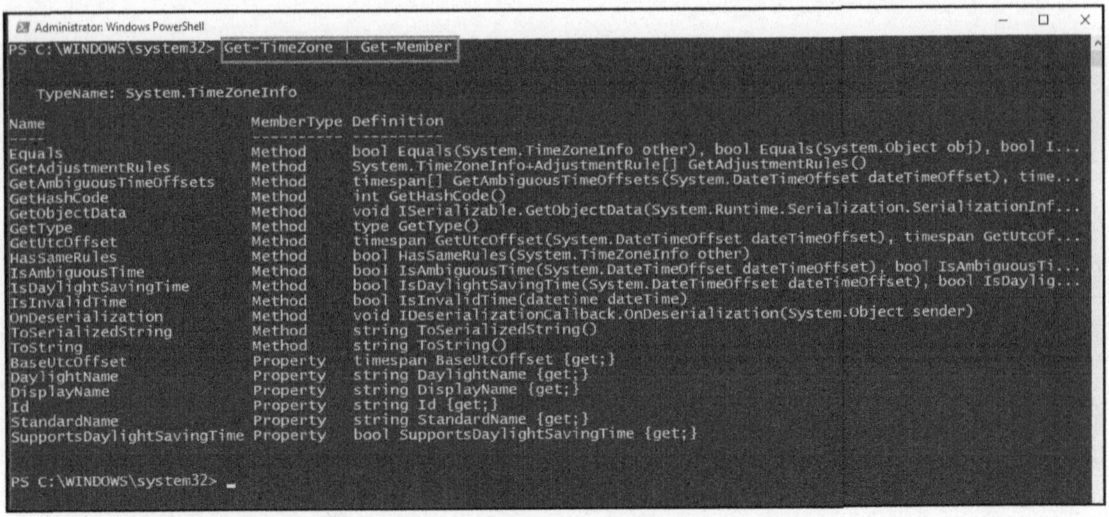

```
Administrator: Windows PowerShell
PS C:\WINDOWS\system32> Get-TimeZone | Get-Member

   TypeName: System.TimeZoneInfo

Name                         MemberType Definition
----                         ---------- ----------
Equals                       Method     bool Equals(System.TimeZoneInfo other), bool Equals(System.Object obj), bool I...
GetAdjustmentRules           Method     System.TimeZoneInfo+AdjustmentRule[] GetAdjustmentRules()
GetAmbiguousTimeOffsets      Method     timespan[] GetAmbiguousTimeOffsets(System.DateTimeOffset dateTimeOffset), time...
GetHashCode                  Method     int GetHashCode()
GetObjectData                Method     void ISerializable.GetObjectData(System.Runtime.Serialization.SerializationInf...
GetType                      Method     type GetType()
GetUtcOffset                 Method     timespan GetUtcOffset(System.DateTimeOffset dateTimeOffset), timespan GetUtcOf...
HasSameRules                 Method     bool HasSameRules(System.TimeZoneInfo other)
IsAmbiguousTime              Method     bool IsAmbiguousTime(System.DateTimeOffset dateTimeOffset), bool IsAmbiguousTi...
IsDaylightSavingTime         Method     bool IsDaylightSavingTime(System.DateTimeOffset dateTimeOffset), bool IsDaylig...
IsInvalidTime                Method     bool IsInvalidTime(datetime dateTime)
OnDeserialization            Method     void IDeserializationCallback.OnDeserialization(System.Object sender)
ToSerializedString           Method     string ToSerializedString()
ToString                     Method     string ToString()
BaseUtcOffset                Property   timespan BaseUtcOffset {get;}
DaylightName                 Property   string DaylightName {get;}
DisplayName                  Property   string DisplayName {get;}
Id                           Property   string Id {get;}
StandardName                 Property   string StandardName {get;}
SupportsDaylightSavingTime   Property   bool SupportsDaylightSavingTime {get;}


PS C:\WINDOWS\system32> _
```

The type of the input is `System.String[]` and the type of the output is `System.TimeZoneInfo[]`.

Using the if and where statements

When writing scripts, we have to implement business logic that will shape the process. The `if` and `where` statements allow us to define logical conditions. For example, if you would like to compare two numbers, you can use the `if` and `else` statements and, based on the comparison, take appropriate action.

Conditional statements are the building blocks of any programming and scripting language.

If a certain condition is true, we can run a block of code. The syntax of an `if...else` is as follows:

```
if (<test1>)
  {<statement list 1>}
elseif (<test2>)
  {<statement list 2>}
else
  {<statement list 3>}
```

Here's an example:

```
$a = 6;
 if( $a -eq 5){
   Write-Host "Variable a is equal to 5"
 }
 elseif( $a -eq 4){
   Write-Host "Variable a is equal to 4"
 }
 else
 {
   Write-host "Variable a is not equal to 5 and 4"
 }
```

The output of this script will be `Variable a is not equal to 5 and 4`.

We can use a combination of the `if...else` statements where in the `if` block we check for a condition: if that condition is true, then we execute a block of code, and if the condition is not true, then we execute another block of code. Sometimes, we can have more than one expected outcome and we can use multiple `elseif` conditions. The comparison operator -`eq` returns Boolean values (`true` or `false`). If the outcome of the comparison is true, then the associated block of code is executed. Since it is a Boolean value, we can use the reverse logic as well.

We have a lot of comparison operators available in PowerShell:

- `-eq`: Equal to
- `-ne`: Not equal to
- `-gt`: Greater than
- `-ge`: Greater than or equal to
- `-lt`: Less than
- `-le`: Less than or equal to
- `-like`: Wildcard match
- `-notlike`: Does not match wildcard
- `-match`: Regular expression matching
- `-notmatch`: Does not match regular expression pattern
- `-contains`: Collection contains item
- `-notcontains`: Collection does not contain item
- `-in`: Item is in a collection

We can use multiple comparison operators in a single `if` statement. This helps you implement complex scenarios.

You can have multiple `if` statements or even use nested `if` statements.

We can **Where-Object** cmdlet to filter data return by other cmdlets. For example, if we would like to find out the processes running on a computer with the name `svcHost` we can use the Where-Object cmdlet with the Get-Process cmdlets as shown below.

```
Get-Process | Where-Object {$_.name -contains "svcHost"}
```

Using the for and while loops

Loops in PowerShell execute a series of commands or cmdlets as long as the condition to run them is true. Loops are helpful for running repetitive tasks inside a PowerShell script. For example, if we need to create five new users, we can use a loop, and inside the loop, we can add the logic to create a new user and execute the loop five times. Loops allow us to write business logic once and then run it repetitively as long as a certain condition is met. To implement loops in PowerShell, we can use the `for`, `foreach`, `while`, `do...while`, and `do...until` loops.

In a `for` loop, we run the command block based on a conditional test. In the following `for` loop, we are running `Write-Host` until the value of variable `$i` is less than `5`. In the beginning, the value of variable `$i` is `0`, and every time the loop is executed, we are incrementing the value of `$i` by `1`. During the execution of the loop, when the value of variable `$i` becomes `5`, the loop stops executing:

```
for ( $i=0; $i -lt 5; $i++)
{
   Write-Host "Value of i is" $i
}
```

The output of this `for` loop is as follows:

```
Administrator: Windows PowerShell
PS C:\Demo> .\Chap01_Demo04.ps1
Value of i is 0
Value of i is 1
Value of i is 2
Value of i is 3
Value of i is 4
PS C:\Demo> _
```

Using the `while`, `do...while`, and `do...until` loops, we can run loops as long as a condition is `true` (it is met).

The `while` loops only use the `while` keyword, followed by the condition and then the script block, as shown here:

```
$i=1
 while ($i -le 10)
 {
   Write-Host "Value of i is" $i
   $i++
 }
```

In this script, the script block inside the `while` loop will run till the value of the variable `$i` is less than `10`. The output of this `while` loop is as follows:

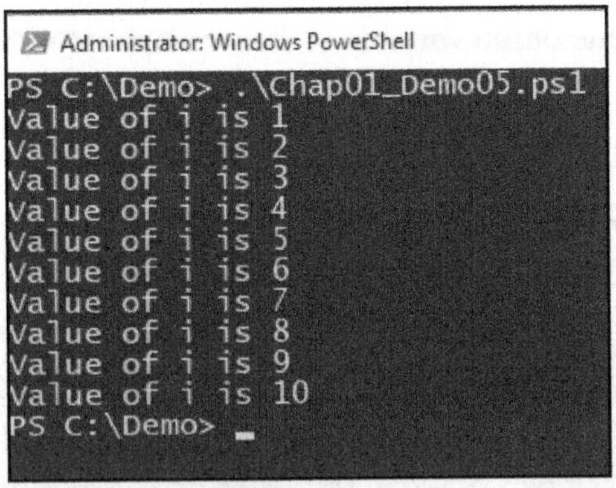

```
Administrator: Windows PowerShell
PS C:\Demo> .\Chap01_Demo05.ps1
Value of i is 1
Value of i is 2
Value of i is 3
Value of i is 4
Value of i is 5
Value of i is 6
Value of i is 7
Value of i is 8
Value of i is 9
Value of i is 10
PS C:\Demo>
```

The `do...while` and `do...until` loops begin with the `do` keyword, followed by the script block and then by the conditional keyword and the condition.

Here's an example of the `do...while` loop:

```
$i=1
 do
 {
   Write-Host "Value of i is" $i
   $i++
 }
 while ($i -le 10)
```

Here's an example of the `do...until` loop:

```
$i=1
 do
 {
   Write-Host "Value of i is" $i
   $i++
 }
 until ($i -gt 10)
```

Both the examples mentioned here basically implement the same business logic using loops, with slightly different comparison methods. In the `do...while` loop, the script block will run until the value of the variable `$i` is less than `10`, and in the `do...until` loop, the script block will run until the value of the variable `$i` becomes greater than `10`. The output of both the loops will be the same as, shown here:

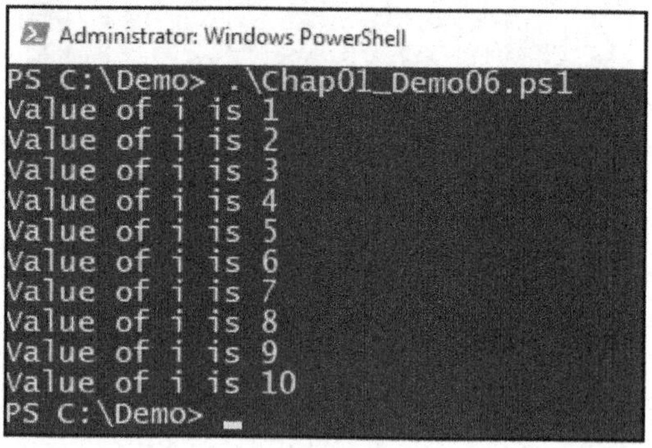

```
Administrator: Windows PowerShell
PS C:\Demo> .\Chap01_Demo06.ps1
Value of i is 1
Value of i is 2
Value of i is 3
Value of i is 4
Value of i is 5
Value of i is 6
Value of i is 7
Value of i is 8
Value of i is 9
Value of i is 10
PS C:\Demo>
```

Creating your first script

To automate tasks, we need to create and run PowerShell scripts. To run a script, we need to follow these steps:

1. **Configure PowerShell to run scripts**: Running a malicious script can harm the computer/server; the default setting for PowerShell is not to run them. We need to change the execution policy of the computer/server to be less restrictive. These steps need to be implemented once.
2. **Store the script**: We need to store the script files with the `.ps1` extension on the file system.
3. **Edit the script**: Add the business logic using commands, cmdlets, variables, and so on.
4. **Run the script**: Run the PowerShell script within the PowerShell Command Prompt or ISE.

Let's create our first PowerShell script. We will be creating a script to read the information from a CSV file and then process the information using the `for` loops and then print it on the screen.

A comma-separated file has information in the form of tables, as shown in the following screenshot. The file has the user's information: their first name, last name, location, and department. We will use this information and create the login names for the users using the format `$firstName + "." + $lastName`.

The CSV file is as follows:

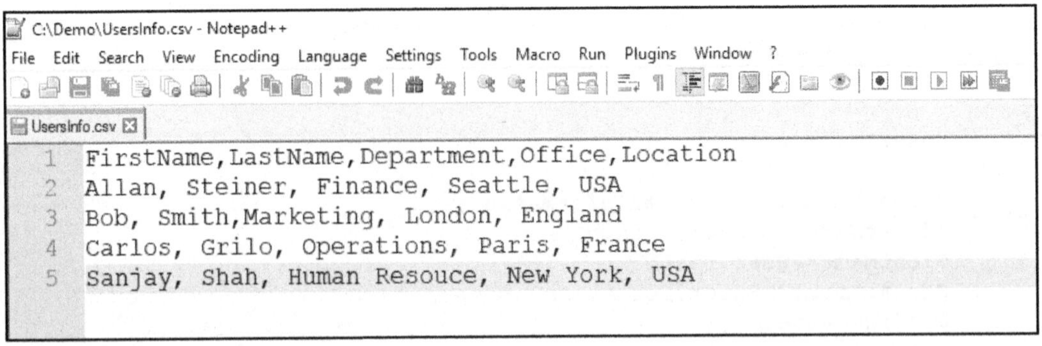

```
FirstName,LastName,Department,Office,Location
Allan, Steiner, Finance, Seattle, USA
Bob, Smith,Marketing, London, England
Carlos, Grilo, Operations, Paris, France
Sanjay, Shah, Human Resouce, New York, USA
```

The script is as follows:

```
Function generateUserName($firstName, $lastName){
  $userName = $firstName + "." + $lastName
  Return $userName;
}

$userInformation = import-csv 'C:\Demo\UsersInfo.csv'

foreach($user in $userInformation){
  $firstName = $user.FirstName
  $lastName=$user.LastName
  $department =$user.Department
  $office=$user.Office
  $Location=$user.Location
  $userName = generateUserName $firstName $lastName
  Write-Host "The generated user name is " $userName
}
```

The following screenshot shows the preceding script:

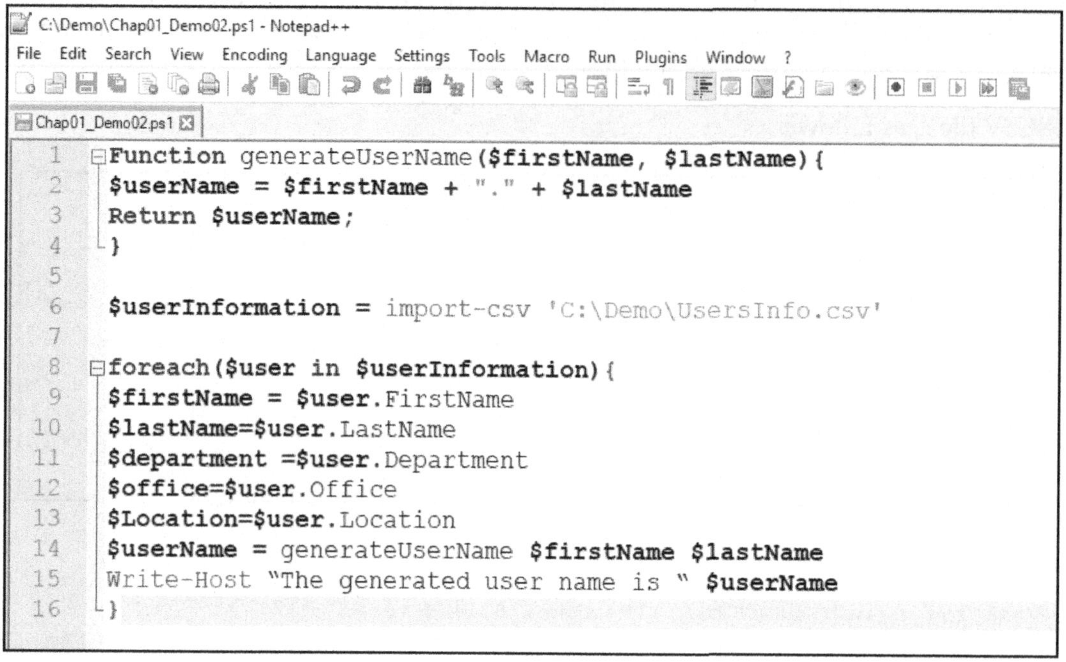

C:\Demo\Chap01_Demo02.ps1 - Notepad++

File Edit Search View Encoding Language Settings Tools Macro Run Plugins Window ?

Chap01_Demo02.ps1

```
1  Function generateUserName($firstName, $lastName){
2  $userName = $firstName + "." + $lastName
3  Return $userName;
4  }
5
6  $userInformation = import-csv 'C:\Demo\UsersInfo.csv'
7
8  foreach($user in $userInformation){
9  $firstName = $user.FirstName
10 $lastName=$user.LastName
11 $department =$user.Department
12 $office=$user.Office
13 $Location=$user.Location
14 $userName = generateUserName $firstName $lastName
15 Write-Host "The generated user name is " $userName
16 }
```

Now let's review this script line by line. As mentioned before, if you are using functions inside a script, it is recommended that you write them at the top of the script. The reason is that when the script is executed, the functions are already loaded.

On **line 1** we have declared the function with the name `generateUserName`, and it accepts two parameters of type string. We can pass complex datatypes as parameters as well.

On **line 2**, we are creating the value for the username using the following logic:

```
$firstname + "." + $lastName
```

On **line 3**, we are returning that value.

On **line 6**, we are reading the contents of the CSV file. The `Import-CSV` cmdlet is a cmdlet to read the contents of a file.

We will be covering this cmdlet in detail because to automate bulk user creation, we can use `$userInformation` stored in CSV files. We can also use information from other sources, such as plain text files or SharePoint lists. But as of now, CSV files are more common.

The `Import-CSV` cmdlet reads the information from the .csv file and stores them in the table-like custom objects. Each column header becomes the property and the subsequent rows become the values of the properties. You can find more information about this cmdlet here `https://msdn.microsoft.com/en-us/powershell/reference/5.0/microsoft.powershell.utility/import-csv`.

Here is the `Import-CSV` command:

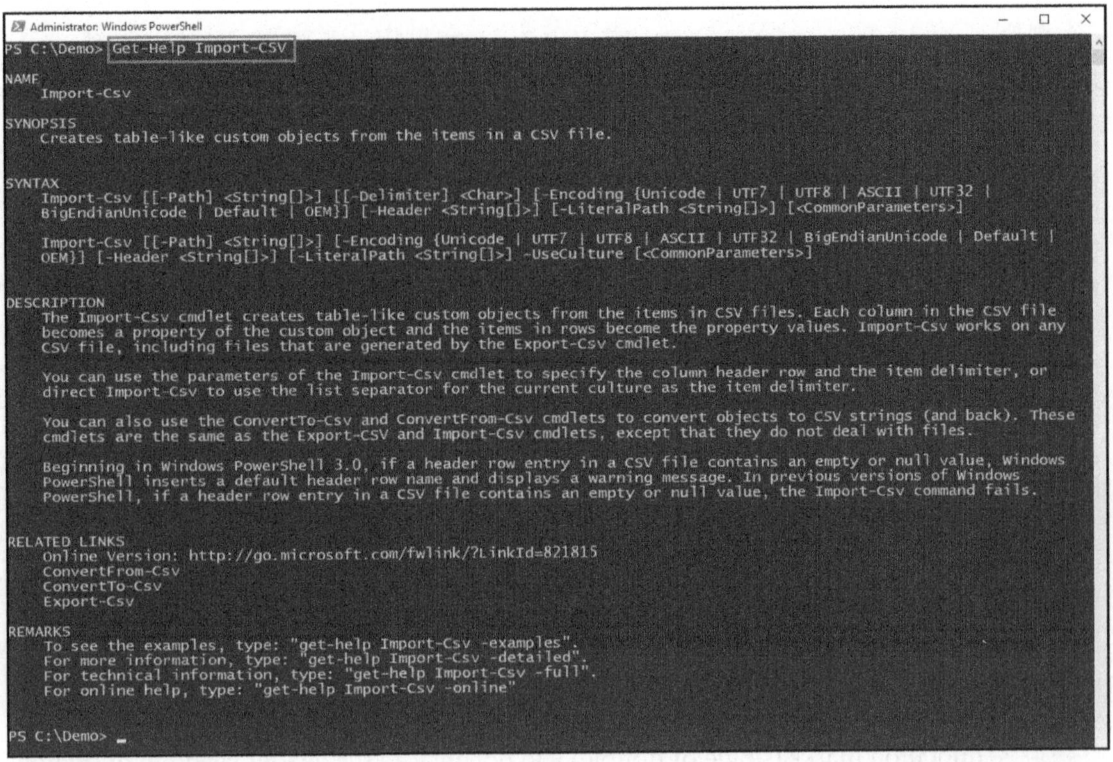

```
Administrator: Windows PowerShell
PS C:\Demo> Get-Help Import-CSV

NAME
    Import-Csv

SYNOPSIS
    Creates table-like custom objects from the items in a CSV file.


SYNTAX
    Import-Csv [[-Path] <String[]>] [[-Delimiter] <Char>] [-Encoding {Unicode | UTF7 | UTF8 | ASCII | UTF32 |
    BigEndianUnicode | Default | OEM}] [-Header <String[]>] [-LiteralPath <String[]>] [<CommonParameters>]

    Import-Csv [[-Path] <String[]>] [-Encoding {Unicode | UTF7 | UTF8 | ASCII | UTF32 | BigEndianUnicode | Default |
    OEM}] [-Header <String[]>] [-LiteralPath <String[]>] -UseCulture [<CommonParameters>]


DESCRIPTION
    The Import-Csv cmdlet creates table-like custom objects from the items in CSV files. Each column in the CSV file
    becomes a property of the custom object and the items in rows become the property values. Import-Csv works on any
    CSV file, including files that are generated by the Export-Csv cmdlet.

    You can use the parameters of the Import-Csv cmdlet to specify the column header row and the item delimiter, or
    direct Import-Csv to use the list separator for the current culture as the item delimiter.

    You can also use the ConvertTo-Csv and ConvertFrom-Csv cmdlets to convert objects to CSV strings (and back). These
    cmdlets are the same as the Export-CSV and Import-Csv cmdlets, except that they do not deal with files.

    Beginning in Windows PowerShell 3.0, if a header row entry in a CSV file contains an empty or null value, Windows
    PowerShell inserts a default header row name and displays a warning message. In previous versions of Windows
    PowerShell, if a header row entry in a CSV file contains an empty or null value, the Import-Csv command fails.


RELATED LINKS
    Online Version: http://go.microsoft.com/fwlink/?LinkId=821815
    ConvertFrom-Csv
    ConvertTo-Csv
    Export-Csv

REMARKS
    To see the examples, type: "get-help Import-Csv -examples".
    For more information, type: "get-help Import-Csv -detailed".
    For technical information, type: "get-help Import-Csv -full".
    For online help, type: "get-help Import-Csv -online"

PS C:\Demo> _
```

This cmdlet accepts the following parameters.

- `[-Delimiter]`: Specifies the delimiter that separates the property values in the CSV file. The default is a comma (`,`). Enter a character, such as a colon (`:`). To specify a semicolon (`;`), enclose it in quotation marks.
  If you specify a character other than the actual string delimiter in the file, `Import-CSV` cannot create objects from the CSV strings. Instead, it returns the strings.

- `[-Encoding]`: Specifies the type of character encoding that was used in the CSV file. Acceptable values for this parameter are as follows:
  - `Unicode`
  - `UTF7`
  - `UTF8`
  - `ASCII`
  - `UTF32`
  - `BigEndianUnicode`
  - `Default`
  - `OEM`

  The default is ASCII.

  This parameter was introduced in Windows PowerShell 3.0.

- `[ -Header]`: Specifies an alternate column header row for the imported file. The column header determines the names of the properties of the object that `Import-CSV` creates.
  Enter a comma-separated list of the column headers. Enclose each item in quotation marks (single or double). Do not enclose the header string in quotation marks. If you enter fewer column headers than there are columns, the remaining columns will have no header. If you enter more headers than there are columns, the extra headers are ignored.
  When using the `Header` parameter, delete the original header row from the CSV file. Otherwise, `Import-CSV` creates an extra object from the items in the header row.

- [-LiteralPath]: Specifies the path to the CSV file to import. Unlike Path, the value of the LiteralPath parameter is used exactly as it is typed. No characters are interpreted as wildcards. If the path includes escape characters, enclose it in single quotation marks. Single quotation marks tell Windows PowerShell not to interpret any characters as escape sequences.
- [-Path]: Specifies the path to the CSV file to import. You can also pipe a path to Import-CSV.
- [-UseCulture]: Indicates that this cmdlet uses the list separator for the current culture as the item delimiter. The default is a comma (,).
- [CommonParameters]: This cmdlet supports the common parameters: -Debug, -ErrorAction, -ErrorVariable, -InformationAction, -InformationVariable, -OutVariable, -OutBuffer, -PipelineVariable, -Verbose, -WarningAction, and -WarningVariable.

Inputs:

[System.String]: You can pipe a string that contains a path to Import-CSV.

Outputs:

[Object]: This cmdlet returns the objects described by the content in the CSV file.

Let's come back to the script. Once we get the contents of the CSV file in the $userInformation object, we process each row and assign the first name, last name, department, and office to the variables. On **line 14**, we call the generateUserName function and capture the return value in the variable and display the username on the script:

```
Administrator: Windows PowerShell
PS C:\Demo> .\Chap01_Demo02.ps1
The generated user name is  Allan.Steiner
The generated user name is  Bob.Smith
The generated user name is  Carlos.Grilo
The generated user name is  Sanjay.Shah
PS C:\Demo> _
```

Using a similar script, we will cover how to create bulk users and assign them licenses in Chapter 3, *Azure AD and Licensing Management.*

Summary

In this chapter, we discussed how PowerShell is a cmdlet-based language with verb-noun syntax. We covered how to pass parameters to cmdlets and store results as variables. We covered how to get help with PowerShell. We covered object-oriented concepts with PowerShell and the concept of objects. We covered how to use the `if` and `where` statements. We covered how to use the `for` and `while` loops. Finally, we created our first script and used the concepts we covered in the earlier sections to read the contents from a CSV file. In the next chapter, we will cover how can manage Office 365 using PowerShell.

2

Managing Office 365 with PowerShell

As we discussed in the first chapter, using PowerShell to manage Office 365 is like driving your own car to reach your destination. In this chapter, we will cover the various admin roles that are available for Office 365 and the installation and configuration of the Office 365 admin tools. Once the tools are installed, we will cover the permissions/roles we need to manage Office 365 using PowerShell. Once these steps are done, we will validate our setup by creating a user account using PowerShell in Office 365.

We will cover the following topics:

- Admin roles for Office 365
- Installing and working with Office 365 admin tools
- Creating the first user account in PowerShell

Admin roles for Office 365

Office 365 is a premium **Software as a Service (SaaS)** offering from Microsoft; Microsoft has done an excellent job of formulating different roles for administrators. Depending on the subscription, you may not see some of the administrator roles. As of today (July 2017), the following are the different types of roles available. The reason for the *as of today* is that, ever since its launch, Microsoft has been adding new services to Office 365 consistently.

Now let's look at the various administrator roles:

- **Global administrator**: This is the highest privileged role. The account you used to sign up for the Office 365 subscription gets this role automatically. The global administrator has access to all the administrative features in the Office 365 suite of services in your plan. For example: create, edit, delete users/groups, manage domains, and so on. To assign this role to other user accounts, you will need to use the global administrator account. Global administrators are the only admins who can assign other admin roles. As a best practice, you should have as few global administrators as possible.
- **Billing administrator**: Members of this role make the purchase, manage subscriptions, manage support tickets, and monitor service health. Members of this role do not have additional privileges in Exchange Online, SharePoint Online, or Skype for Business Online.
- **Exchange administrator**: Members of this role can manage mailboxes and anti-spam policies of your business using the Exchange admin center. It is recommended that, when you assign someone the Exchange admin role, you assign them to the service administrator role as well. This way, the Exchange administrator can see the important information in the Office 365 admin center, such as the health of the Exchange Online service, and change release notifications.
- **SharePoint administrator**: Members of this role manage SharePoint Online using the SharePoint admin center. Members of this role can assign other people as site collection administrators and term store administrators.
- **Password administrator**: This is a limited role, and members of this role can reset the passwords of nonprivileged users and other members of the password administrator role, manage service requests, and monitor service health.
- **Skype for Business administrator**: Members of this role can configure Skype for Business for your organization and view all activity reports in the Office 365 admin center.
- **Compliance administrator**: Members of this role manage security and compliance policies for your organization. Compliance admins have permissions for the Office 365 admin center, Security & Compliance Center, Exchange Online admin center, and the Azure AD admin portal.

- **Service administrator**: Members of this role openly support requests with Microsoft and view the service dashboard and message center. They have the **View Only** permissions except for opening support tickets and reading them. Users who are assigned to the Exchange Online, SharePoint Online, and Skype for Business admin roles should be assigned to the service admin role. This way, these users can see important information in the Office 365 admin center, for example, the health of the service, changes, and release information.
- **User management administrator**: Members of this role can reset a user's password, monitor service health, and manage (add/delete) some user accounts, groups, and service requests. Members of this role cannot delete a global admin, create other admin roles, or reset the passwords for global, billing, Exchange, SharePoint, compliance, and Skype for Business administrators.
- **Power BI administrator**: Members of this role will have access to the Office 365 Power BI usage metrics. They can control the organization's usage of Power BI features.
- **Delegated administrator**: Members of this role are users outside the organization who perform administrative tasks in your Office 365 tenant. To be the delegated administrator, the user needs to have an account in their organization's Office 365 tenant. If your company has multiple tenants or you are managing multiple tenants for your clients, instead of using the separate account for each Office 365 tenant, we can assign an account delegated administrator rights to other tenants. Using this approach, we can use a single account across multiple Office 365 tenants. The delegated administrator can have the following two permission levels:
    - **Full administration**: This delegated administrator has full rights as a global administrator
    - **Limited administration**: This delegated administrator has the same rights as a password administrator

Depending on the type of operation you would like to perform, your account needs to have the corresponding admin role assigned.

For example, if you would like to create a user account, your account needs to be a part of global administrator role or a user management administrator role. The general rule of permissions should be followed while assigning the user roles. You should always start with the least privileged role and elevate the role based on the operation the user would like to do. If the user is only going to change passwords, then it does not make sense to make that user the global admin. Instead, assign the user the password administrator role. We can use either Office 365 admin center or PowerShell to assign the admin roles.

Installing and working with the Office 365 admin tools

In this section, we will cover the installation and configuration of the Office 365 admin tools.

Office 365 is a premier SaaS offering from Microsoft, and they host the services for us. We don't have direct access to the servers that host Exchange, SharePoint, Skype for Business, and so on. So, we need to use the remote management tool. PowerShell for Office 365 is a remote management tool. Even though the new *Microsoft* under Satya Nadella's leadership has embraced open source technologies, in order to manage Office 365 using PowerShell, we need a 64-bit Windows machine as of today. I expect this to change in future, and Microsoft may add support for Linux distributions as well. When Office 365 was launched in 2013, the *Windows Azure Active Directory Module for Windows PowerShell* was supported on 32-bit machines. However, this support was discontinued in October 2014.

To manage Office 365 using PowerShell, we need to install *Microsoft Online Services Sign-In Assistant* and *Windows Azure Active Directory Module for Windows PowerShell*. To install these Office 365 admin tools, we need a 64-bit machine with Windows 7 **Service Pack 1 (SP1)** or higher or Windows Server 2008 R2 SP1 or higher.

This means the supported Windows operating systems are as follows:

- Windows 7 SP1
- Windows 8
- Windows 10
- Windows Server 2008 R2 SP1
- Windows Server 2012
- Windows Server 2012 R2
- Windows Server 2016

There is no predefined sequence, and we can install the tools in any order.

Installing Microsoft Online Service Sign-In Assistant

First, let's install the Microsoft Online Services Sign-In Assistant:

1. Download the 64-bit setup from `https://www.microsoft.com/en-us/download/details.aspx?id=41950` and ensure that the correct language is selected:

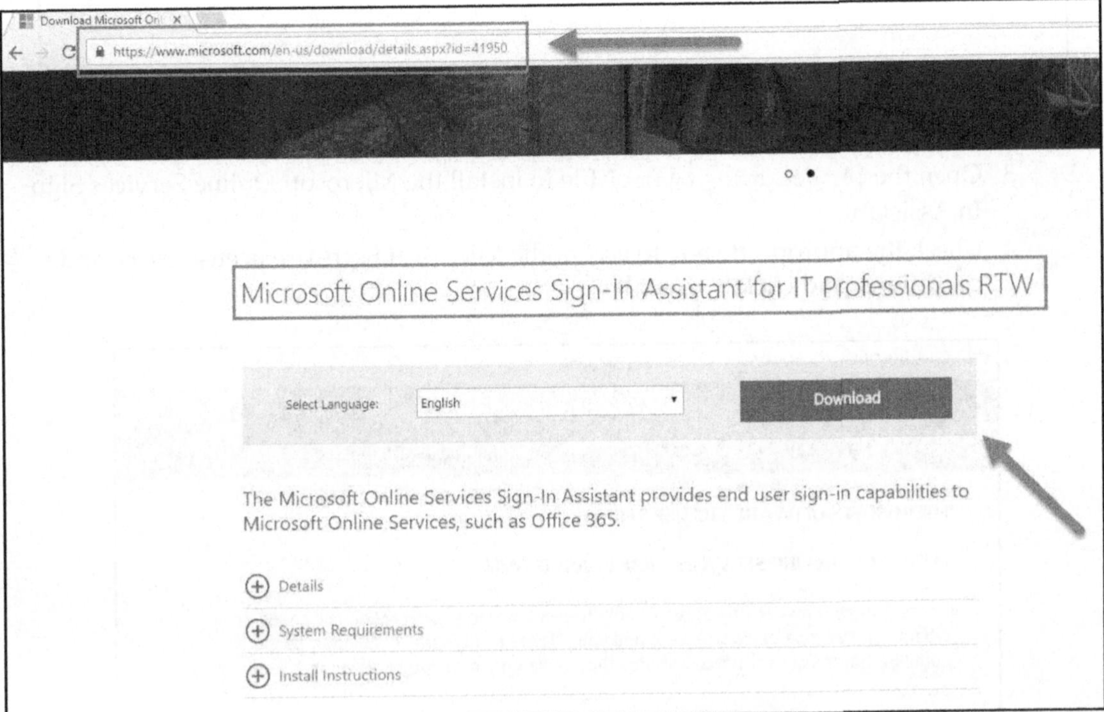

2. Select the 64-bit `.\msoidcli_64.msi` file:

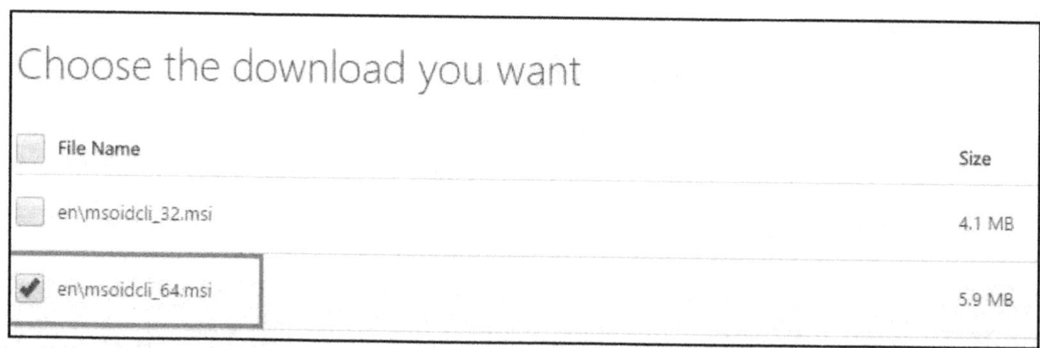

3. Open the `.\msoidcli_64.msi` file to install the Microsoft Online Services Sign-In Assistant.
4. Check the appropriate box to accept the Microsoft Software license terms and conditions, and click on **Install**:

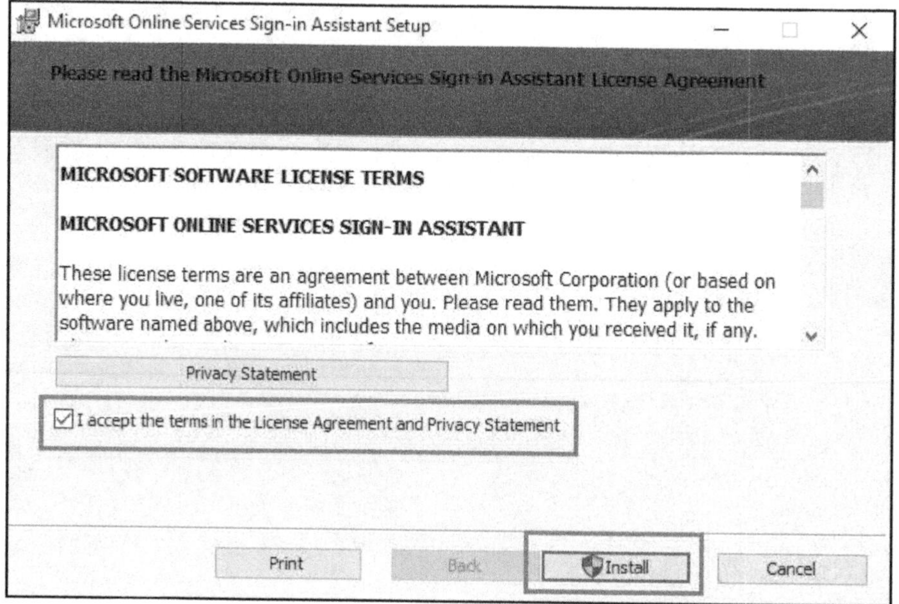

Installing the Windows Azure Active Directory Module for PowerShell

The next step is to install the Windows Azure Active Directory Module for PowerShell. You may be wondering why we need to install the Azure Active Directory Module for PowerShell. The reason is every Office 365 tenant gets Azure Active Directory by default, and Microsoft stores the user information in Azure Active Directory. To execute PowerShell cmdlets for Office 365, we first need to authenticate against the Azure Active Directory. Let's install the Windows Azure Active Directory Module for PowerShell:

1. Download the 64-bit setup from `http://go.microsoft.com/fwlink/p/?linkid=236297`:

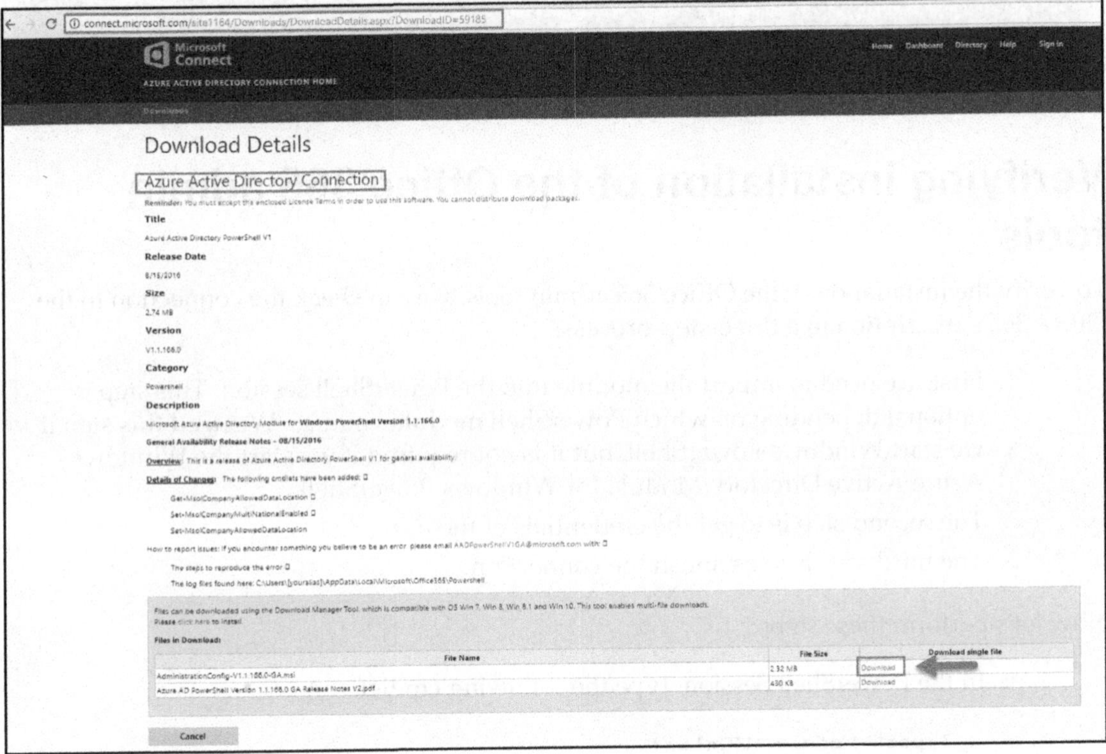

2. After successful installation of the setup, you may find a shortcut named **Windows Azure Active Directory Module for Windows PowerShell** on the desktop.

3. If the shortcut is not present, either search for Windows Azure Active Directory in the Start menu, or locate it in the installed programs, and launch the **Windows Azure Active Directory Module** application.
4. We can also use the following PowerShell cmdlet to verify the installation:

```
Get-Module | Select-Object Name, Path
```

5. If you see the `MSOnline` module, then the installation is successful:

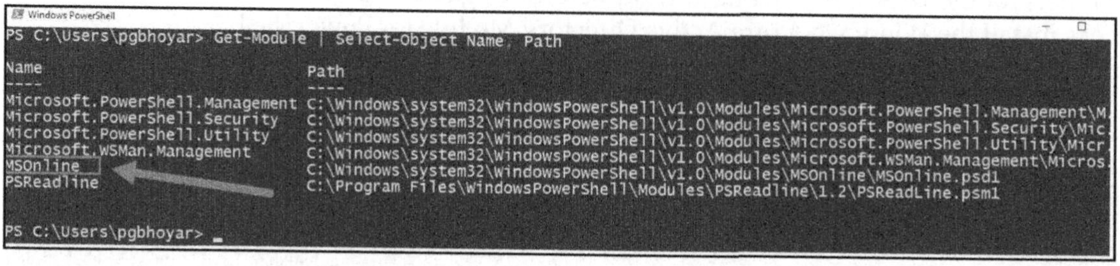

```
PS C:\Users\pgbhoyar> Get-Module | Select-Object Name, Path

Name                            Path
----                            ----
Microsoft.PowerShell.Management C:\Windows\system32\WindowsPowerShell\v1.0\Modules\Microsoft.PowerShell.Management\M
Microsoft.PowerShell.Security   C:\Windows\system32\WindowsPowerShell\v1.0\Modules\Microsoft.PowerShell.Security\Mic
Microsoft.PowerShell.Utility    C:\Windows\system32\WindowsPowerShell\v1.0\Modules\Microsoft.PowerShell.Utility\Micr
Microsoft.WSMan.Management      C:\Windows\system32\WindowsPowerShell\v1.0\Modules\Microsoft.WSMan.Management\Micros
MSOnline                        C:\Windows\system32\WindowsPowerShell\v1.0\Modules\MSOnline\MSOnline.psd1
PSReadline                      C:\Program Files\WindowsPowerShell\Modules\PSReadline\1.2\PSReadLine.psm1

PS C:\Users\pgbhoyar> _
```

Verifying installation of the Office 365 admin tools

To verify the installation of the Office 365 admin tools, we can check the connection to the Office 365 subscription in a three-step process:

1. First, we need to import the module into the PowerShell session. This step is optional depending on which PowerShell module you use. We need this step if we start Windows PowerShell, but it is not required if we start the Windows Azure Active Directory Module for Windows PowerShell.
2. The second step is to get the credentials of the user.
3. The third step is to establish the connection.

Now let's perform these steps:

1. In the PowerShell Session, type the following cmdlet:

```
Import-Module MSOnline
```

2. In the PowerShell session, type this cmdlet:

```
$cred = Get-Credential
```

The following screenshot shows the output of the preceding command:

```
Windows Azure Active Directory Module for Windows PowerShell
PS C:\Users\pgbhoyar\Desktop> $cred = Get-Credential
```

- This will launch the **Windows PowerShell credential request** dialog box.
- Enter the valid Office 365 work or school username and password and click on **OK**:

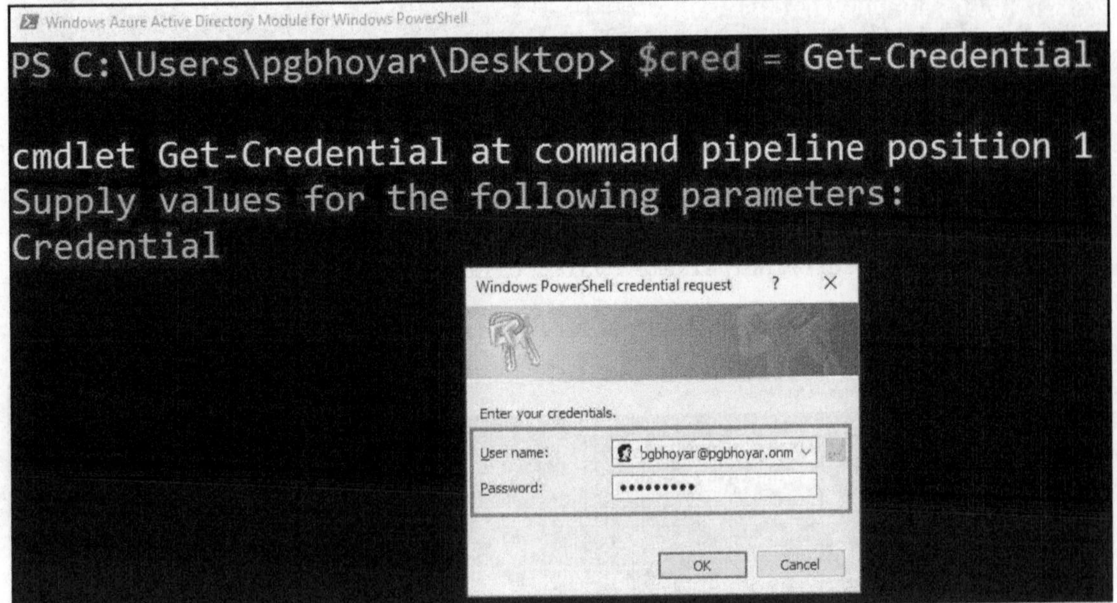

- The `Get-Credential` cmdlet does not tell us whether the username and password are correct or not.

3. Now run the cmdlet:

```
Connect-MsolService -Credential $cred
```

The following screenshot shows the output for the preceding command:

```
Windows Azure Active Directory Module for Windows PowerShell
PS C:\Users\pgbhoyar\Desktop> $cred = Get-Credential

cmdlet Get-Credential at command pipeline position 1
Supply values for the following parameters:
Credential
PS C:\Users\pgbhoyar\Desktop> Connect-MsolService -Credential $cred
PS C:\Users\pgbhoyar\Desktop>
```

This cmdlet initiates a connection to the Azure Active Directory.

If the cmdlet is successful, it will not display the error message. This should be enough to verify the connection; if you prefer additional confirmation, get the details of the user account for which we provided the credentials in *Step 2* using the following cmdlet:

```
Get-MsolUser -UserPrincipalName "valid Office 365 work or school user name"
```

The following screenshot shows the output for the preceding command:

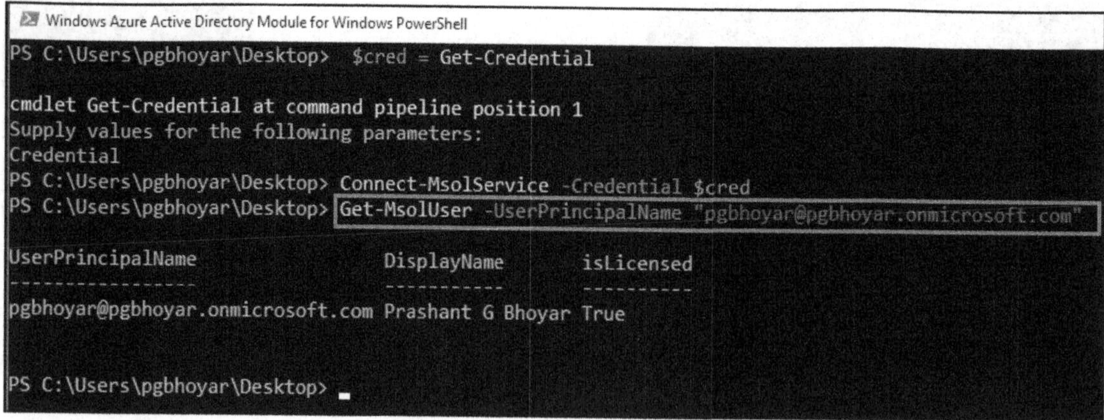

If the cmdlet displays the Office 365 user information, then the connection is successful.

Creating the first user account in PowerShell

If you have an account in Office 365 (even if there is no license assigned to it), using that account you can connect to Office 365 using PowerShell. The operations or cmdlets that you can execute vary depending on the permissions and licenses assigned to that account.

PowerShell cmdlets for Office 365 use the following pattern:

```
<Verb>-Msol<noun>
```

For example, take a look at this:

```
Get-MsolUser
```

Here, `MSOL` = Microsoft Online.

To find out about all the commands, use `Get-Command *Msol*`.

Once the connection is established successfully, let's create a new user account. To create the user account, the account that we will be using needs to be part of the global administrator role or the user management role.

Ensuring user account permissions

Let's check whether the account has the necessary permissions using the following PowerShell cmdlet:

```
Get-MsolUserRole
```

This cmdlet gets all the administrator roles that the specified user belongs to. It will also return the roles that the user is a member of through security group membership.

The cmdlet accepts the following three parameters. `ObjectId` and `UserPrincipalName` are the required parameters, and we need to pass/provide at least one of them:

- `[-ObjectId <Guid>]`: Specifies the unique ID of the user to retrieve roles for.
- `[-TenantId <Guid>]`: Specifies the unique ID of the tenant on which the operation is to be performed. The default value is the tenant of the current user. This parameter applies only to partner users.
- `[-UserPrincipalName <String>]`: Specifies the `UserPrincipalName` of the user to retrieve roles for.

The following cmdlet will display the administrative role for a user:

```
Get-MsolUserRole -UserPrincipalName "pgbhoyar@pgbhoyar.onmicrosoft.com"
```

The following screenshot shows the output for the preceding command:

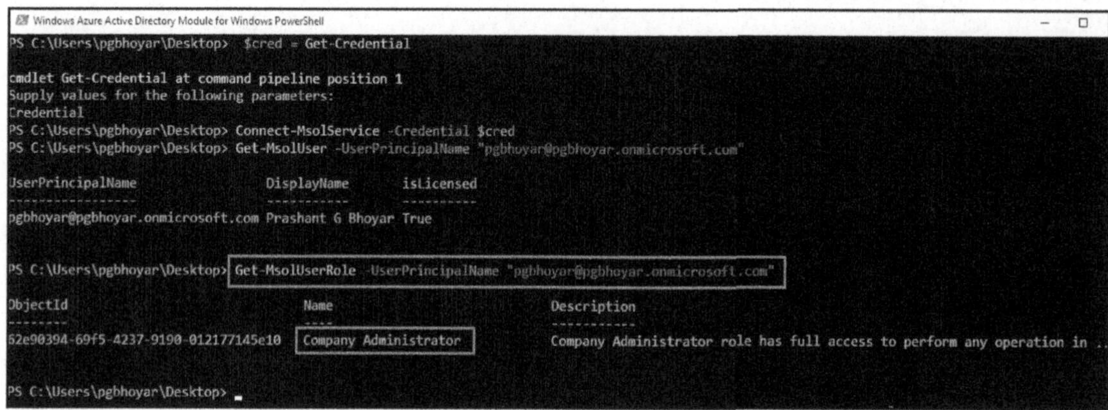

Here, the `Company Administrator` is the same as global administrator.

To grant additional accounts admin roles, we can use the following PowerShell cmdlet:

```
Add-MsolRoleMember
```

To get the available administrative roles, we can use the following PowerShell cmdlet:

```
Get-MsolRole
```

The following screenshot shows the output for the preceding command:

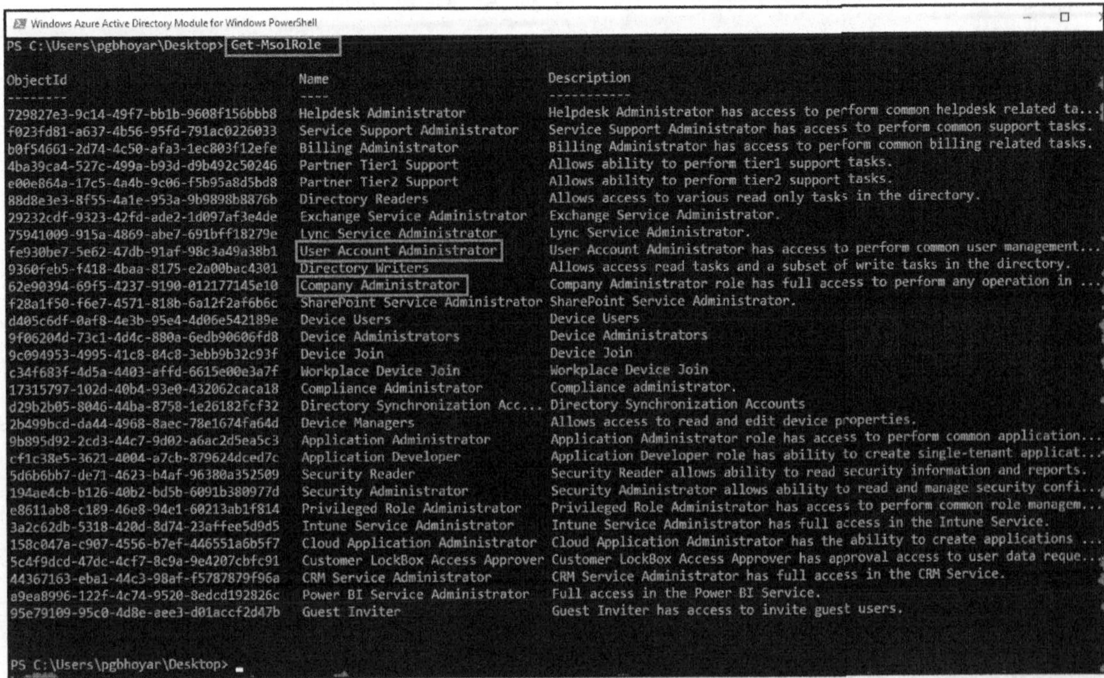

If we need to grant the user *global administrator/company administrator role,* we can use the following PowerShell cmdlet:

```
Add-MsolRoleMember -RoleName "Company Administrator"
  -RoleMemberEmailAddress "prashant-admin@pgbhoyar.onmicrosoft.com"
```

To verify that the user has the admin role now, we can use the PowerShell `Get-MsolUserRole` cmdlet mentioned earlier.

Checking license availability

Once we have verified that the user has the correct role assigned, as a best practice check whether you have the license available. This step is not required if you are just creating the users but not assigning the license.

When we create a new account in Office 365, the account will not count against the subscription until we assign the license.

To check the available licenses, use the following PowerShell Cmdlet:

```
Get-MsolAccountSku
```

The following screenshot shows the output for the preceding command:

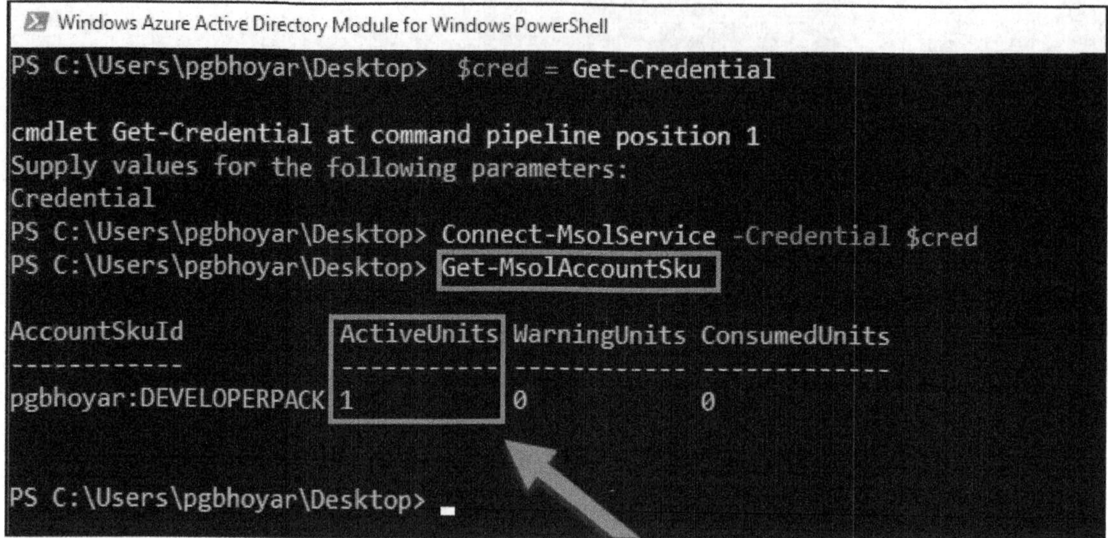

`ActiveUnits` will give you information about the available licenses.

Creating a new user

Now let's create a new user in Office 365. The PowerShell cmdlet to create the new user is as follows:

```
New-MsolUser
```

This cmdlet creates a user in Azure Active Directory. This cmdlet accepts 35 parameters, as shown in the following list. Out of these 35 parameters, only `DisplayName` and `UserPrincipalName` are required parameters:

- `[-AlternateEmailAddresses <String[]>]`: Specifies alternate email addresses for the user.
- `[-AlternateMobilePhones <String[]>]`: Specifies alternate mobile phone numbers for the user.
- `[-BlockCredential <Boolean>]`: Specifies whether the user is able to log on using their user ID.
- `[-City <String>]`: Specifies the city of the user.
- `[-Country <String>]`: Specifies the country of the user.
- `[-Department <String>]`: Specifies the department of the user.
- `[-DisplayName <String>]`: Specifies the display name of the user.
- `[-Fax <String>]`: Specifies the fax number of the user.
- `[-FirstName <String>]`: Specifies the first name of the user.
- `[-ForceChangePassword <Boolean>]`: Indicates that the user is required to change the password during the next sign-in.
- `[-ImmutableId <String>]`: Specifies the immutable ID of the federated identity of the user. This should be omitted for users with standard identities.
- `[-LastName <String>]`: Specifies the last name of the user.
- `[-LicenseAssignment <String[]>]`: Specifies an array of licenses to assign to the user.
- `[-LicenseOptions <LicenseOption[]>]`: Specifies the options for license assignment. Used to selectively disable individual service plans within an SKU.
- `[-MobilePhone <String>]`: Specifies the mobile phone number of the user.
- `[-Office <String>]`: Specifies the office of the user.
- `[-Password <String>]`: Specifies the new password for the user.
- `[-PasswordNeverExpires <Boolean>]`: Specifies whether the user password expires periodically.
- `[-PhoneNumber <String>]`: Specifies the phone number of the user.
- `[-PostalCode <String>]`: Specifies the postal code of the user.
- `[-PreferredDataLocation <String>]`: Specifies the preferred data location for the user.
- `[-PreferredLanguage <String>]`: Specifies the preferred language of the user.

- [-State <String>]: Specifies the state or province where the user is located.
- [-StreetAddress <String>]: Specifies the street address of the user.
- [-StrongPasswordRequired <Boolean>]: Specifies whether you require a strong password for the user.
- [-TenantId <Guid>]: Specifies the unique ID of the tenant on which the operation is to be performed. The default value is the tenant of the current user. This parameter applies only to partner users.
- [-Title <String>]: Specifies the title of the user.
- [-UsageLocation <String>]: Specifies the location of the user where services are consumed. Specifies a two-letter country code.
- [-UserPrincipalName <String>]: Specifies the user ID for this user. This is required.
- [-LastPasswordChangeTimestamp <DateTime>]: Specifies the time when the password was last changed.
- [-SoftDeletionTimestamp <DateTime>]: Specifies a time for soft deletion.
- [-StrongAuthenticationMethods <StrongAuthenticationMethod[]>]: Specifies an array of strong authentication methods.
- [-StrongAuthenticationRequirements <StrongAuthenticationRequirement[]>]: Specifies an array of strong authentication requirements.
- [-StsRefreshTokensValidFrom <DateTime>]: Specifies a StsRefreshTokensValidFrom value.
- [-UserType <UserType>] [<CommonParameters>]: Specifies the user type.

The following cmdlet will create a new user with minimum information:

```
New-MsolUser -UserPrincipalName "pbhoyar@pgbhoyar.onmicrosoft.com"
 -DisplayName "Prashant G Bhoyar"
```

The following screenshot shows the output for the preceding command:

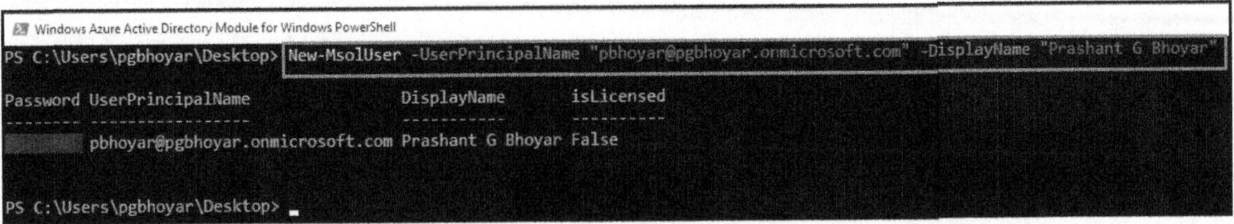

After the successful creation of the account, the temporary password will get generated/displayed. So far, we have not assigned a license to this user. We will cover this part in detail in the next chapter.

Summary

In this chapter, we covered the different administrative roles available in Office 365. We covered the steps we need to take in order to set up the Office 365 admin tools. We covered the steps that we need to take to connect to Office 365 using PowerShell. Finally, we tested the setup by creating a new user account in Office 365. In the next chapter, we will walk users through common administrative cmdlets that are used for managing accounts and licensing.

3

Azure AD and Licensing Management

In the previous chapter, we connected to Office 365 using PowerShell and created a new user. In this chapter, we will cover in detail bulk user creation, the updating and deletion of users, license assignments, and license updates using PowerShell.

Specifically, we will cover the following topics:

- Common administrative cmdlets that are used for managing accounts and licensing
- Formatting data to be used for bulk account management
- How to change licenses for existing users?
- How to remove accounts and licenses?
- How to reset account passwords?
- How to update user account details?
- Working with Office 365 groups

Common administrative cmdlets that are used for managing accounts and licensing

Office 365 is a subscription-based service, and it is important for organizations to manage the licenses of users, such as assigning a license to a new user, removing licenses, and activating new licenses in bulk.

Before assigning the license, let's see how we can filter users based on some criteria. For example, if you have users in multiple locations, we can use the following cmdlets to filter users based on the location *Bethesda*:

1. Since PowerShell for Office 365 is used via remote management, as always the first step will be to connect to Office 365 and prove our identity:

   ```
   Import-Module MSOnline
   $cred = Get-Credential
   ```

   This will launch the **Windows PowerShell credential request** dialog.

2. Enter a valid Office 365 work or school **User name** and **Password** and click on **OK**:

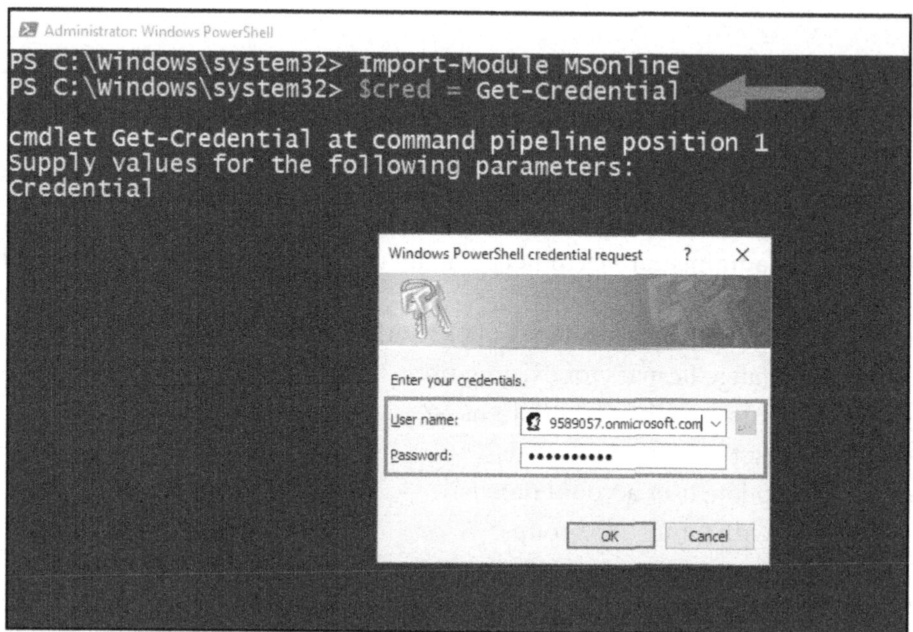

3. Now run the cmdlet:

   ```
   Connect-MsolService -Credential $cred
   ```

   If the cmdlet is successful, it will not display an error message. This should be enough to verify that we have established the connection:

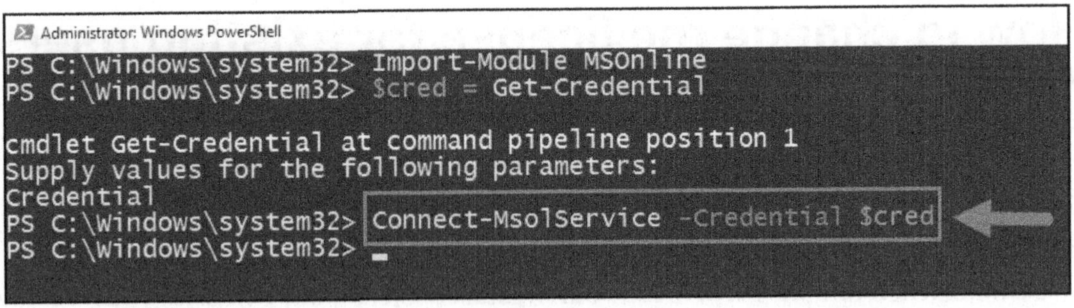

```
Administrator: Windows PowerShell
PS C:\Windows\system32> Import-Module MSOnline
PS C:\Windows\system32> $cred = Get-Credential

cmdlet Get-Credential at command pipeline position 1
Supply values for the following parameters:
Credential
PS C:\Windows\system32> Connect-MsolService -Credential $cred
PS C:\Windows\system32>
```

4. To filter users based on location, we can use the following cmdlet:

```
Get-MSOLUser -City Bethesda
```

5. If we would like to filter users based on department, we can use something like this:

```
Get-MsolUser -Department 'Corporate Marketing'
```

The output for the preceding command is shown in the following screenshot:

```
PS C:\Windows\system32> get-MSOlUser -Department 'Corporate Marketing'

UserPrincipalName                 DisplayName  isLicensed
-----------------                 -----------  ----------
alans@CIE9589057.onmicrosoft.com Alan Steiner True
```

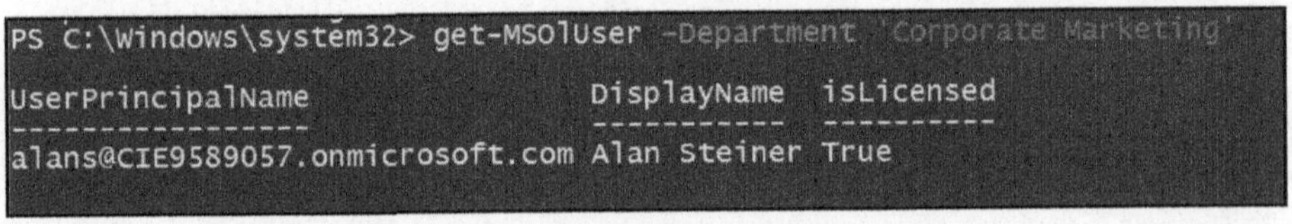

6. As mentioned in `Chapter 1`, *PowerShell Fundamentals*, if we would like to collect this information in a text or CSV file, we can use the following cmdlet:

```
Get-MsolUser -Department "Corporate Marketing"
 >Corporate MarketingUsers.csv
```

We can even use a text file, as shown here:

```
Get-MsolUser -Department "Corporate Marketing"
 >Corporate MarketingUsers.txt
```

The following screenshot shows the output for the preceding command:

```
Administrator: Windows PowerShell
PS C:\Windows\system32> Get-MsolUser -Department 'Corporate Marketing' > CorporateMarketingUsers.txt
PS C:\Windows\system32> Get-MsolUser -Department 'Corporate Marketing' > CorporateMarketingUsers.csv
PS C:\Windows\system32>
```

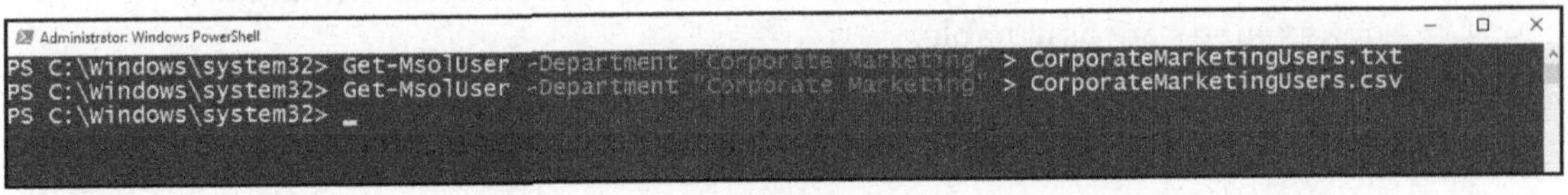

How to change the license for existing users

Before assigning licenses to users, it is good practice to check how many licenses are available unless you remember this information off the top of your head.

To check available licenses, we need to use following cmdlet:

```
Get-MSolAccountSku
```

This cmdlet will return the list of SKUs your organization/company owns. As you may have noticed, there is no required parameter for this cmdlet. An optional parameter is `TenantId`.

`[-TenantId <Guid>]` specifies the unique ID of the tenant.

By default, if the `TenantId` is not specified, the cmdlet will use the ID of the current user. `TenantId` is applicable for partner users (users who are registered partners and manage multiple tenants).

This cmdlet returns the `AccountSku` object, which contains the following information:

- `[AccountName]`: The name of the account this SKU belongs to.
- `[AccountObjectId]`: The unique ID of the account this SKU belongs to.
- `[AccountSkuId]`: The unique string ID of the account/SKU combination. This value should be used when assigning or updating licenses.
- `[ActiveUnits]`: The number of active licenses.
- `[ConsumedUnits]`: The number of licenses consumed.
- `[ServiceStatus]`: The provisioning status of individual services belonging to this SKU.
- `[SkuId]`: The unique ID for the SKU.
- `[SkuPartNumber]`: The partner number of this SKU.
- `[SubscriptionIds]`: A list of all subscriptions associated with this SKU. For the purposes of assigning licenses, all subscriptions with the same SKU will be grouped into a single license pool.
- `[SuspendedUnits]`: The number of suspended licenses. These licenses are not available for assignment.
- `[TargetClass]`: The target class of this SKU. Only SKUs with target `class=user` are assignable.
- `[WarningUnits]`: The number of warning units.

The following figure shows the output of the preceding command:

```
PS C:\Windows\system32> Get-MsolAccountSku

AccountSkuId                                  ActiveUnits WarningUnits ConsumedUnits
------------                                  ----------- ------------ -------------
CIE9589057:ENTERPRISEPREMIUM                  25          0            23
CIE9589057:PROJECTPREMIUM                     25          0            23
CIE9589057:EMS                                25          0            23
CIE9589057:PROJECT_MADEIRA_PREVIEW_IW_SKU     10000       0            23

PS C:\Windows\system32> _
```

We can find out the available licenses by subtracting `ConsumedUnits` from `ActiveUnits`. For example, in this case, we have two Enterprise licenses available. If we run out of licenses, we need to purchase more; depending on your organization, you can make that decision or you may need to go through a procurement process.

If you have Active Directory Sync on, you will not need to create the new users in Azure Active Directory. The new users will get added to Azure Active Directory via the sync process, and we will need to assign the appropriate licenses.

Depending on the Azure subscription, you may automatically assign the license if you add the users to a specific group. This feature is still in preview at the time of writing.

In this case Active Directory Sync is not on, so we can use the PowerShell or Office 365 admin center to create a new user. In the previous chapter, we covered the cmdlet to create a new user in detail.

Now let's create the new user `Bob Smith`:

```
New-MsolUser -UserPrincipalName "bobsmith@CIE9589057.onmicrosoft.com"
  -DisplayName "Bob Smith" -FirstName "Bob" -LastName "Smith"
  -UsageLocation "US"
```

The following screenshot shows the output for the preceding command:

```
PS C:\Windows\system32> New-MsolUser -UserPrincipalName "bobsmith@CIE9589057.onmicrosoft.com" -DisplayName "Bo
FirstName "Bob" -LastName "Smith" -UsageLocation "US"

Password UserPrincipalName                   DisplayName isLicensed
-------- -----------------                   ----------- ----------
         bobsmith@CIE9589057.onmicrosoft.com Bob Smith   False

PS C:\Windows\system32> _
```

If the user gets created successfully, then it will return the `UserPrincipalName` variable and a temporary password. The user will need to change this password after the first successful login.

We can assign a license when we create a new user or after. Without the license, the new user will not be able to access the different services available in the Office 365 tenant. They can still log in to `https://portal.office.com`, but will not have access to Exchange Online, SharePoint Online, Skype For Business Online, Planner, and so on unless we assign the appropriate license to them.

To assign the license while creating a new user, we can use the following command. Note that the value for the `LicenseAssignment` parameter can be obtained with the cmdlet `Get-MSolAccountSku`:

```
New-MsolUser -UserPrincipalName "bobsmith@CIE9589057.onmicrosoft.com"
 -DisplayName "Bob Smith" -FirstName "Bob" -LastName "Smith"
 -UsageLocation "US" -LicenseAssignment "CIE9589057:ENTERPRISEPREMIUM"
```

The following screenshot shows the output of the preceding command:

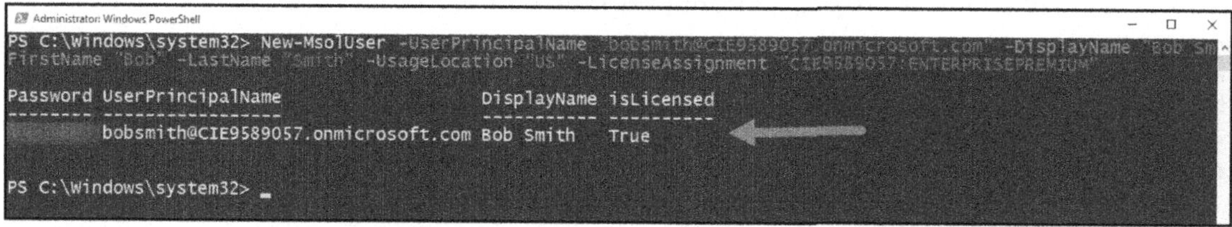

After the user account is created, we can check it via PowerShell:

```
Get-MsolUser -userprincipalname "bobsmith@CIE9589057.onmicrosoft.com"
```

The following figure shows the output for the preceding command:

```
Administrator: Windows PowerShell
PS C:\Windows\system32> Get-MsolUser -userprincipalname bobsmith@CIE9589057.onmicrosoft.com
UserPrincipalName                   DisplayName isLicensed
-----------------                   ----------- ----------
bobsmith@CIE9589057.onmicrosoft.com Bob Smith   True

PS C:\Windows\system32> _
```

We can also check the new user via the Office 365 admin center:

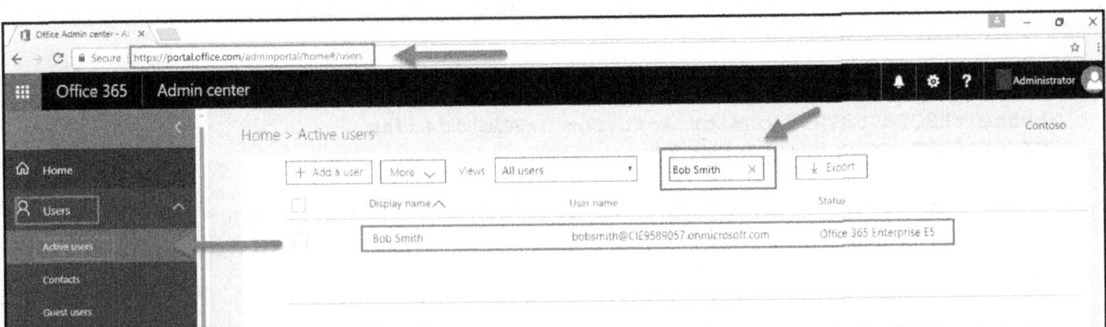

To assign a license after the user has been created, we need to use the following cmdlet along with the `AccountSkuId` parameter:

```
Set-MsolUserLicense
```

This cmdlet updates (add/update/remove) the license assignment for a user. Updating encompasses adding a new license, removing a license, updating license options, or any combination of these actions. This cmdlet accepts five parameters, as shown in the following list. Out of these five parameters, either `UserPrincipalName` or `ObjectId` is required.

- `[-AddLicenses <String[]>]`: Specifies an array of licenses to assign to the user.
- `[-LicenseOptions <LicenseOption[]>]`: Specifies an array of license- or SKU-specific settings. This is used to disable individual services when assigning a license.
- `[-ObjectId <Guid>]`: Specifies the unique object ID of the user for whom to update licenses.
- `[-UserPrincipalName <String>]`: Specifies the `UserPrincipalName` of the user to update.
- `[-RemoveLicenses <String[]>]`: Specifies an array of licenses to remove from the user.
- `[-TenantId <Guid>]`: Specifies the unique ID of the tenant on which to perform the operation. The default value is the tenant of the current user. This parameter applies only to partner users.

To assign the license to `Bob Smith`, we can use the following command. Note that the value for the `AddLicense` parameter can be obtained using the cmdlet `Get-MSolAccountSku`.

```
Set-MSOLUserLicense -UserPrincipalName
"bobsmith@CIE9589057.onmicrosoft.com" -AddLicenses
"CIE9589057:ENTERPRISEPREMIUM"
```

After successful execution of the command, there will be no return message notifying that the license was assigned successfully. You can verify the license using the following command:

```
Get-MsolUser -userprincipalName "bobsmith@CIE9589057.onmicrosoft.com"
```

The following figure shows the output of the preceding command:

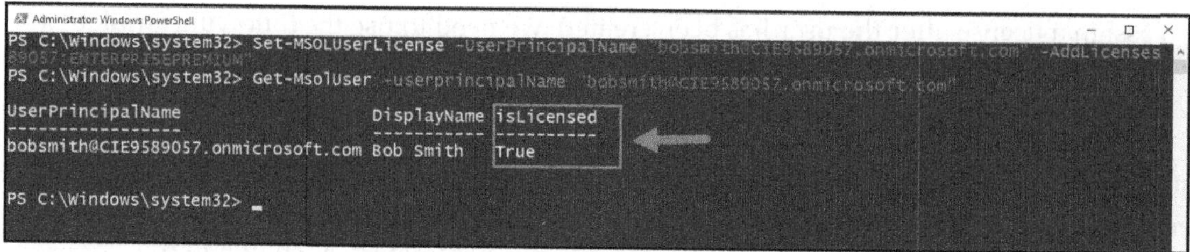

To remove the license, we can use the following command:

```
Set-MsolUserLicense -UserPrincipalName
"bobsmith@CIE9589057.onmicrosoft.com" -RemoveLicenses
"CIE9589057:ENTERPRISEPREMIUM"
```

Remember; when we remove a license from a user, the user's data may get removed from the respective service:

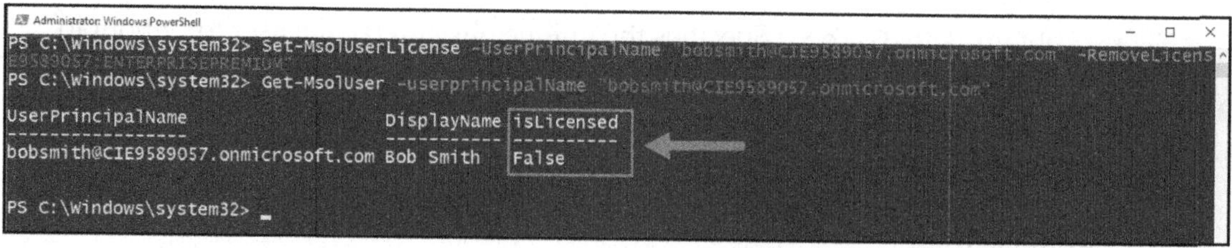

If by mistake we assign an incorrect license and we need to update the license information, we can use the following cmdlet. To get information about the available licenses, you will need to use the cmdlet `Get-MsolAccountSku`:

```
Set-MsolUserLicense -UserPrincipalName
"bobsmith@CIE9589057.onmicrosoft.com" -AddLicenses "CIE9589057:EMS"
 -RemoveLicenses "CIE9589057:PROJECTPREMIUM"
```

The following screenshot shows the output of the preceding command:

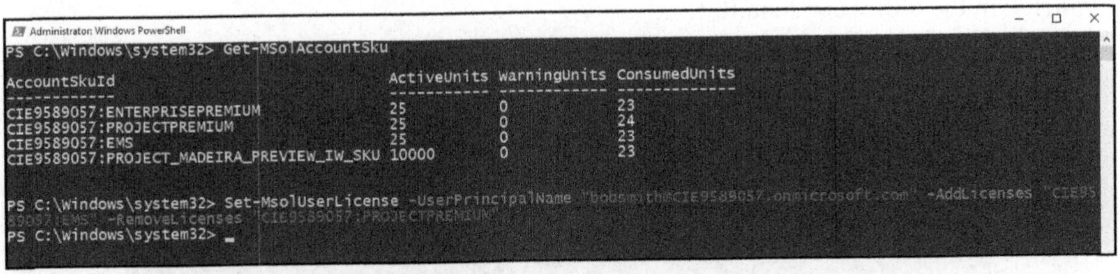

```
Administrator: Windows PowerShell
PS C:\Windows\system32> Get-MSolAccountSku

AccountSkuId                                 ActiveUnits WarningUnits ConsumedUnits
------------                                 ----------- ------------ -------------
CIE9589057:ENTERPRISEPREMIUM                 25          0            23
CIE9589057:PROJECTPREMIUM                    25          0            24
CIE9589057:EMS                               25          0            23
CIE9589057:PROJECT_MADEIRA_PREVIEW_IW_SKU    10000       0            23

PS C:\Windows\system32> Set-MsolUserLicense -UserPrincipalName "bobsmith@CIE9589057.onmicrosoft.com" -AddLicenses "CIE95
89057:EMS" -RemoveLicenses "CIE9589057:PROJECTPREMIUM"
PS C:\Windows\system32> _
```

This command replaces the Office 365 *Project Online Premium* license with an *Enterprise Mobility + Security E3* license. These changes are made in a single operation, and the user does not end up in an intermediate stage where one license is removed without the other being added.

Sometimes, we may require that, instead of assigning licenses to all the services in a license pack, we need to assign the licenses to a few selected services, for example, Exchange and SharePoint only.

To implement this, we need to create a custom license pack using the following cmdlet:

```
New-MSOLLicenseOptions
```

This cmdlet creates a `LicenseOptions` object and accepts two parameters, `AccountSkuId` (required parameter) and `DisabledPlans`:

- `[-AccountSkuId <String>]`: Specifies the license, or account's SKU ID, for these options
- `[-LicenseOptions System.Collections.Generic.List`1[System.String]`: Specifies a list of service plans to disable when assigning this license to the user

To create a custom license pack, we will first create a variable `$sku` and assign it the existing SKUs available in the tenant. Then we will create a custom license pack and assign it to a variable `$newSku`. While assigning the license, we will use the custom license pack assigned to the variable `$newSku`.

```
$sku = Get-MSolAccountSku
$sku.ServiceStatus
```

`$sku.ServiceStatus` will display all the individual service plans that are currently available in the Office 365 tenant.

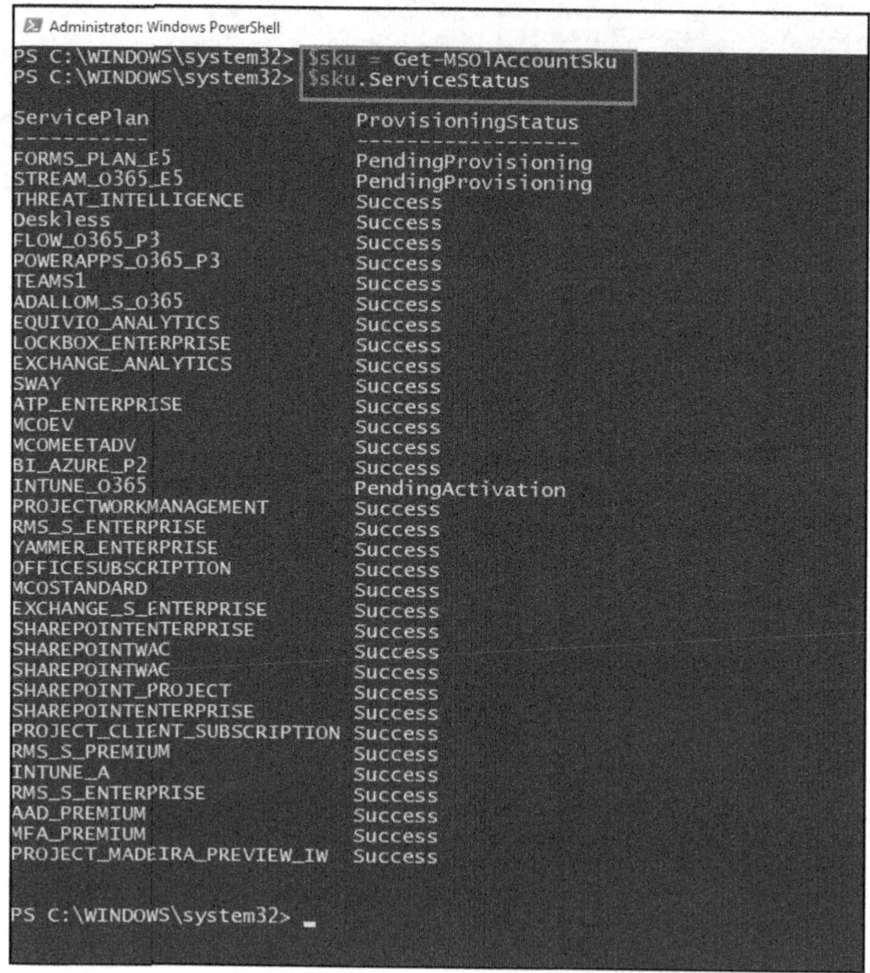

To create the new license SKU, we will need to pick and choose the service plans that are available and are active. The `ProvisioningStatus` is `Success` tells us that a service plan is ready for the use or not. Now let's create a new license SKU where we will not be assigning the license of Yammer and Sway to the newly created user `Bob Smith`. We can get the plan names from the `$sku.ServiceStatus` display.

```
$newSku = New-MSOLLicenseOptions -AccountSkuId
"CIE9589057:ENTERPRISEPREMIUM"
 -DisabledPlans "YAMMER_ENTERPRISE", "SWAY"
```

After this new SKU is created, we need to apply it to the user using the `Set-MSOLUserLicense` cmdlet:

```
Set-MsolUserLicense -userprincipalname
"bobsmith@CIE9589057.onmicrosoft.com" -LicenseOptions $newsku
```

Formatting data to be used for bulk account management

To create multiple users, assign licenses to multiple users, or do both at the same time, we can use data stored in a CSV file, text file, or even a SharePoint list.

In the following example, we will cover bulk user creation using a CSV file.

As mentioned previously, to create a new user the mandatory parameters are `userprincipalname` and `DisplayName`.

The CSV will need to be in the following format:

- `FirstName, LastName, Country`
- `Bob, Smith, USA`
- `Sanjay, Shah, UK`

To implement this, we will need to connect to the Office 365 service first and import the input file; the next step is to store the info in variables, and the last step is to create the users in Office 365:

```
$users = Import-CSV "C:\Users.csv"
foreach ( $user in $users){
  $FirstName = $user.FirstName
  $LastName = $user.LastName
```

```
        $DisplayName = build it as per company policy
        $userName = build it as per company policy
        New-MSOLUser -UserPrincipalName $userName -DisplayName $DisplayName
        -FirstName $FirstName -LastName $LastName -Country $user.Country
    }
```

When we run the preceding script, all the users get created in less than a minute. The Office 365 admin center would definitely have taken more time. The passwords of the newly created users will be displayed on the screen.

Once we refresh the Office 365 admin center, we can find the newly created users under the **Active users** section:

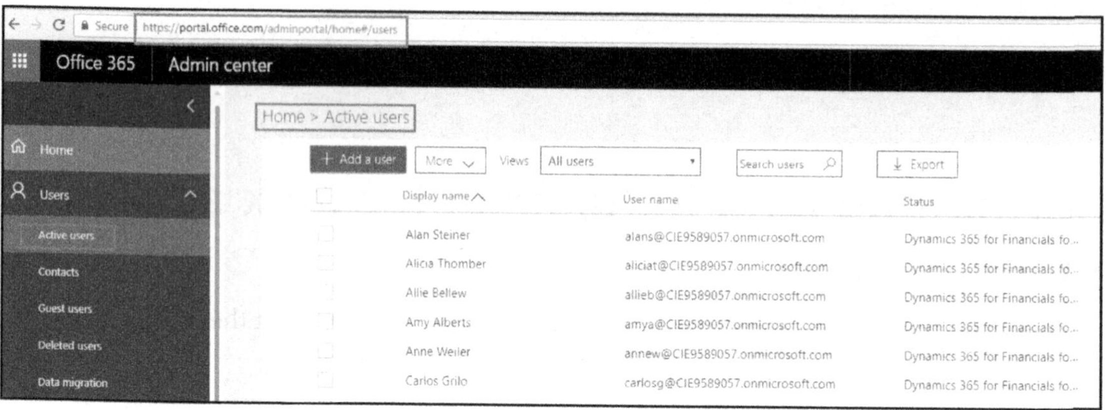

If we would like to assign the licenses to multiple users, we can use the following script. For example, if five to six interns join your organization, and you would like to assign identical licenses to them, we can use the following four steps and scripts:

1. Get all unlicensed users:

```
$unlicensed = Get-MsolUser -UnlicensedUsersOnly
```

2. Save them in a CSV file:

```
$unlicensed | Select-Object UserPrincipalName, DisplayName
 | Export-CSV unlicensed.csv -NoTypeInformation
```

3. Decide which users need licenses and manually delete the users we don't need.
4. Assign licenses:

```
$users = Import-CSV "unlicensed.csv"
 foreach ( $user in $users){
   Set-MSOLUserLicense
   -userprincipalname $user.UserPrincipalName
   -AddLicenses "Contoso:ENTERPRISEPACK"
 }
```

How to reset account passwords

To reset passwords, we need to use the following cmdlet:

```
Set-MsolUserPassword
```

This cmdlet resets the password for a user. It can be used for users with standard identities. The cmdlet accepts six parameters, as shown in the following list. Out of these six parameters, either `UserPrincipalName` or `ObjectId` is required:

- `[-ForceChangePassword <Boolean>]`: Indicates whether the user must change their password the next time they sign in.
- `[-ObjectId <Guid>]`: Specifies the unique ID of the user for whom to set the password.
- `[-UserPrincipalName <String>]`: Specifies the UserPrincipalName of the user for whom to set the password.
- `[-TenantId <Guid>]`: Specifies the unique ID of the tenant on which to perform the operation. The default value is the tenant of the current user. This parameter applies only to partner users.
- `[-ForceChangePasswordOnly <Boolean>]`: This will force the user to change the password.
- `[-NewPassword <String>]`: Specifies a new password for the user. If the user is set to require a strong password, then all of the following rules must be met:
    - The password must contain at least one lowercase letter.
    - The password must contain at least one uppercase letter.
    - The password must contain at least one non-alphanumeric character.

- The password cannot contain any spaces, tabs, or line breaks.
- The length of the password must be 8-16 characters.
- The username cannot be contained in the password. If you do not specify a password, the cmdlet generates a random password for the user.

To reset the password of the user `bob.smith@contoso.com` and generate a random password, we can use the following command. After the first sign in, the user will need to change the password:

```
Set-MsolUserPassword -UserPrincipalName "bob.smith@contoso.com"
 -ForceChangePassword $true
```

To change the password to a given password, we can use the following command. After the the first sign in, the user will need to change the password:

```
Set-MsolUserPassword -UserPrincipalName "bob.smith@consoso.com"
 -NewPassword "3&gEf[8bVC[5jSYr"
```

How to update user account details

So far we have seen how can we assign/remove bulk licenses for users. In this section, we will see how we can update user information such as `DisplayName`, `FirstName`, and `LastName`.

Let's take an example of a user who recently got married and would like to change their last name, or a user who changed departments. The following command will work if you are storing accounts in the cloud only. If you have directory sync or don't have two-way sync, then you will need to do these kinds of change in local Active Directory:

```
Set-MSOLUser -UserPrincipalName bob.smith@consoso.com -LastName
"NewLastName" -DisplayName "First Name New Last Name"
```

To verify the changes, use the following command:

```
Get-MSOLUser -UserPrincipalName "bob.smith@consoso.com"
```

You can also check this change out in the Office 365 admin center.

Summary

In this chapter, we covered how can we use PowerShell to automate user management and went through licensing-management tasks, for example, how to change licenses for existing users, how to remove accounts and licenses, how to reset account passwords, and how to update user account details.

In the next chapter, we will cover using PowerShell for Exchange Online.

4

Managing SharePoint Online Using PowerShell

In this chapter, we will go over the SharePoint Online API, but we would be remiss not to review the other APIs. They will be needed in order to configure and manage your SharePoint deployment.

As one of the most mature products in the Office 365 lineup, SharePoint has been instrumental in--if not the cornerstone of--Microsoft's online collaboration strategy. Over the years, SharePoint has expanded and gone through several transformations, accumulating several APIs in the process.

By the end of this chapter, you will learn how to use the SharePoint Online API and take advantage of the CSOM and REST APIs using PowerShell.

We will cover the following topics:

- Making sense of all the available APIs for SharePoint management
- Setting up your environment
- Administration tasks
- Additional tasks using CSOM/REST APIs

A brief overview of the SharePoint APIs

While learning SharePoint, you may find alternative solutions using different APIs. Although most will be conceptually useful, some may not be applicable to SharePoint Online. In this section, we will quickly recap what is available and how to leverage it.

The SharePoint web services API

Available since version 1, the SharePoint web services are implemented using SOAP. This protocol is intended for machine-to-machine communication and requires tedious XML message crafting. You can easily identify a web service example as it is hosted under the path `/_vti_bin` and uses the extension `.asmx`.
The SPServices project offers a JavaScript API that simplifies the use of SharePoint web services. It has many examples and a large community (`http://sympmarc.github.io/SPServices/`).

Even though web services can used in SharePoint Online, newer APIs are usually easier to use from PowerShell.

The SharePoint server-side API and PowerShell API

The server-side API was the method of choice for developers. The advantages include full access to all APIs and features of the platform and low latency as the scripts have to run on the SharePoint server. The deployment of server-side code entails small periods of unavailability and a slow development life cycle. Moreover, poor implementations can impact farm health. With the availability of sandboxed solutions (locked down server-side code, both in operations access and volume) and later with the move to client-side implementations, the server-side approach has lost a lot of traction.
Server-side examples can be ported to CSOM, but you will need some investments in learning C# and development concepts. Most examples will include references to *SPSite* (for site collections) and *SPWeb* (for websites).

Before PowerShell, administrators had to rely on `stsadm.exe`, a command-line tool that, although versatile, had limited access to the API. The PowerShell API was quickly adopted for administrative tasks as it provides a dynamic terminal for developers and administrators to deploy and maintain customizations.

On-premise PowerShell examples will reference `Get-SPSite` and `Get-SPWeb` for site collections and websites. The concepts can also be migrated to remote APIs, but none of the commands are available in the SharePoint Online API.

The client-side object model

The **client-side object model** (**CSOM**) is meant for remote scripting and was released to replace the cumbersome web services SOAP implementation. You will find examples in two flavors: the **JavaScript object model** (**JSOM**) and the C# implementation (CSOM). All examples are useful but only the C# version can be used from PowerShell. CSOM examples can be used in SharePoint Online, but not through the SharePoint Online API. Later on in this chapter we will go over how to work with it.

CSOM and JSOM make use of a batched request system (so that the user can package as many operations as possible in one single request to the server). You can recognize examples as both rely on the class `ClientContext` to manage the connection with the server.

The REST API

The REST API lets you use simple HTTP requests to achieve the same results as previous APIs. You can accomplish a lot by crafting a simple URL. We will review an example of how to use it because its adoption among developers has been significant. For administrators, its use is somewhat impractical as, in general parsing, the result is a cumbersome task in PowerShell.

You can identify REST API examples as the endpoint is hosted under the `/_api` path.

The SharePoint Online API

The Online API contains a subset of the options of the server-side implementation. One of the benefits of a managed deployment is delegating maintenance tasks, so it is expected that some tasks will simply not be needed. As the online platform matures, some *online-only* features have been rolled out and several methods are available only in this version.

All methods of the API follow this syntax: `verb-SPONoun`

Setting up your environment

Preparing your environment for SharePoint Online scripting is very simple.

PowerShell execution policy

As the preferred scripting tool for administrators, PowerShell security is paramount. We will review the execution policy in depth in `Chapter 6`, *Script Automation*, but by default it restricts scripts to running only in an interactive session.
In this mode, you cannot execute scripts in `.ps1` files (not even in the interactive mode) and unattended scripts will be blocked.

In the following example, we attempt to execute the `HelloWorld.ps1` file. The call is blocked and the error message suggests that you look into the execution policy setting.

In the next line, we use the `Get-ExecutionPolicy` command to get a list of settings for all the different execution scopes.

The execution policy is effective on a certain context. The default scope is `CurrentUser`, this means that your policy changes will only apply to your account unless a specific scope is set. This is important when unattended scripts with service accounts and we will review it again in the `Chapter 6`, *Script Automation*. As you might expect, we can modify the scope value to run script files in interactive mode:

```
Set-ExecutionPolicy Unrestricted -Scope CurrentUser
```

You will be prompted for confirmation and then we can verify that the change is effective with the `Get-ExecutionPolicy` command:

```
Windows PowerShell
PS C:\temp> Set-ExecutionPolicy Unrestricted -Scope CurrentUser

Execution Policy Change
The execution policy helps protect you from scripts that you do not trust. Changing the execution policy might expose
you to the security risks described in the about_Execution_Policies help topic at
http://go.microsoft.com/fwlink/?LinkID=135170. Do you want to change the execution policy?
[Y] Yes  [A] Yes to All  [N] No  [L] No to All  [S] Suspend  [?] Help (default is "N"): y
PS C:\temp> Get-ExecutionPolicy
Unrestricted
PS C:\temp> _
```

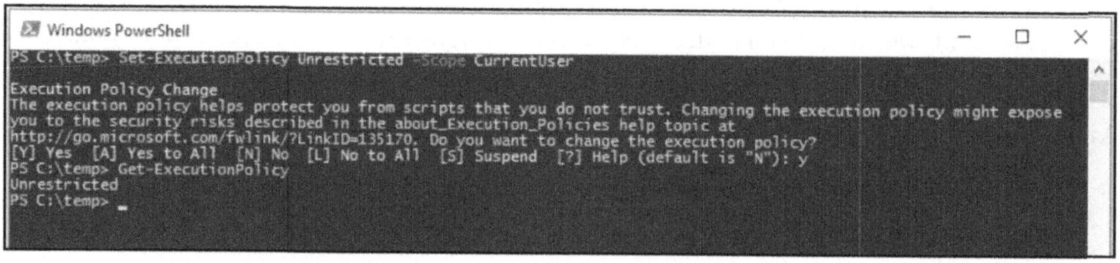

In the context of this chapter, we'll set the value to `Unrestricted`, which will allow us to execute scripts. But note that for unattended or production scenarios, `AllSigned` or `RemoteSigned` are preferable.

The PowerShell version
PowerShell version 3 is required for the SharePoint Online module. This version is bundled in modern operating systems, but you may run into dependency issues if you mistakenly open an older version or if PowerShell 3 is not available.
In the following script, we use the `$PSVersionTable` global variable and exit the script if the version is less than 3.

The following screenshot shows the output for `$PSVersionTable`:

```
Windows PowerShell
PS C:\temp> if ($PSVersionTable.PSVersion.Major -lt 4) {
>> Write-Error "PowerShell 3 is required!"
>> return;
>> }
PS C:\temp> $PSVersionTable

Name                           Value
----                           -----
PSVersion                      5.1.14393.693
PSEdition                      Desktop
PSCompatibleVersions           {1.0, 2.0, 3.0, 4.0...}
BuildVersion                   10.0.14393.693
CLRVersion                     4.0.30319.42000
WSManStackVersion              3.0
PSRemotingProtocolVersion      2.3
SerializationVersion           1.1.0.1
```

SharePoint Online Management Shell

The Management Shell installer (`http://go.microsoft.com/fwlink/p/?LinkId=255251`) will copy the modules to your machine and set up a **SharePoint Online Management Shell** shortcut.

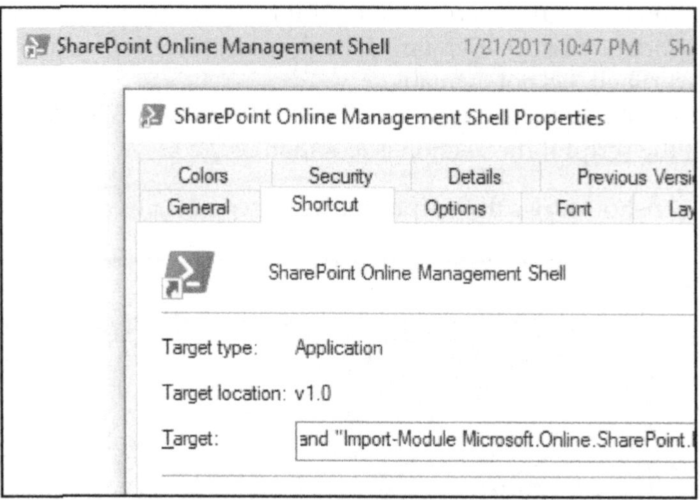

The shortcut will open PowerShell and preload the SharePoint Online module. The shortcut's target shows how this is done and introduces us to the `Import-Module` command:

```
powershell.exe -NoExit -Command "Import-Module
Microsoft.Online.SharePoint.PowerShell `
-DisableNameChecking;"
```

The `Import-Module` command allows us to load modules on demand and will be necessary when creating unattended scripts. We will review this and other related commands in a later chapter.

For the time being, the following script shows how to check whether the module is available and load it if necessary:

```
if ((Get-Module Microsoft.Online.SharePoint.PowerShell).Count -eq 0) {
    Write-Host 'Loading SharePoint.Powershell'
    Import-Module Microsoft.Online.SharePoint.PowerShell -
DisableNameChecking
}
```

Because SharePoint Online is in constant evolution, the cadence of API updates is much faster than for on-premise. If a command is not available or the parameters do not match the documentation, you probably have an older version of the API. The following example shows how to retrieve version information for the module:

```
Windows PowerShell
PS C:\temp> $module = Get-Module Microsoft.Online.SharePoint.PowerShell
PS C:\temp> $module.Version

Major  Minor  Build  Revision
-----  -----  -----  --------
16     0      6008   0

PS C:\temp> _
```

Security requirements

The minimum privilege required for SPO API access is being a SharePoint Online **Global Administrator**. Tenant administrators will also be able to use the API. However, it is good practice to set up a dedicated scripting account with that specific role. If the account is only going to be used for that purpose, you do not need to assign it a license:

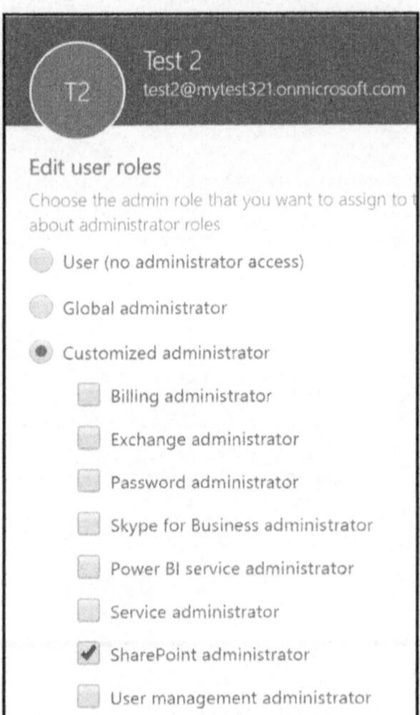

You can assign the permission to individual accounts in the tenant administrator site.

The SharePoint Online API supports multi-factor authentication in an interactive session. However, an account with multi-factor authentication cannot be used for unattended scripting.

Now that we have covered the requirements, we can finally start using the API.

SharePoint Online scripting

To be able to connect to your tenant, you will use the `Connect-SPOService` command. The command takes the URL of the admin site of your tenant and the credentials for the session.
The admin URL is usually of the `yourdomain-admin.sharepoint.com` form, but you can get the actual URL by going to the site through the Office 365 admin center:

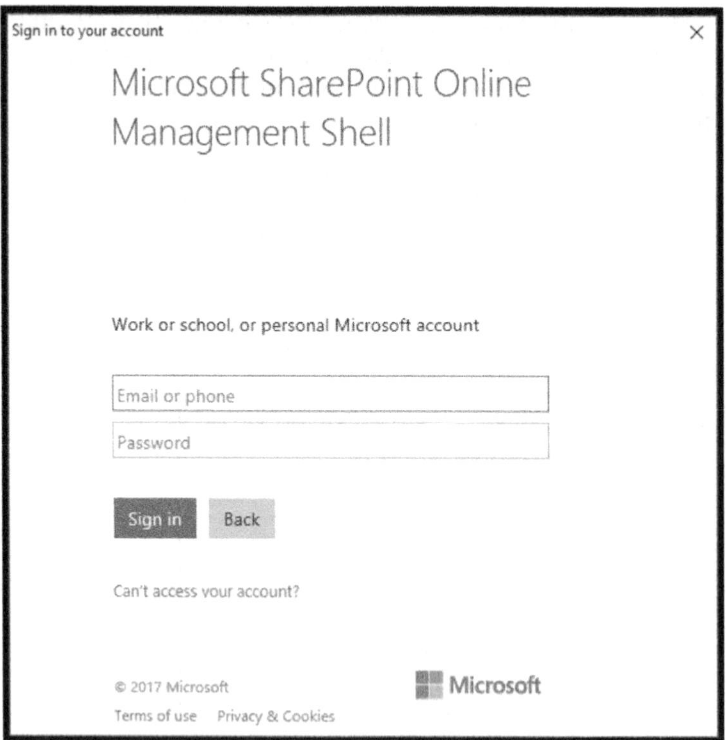

The prompt is displayed when connecting to SharePoint Online. Not all the APIs support it, but SharePoint Online will prompt for credentials, allowing you to go through the MFS workflow if needed.

If you run the command without parameters, the credential prompt will be used.

It is good practice to store credentials in a variable, as it is often reused when connecting to other APIs.

```
$credentials = Get-Credential Connect-SPOService `
 -Url https://mytest321-admin.sharepoint.com `
 -Credential $credentials
```

The `Connect-SPOService` command will establish a connection that will live throughout the current PowerShell session or until the user runs the `Disconnect-SPOService` command. Executing `Connect-SPOService` will also disconnect an active connection before establishing a new one. This presents a challenge when working on multi-tenant scenarios. You will only be able to connect to one tenant at a time, which implies having to save information to the filesystem or elsewhere between connections.

Before we start with the different scripting scenarios, let's combine the methods we reviewed to create a connection script:

```
if ($PSVersionTable.PSVersion.Major -lt 3){
    Write-Error 'PowerShell 3 is required!'
    return;
}

if ((Get-Module Microsoft.Online.SharePoint.PowerShell).Count -eq 0) {
    Write-Host 'Loading SharePoint.Powershell'
    Import-Module Microsoft.Online.SharePoint.PowerShell -DisableNameChecking
}

$adminUrl = 'https://mytest321-admin.sharepoint.com'

Connect-SPOService -Url $adminUrl

Write-Host "Connected to $adminUrl" -ForegroundColor Green
```

The `Connect.ps1` file is far from perfect. For example, we could set up a parameter for the tenant URL and provide an option to cache the credentials. We will improve this script in the `Chapter 6`, *Script Automation*.

Further examples will assume that you already have an active connection and that you will dispose of the connection when done.

In the following scenarios, we cover the most common situations, but there are too many parameters to completely cover all of them. Fortunately, you have many resources to fill in any gaps and cover future features. PowerShell has a `Get-Help` command that is very handy since you can get help directly on the console. We encourage you to explore the different options of this command, but our favorite is the `-Online` parameter, as it will open the help web page for the selected command. In our writing experience, we found that the online documentation is updated more frequently than the PowerShell version.

Here are a few examples of how to use the `Get-Help` command:

```
Get-Help Command -Examples
Get-Help Command -Detailed
Get-Help Command -Parameter ParameterName
Get-Help Command -Online
```

At the time of writing, both examples and parameter documentation are scarce in the SPO documentation. Your best bet is to use the `-Online` parameter, yet we found that in some situations, the URL is not set on the command but the help page exists.

Scenario 1 - getting to know the API

The SharePoint Online API has about 60 commands. This is a low number in comparison to other modules. This is because there are other SharePoint APIs available and the Online API focuses on tenant and site collection operations.

In this sample, we will try to visualize the entire command set. The end result might be a useful reference, but the script itself is a good example of how to manipulate collections in PowerShell. Take a moment to review the list of commands. The first command in the list is `Get-SPOAppErrors`:

```
SharePoint Online Command Count (build: 6323): 65

Noun                                Verbs
----                                -----
SPOAppErrors                        Get
SPOAppInfo                          Get
```

```
SPOCrossGeoMovedUsers                    Get
SPOCrossGeoUsers                         Get
SPODeletedSite                           Get, Remove, Restore
SPOExternalUser                          Get, Remove
SPOMigrationEncryptedPackage             ConvertTo
SPOMigrationEncryptionParameters         New
SPOMigrationEncryptUploadSubmit          Invoke
SPOMigrationJob                          Remove, Submit
SPOMigrationJobProgress                  Get
SPOMigrationJobStatus                    Get
SPOMigrationPackage                      New
SPOMigrationPackageAzureSource           Set
SPOMigrationTargetedPackage              ConvertTo
SPOPersonalSite                          Request
SPOPublicCdnOrigin                       New, Remove
SPOPublicCdnOrigins                      Get
SPOSdnProvider                           New, Remove
SPOService                               Connect, Disconnect
SPOSite                                  Get, New, Remove, Repair, Set, Test,
Upgrade
SPOSiteGroup                             Get, New, Remove, Set
SPOTenant                                Get, Set
SPOTenantCdnEnabled                      Get, Set
SPOTenantCdnOrigin                       Add, Remove
SPOTenantCdnOrigins                      Get
SPOTenantCdnPolicies                     Get
SPOTenantCdnPolicy                       Set
SPOTenantLogEntry                        Get
SPOTenantLogLastAvailableTimeInUtc       Get
SPOTenantSyncClientRestriction           Get, Remove, Set
SPOTenantTaxonomyReplicationParameters Get, Set
SPOUpgradeEvaluationSite                 Request
SPOUser                                  Add, Get, Remove, Set
SPOUserAndContentMove                    Start, Stop
SPOUserAndContentMoveState               Get
SPOUserOneDriveLocation                  Get
SPOUserSession                           Revoke
SPOWebTemplate                           Get
```

From build `16.0.6008` to `16.0.6323`, the command count went from `59` to `65`. This script takes advantage of the fact that the methods of the API follow the syntax: `<<verb>> -SPO <<noun>>`.

We will group scripts by nouns and display all available verbs in a table. The first step is to get a list of all the methods. To be certain that we have all the methods, we use the `ExportedCommands` property of the module:

```
$module = Get-Module Microsoft.Online.SharePoint.PowerShell
$commands = $module.ExportedCommands.Values
```

In practice, a better approach is to use `Get-Command`, as it will let you search across all loaded modules and make use of wildcards. This command is particularly helpful when you do not remember the exact command name:

```
Get-Command *-SPO*
```

What follows could be considered advanced PowerShell, so do not get discouraged if it is difficult to understand at first. It is representative of the types of manipulation that are common and that PowerShell excels in.

In the next line, we make use of `Select` to create calculated properties for each command. The `Verb` and `Noun` columns are the values before and after the `'-'` of the command name. Each calculated property has a `Name` and an `Expression` property that can be set as needed. In the `Expression` property, we get a reference to the command using the `$_` variable.

We then pipe the results through the `Sort` and `Group` commands that help in organizing the results:

```
# group commands by noun and create a 'Verb' property
$gs = $commands | Select @{ Name = 'Noun'; Expression = { `
$_.Name.Split('-')[-1] }} , # the -1 index will return the last item  of
the array @{ Name = 'Verb'; `
Expression = { $_.Name.Split('-')[0] }} `
Sort-Object Noun, Verb | Group-Object Noun
```

At this point, `$gs` has a record for each `Noun` group. We will create a calculated `Verbs` property that aggregates all the verbs within each group. Verbs are of particular interest because their expression loops through the group's items and aggregates the `Verb` property of command. In this case, we are using a `ForEach` loop with the `-Begin`, `-Process`, and `-End` options. Within the loop, we set the value of a property `$vs` that will hold the aggregation of all the verbs as a string.

To complete the script, we pipe the results to the `Format-Table` command. This command takes care of formatting the results as a table:

```
# print command groups and list available verbs
$gs | Select @{N = 'Noun'; E = {$_.Name}},
# N and E are shorthand for Name and Expression
@{ Name = 'Verbs'; Expression={$_.Group | `
# Aggregate the Verb property of each command into the new calculated
'Verbs' column
ForEach-Object -Begin {$vs='';} -Process { $vs += $_.Verb + ', ';} -End
{$vs.Trim(', ')}}} | `
Format-Table
```

The following is the complete script:

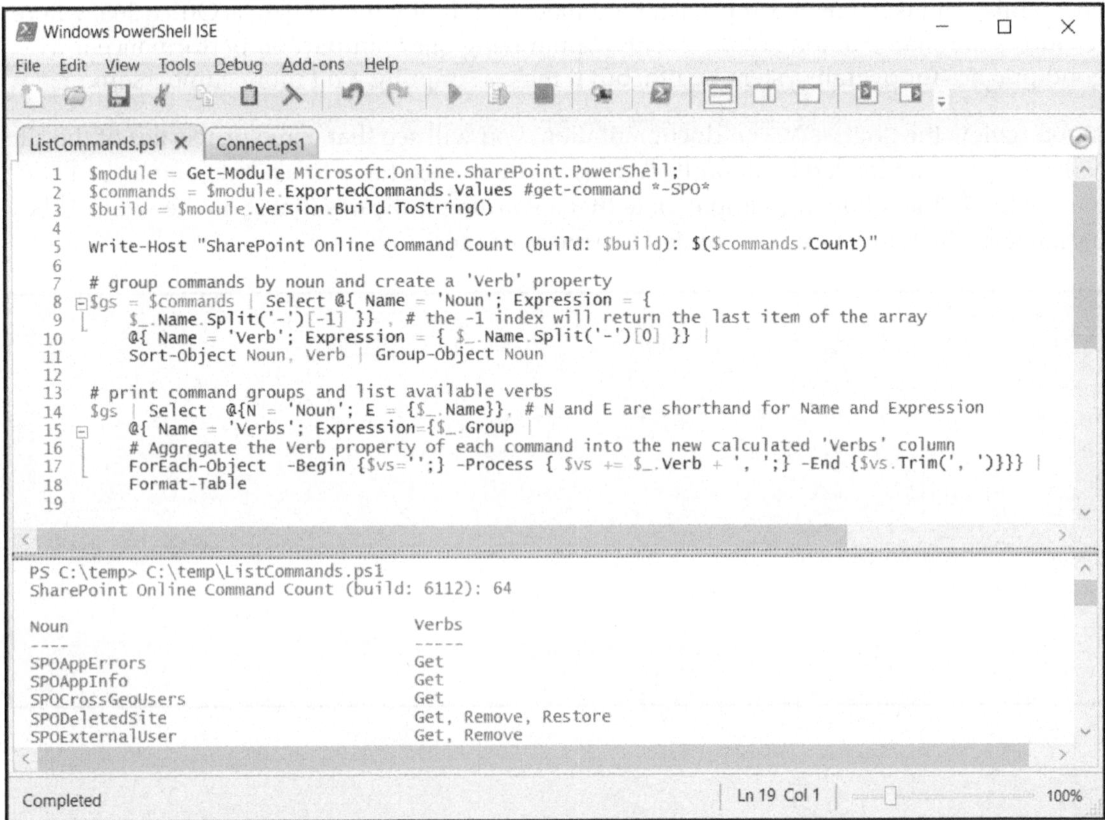

Scenario 2 - site collection information

Aside from global settings, site collections are the primary target of the SharePoint Online administrator.

Let's use the `Get-SPOSite` command to list all the site collections in the tenant. In this example, we are filtering out sites that contain `contentTypeHub` in their URL and using the `IncludePersonalSite` option so that personal sites are not excluded:

```
Get-SPOSite -Filter { Url -notlike 'contentTypeHub'} `
-IncludePersonalSite $true
```

The fact that personal sites are excluded by default is an indication of how the API tries to avoid loading information unless necessary or explicitly requested. This is a deviation from on-premise and is a sensible approach for a managed deployment such as Office 365, where resources are shared among many clients. Minimizing query impact on performance is a good practice for overall system health, but it makes scripting a bit more cumbersome.

If you review the `Get-SPOSite` documentation, you will see that some properties of the site collections are not loaded by default. To retrieve them, you have to use the `-Detailed` parameter. In the following sample, note that a warning indicates that soon the `-Detailed` parameter will not work when applied to groups of sites:

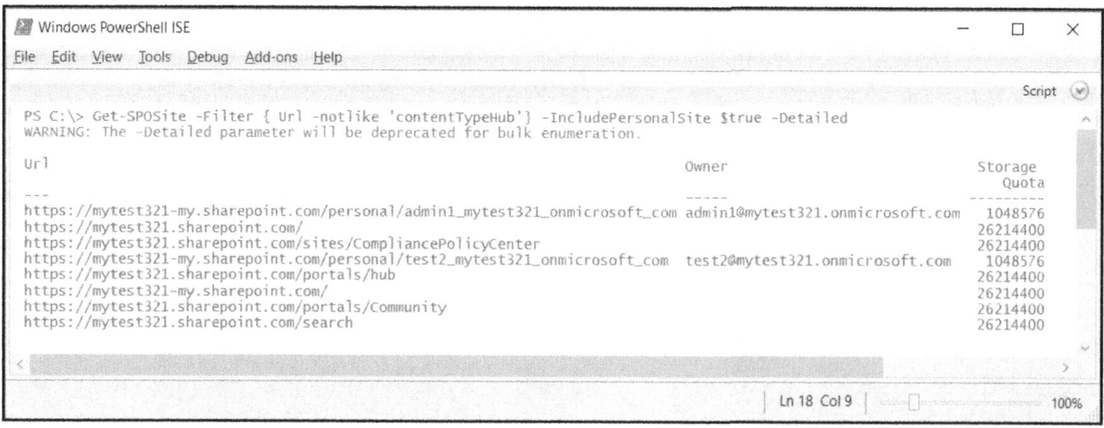

The warning indicates that a better approach is needed. The adjusted sample gets all site collections and then iterates over them, retrieving them with the `-Detailed` parameter individually:

```
$allSites = Get-SPOSite -Filter { Url -notlike 'contentTypeHub'} `
 -IncludePersonalSite $true

$allSites | foreach { $allSites[$allSites.IndexOf($_)] = Get-SPOSite
 $_ ` -Detailed };
```

The end result of the script is the same as the previous one. This script is actually noticeably slower because it is making *n+1* requests instead of just one. This chatty approach is preferred because it spreads out the task into multiple queries, thus minimizing the resources needed to service each individual request:

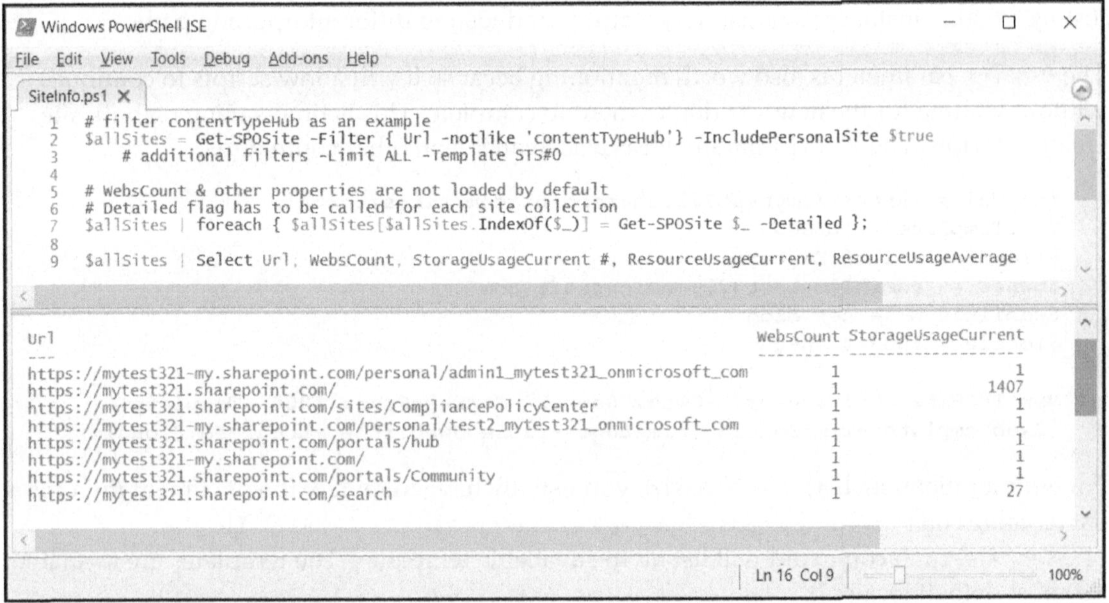

Scenario 3 - site collection maintenance

In this scenario, we will cover typical maintenance operations when working with site collections. The following is the syntax for the `New-SPOSite` command:

```
New-SPOSite [-Url] <UrlCmdletPipeBind> -Owner <String> -StorageQuota
<Int64> `
[-CompatibilityLevel <Int32>] [-LocaleId <UInt32>] `
[-NoWait <SwitchParameter>] `
[-ResourceQuota <Double>] [-Template <String>] `
[-TimeZoneId <Int32>] [-Title <String>]
```

At the time of writing, the `CompatibilityLevel` parameter accepts only the current value, `15`. With the next major release, both `15` and `16` will be temporarily available. Administrators will find this parameter and other related commands that are useful in testing existing instances against new features and testing different upgrade paths.

The `NoWait` parameter is also worth mentioning because it will allow scripts to continue without waiting for the new site deployment to complete. This is time-saving on bulk site creation scripts. The `NoWait` parameter is also available in other commands:

```
$newUrl = 'https://mytest321.sharepoint.com/sites/testA'
$webTemplate = 'BLOG#0'
$timeZone = 10 # Eastern
$owner = 'admin1@mytest321.onmicrosoft.com'
$webTitle = 'A new Blog'
$locale = 1033 # en-US

New-SPOSite -Url $newUrl -Owner $owner -StorageQuota 1000 -Template `
 $webTemplate -TimeZoneId $timeZone -Title $webTitle -LocaleId $locale
```

For enumerations such as `TimeZoneId`, you usually have to review the documentation for a list of values (`http://go.microsoft.com/fwlink/p/?LinkId=242912`). The `Get-SPOWebTemplate` command will list all the available templates. The templates are available for most default locales (`https://msdn.microsoft.com/en-us/library/ms912047(v=winembedded.10).aspx`), but you can verify that the template/locale combination is valid with the `LocaleId` parameter.

Next, we will update the site with the `Set-SPOSite` command:

```
$siteUrl = 'https://mytest321.sharepoint.com/sites/testA1' `
Set-SPOSite -Identity $siteUrl -Title 'Blog A1' -Owner 1 `
'test2@mytest321.onmicrosoft.com'
```

Some operations (such as `Test-SPOSite`) require the scripting account to also be a site collection administrator. If you want to add an additional site collection administrator instead of changing the site owner, you use the `Set-SPOUser` command:

```
Set-SPOUser $siteUrl -LoginName test2@mytest321.onmicrosoft.com `
 -IsSiteCollectionAdmin $true
```

When using `Set-SPOSite`, you will run into issues that are not documented. For example, the `NewUrl` parameter was used to migrate legacy (BPOS) sites to the new SharePoint Online domain (`https://products.office.com/en-IN/sharepoint/collaboration?ms.officeurl=sharepoint`) and cannot be used to change the URL of an existing site collection. Not being able to change a site collection URL is a major problem for administrators. Keep this in mind when planning your deployment. Another issue is that the `LocaleId` parameter cannot be used for sites that already have a template assigned. It is understandable that changing the language of a site is not supported since several files and other resources get deployed when a site template is applied. Changing the URL of a site collection, however, is something that the administrator can do on the premises, and it was removed from the online platform. There are good reasons behind this, but if you think it is something that should be part of SharePoint Online, use the user voice to get the feature added.

Testing site health

As an administrator, you will be faced with troubleshooting a broken site. Often, changes and customizations by developers or administrators lead to problems that may not be evident immediately. Often, issues are not addressed until a breaking change is found during an upgrade. The first of the tools at our disposal to help us in troubleshooting is the `Test-SPOSite` command.

The command allows you to check several rules against your site collection, producing a report that will help you to take action. By default, the command will return a result with an array of all the rules tested and individual results:

```
Test-SPOSite -Identity $siteUrl

SiteUrl : https://mytest321.sharepoint.com/sites/testA1
Results : {
 SPSiteHealthResult Status=Passed RuleName="Conflicting Content Types"
 RuleId=befe203b-a8c0-48c2-b5f0-27c10f9e1622,
 SPSiteHealthResult Status=FailedWarning RuleName="Customized Files"
 RuleId=cd839b0d-9707-4950-8fac-f306cb920f6c,
 SPSiteHealthResult Status=Passed RuleName="Missing Galleries"
 RuleId=ee967197-ccbe-4c00-88e4-e6fab81145e1,
```

```
 SPSiteHealthResult Status=Passed RuleName="Missing Parent Content Types"
 RuleId=a9a6769f-7289-4b9f-ae7f-5db4b997d284...}
PassedCount : 6
FailedWarningCount : 1
FailedErrorCount : 0
```

The response shows us that one of the rules has a warning; let's produce a list of all the rules tested first, and we will dig further on the rule with the issue.

In the following code, we iterate over the results and select the rule's name and ID:

```
$testResult = Test-SPOSite -Identity $siteUrl

$testResult.Results | Select @{N='Name'; E= {$_.Rule.Name}}, @{N='Id'; E= `
{$_.Rule.Id}}

Name                                             Id
----                                             --
Conflicting Content Types                        befe203b-a8c0-48c2-
b5f0-27c10f9e1622
Customized Files                                 cd839b0d-9707-4950-8fac-
f306cb920f6c
Missing Galleries                                ee967197-ccbe-4c00-88e4-
e6fab81145e1
Missing Parent Content Types                     a9a6769f-7289-4b9f-
ae7f-5db4b997d284
Missing Site Templates                           5258ccf5-e7d6-4df7-
b8ae-12fcc0513ebd
Unsupported Language Pack References             99c946f7-5751-417c-89d3-
b9c8bb2d1f66
Unsupported MUI References                       6da06aab-c539-4e0d-b111-
b1da4408859a
```

Now let's identify the rule that failed and print its description:

```
ForEach ($rule in $testResult.Results | Where { $_.Status -ne 'Passed' }) {
 Write-Host $rule.Message
}
The following files have been customized from their default and may present
some unexpected visuals or behavior after upgrade:
 - https://mytest321.sharepoint.com/sites/testA1/default.aspx - <a
href="...">Reset page to default</a>
Reset specific pages to default to make the page lose customizations and
any embedded data. Normally, you should do this only if you are having
difficulty using the page after upgrade.
```

Customized or *unghosted* pages are one of the most common issues that affect an upgrade. The preceding message shows the URL of the customized page and the suggested action.

Often, addressing individual pages or items individually is impossible due to availability resources, or the number of occurrences. Alternatively, the `Request-SPOUpgradeEvaluationSite` command will create a copy of the site collection so you can attempt the upgrade without affecting the original site collection. This approach is often helpful in identifying false positives (customized pages may work depending on many factors) and often shows issues that a simple test was not able to identify:

```
Request-SPOUpgradeEvaluationSite [-Identity] <SpoSitePipeBind> ^
[-Confirm [<SwitchParameter>]] [-NoEmail <SwitchParameter>] ^
[-NoUpgrade <SwitchParameter>] [-WhatIf [<SwitchParameter>]]
```

The command will send an email to the administrator unless the `NoEmail` parameter is used. The `NoUpgrade` command allows you to make changes before scheduling the upgrade. To perform an upgrade, we will use the `Upgrade-SPOSite` command:

```
Upgrade-SPOSite [-Identity] <SPOSitePipeBind> [-VersionUpgrade] `
[-NoEmail] [-WhatIf] [-Confirm]
```

This is another command that requires the scripting account to be a site collection administrator. At the time of writing, we cannot test this method since only one version is allowed. Since SharePoint Online changes have been pushed at a much faster pace, it is conceivable that we will not see a major version in the foreseeable future. The relevance of the upgrade methods will most likely diminish as Microsoft switches to small but steady functionality deployments.

We will finish this section with the methods related to deleting site collections. On-premise site collection deletions used to be unrecoverable unless you had backups. In Office 365, the Recycle Bin concept has been implemented for site collections. Deleting a site moves it to the Recycle Bin, making the site unavailable. You have 30 days to restore the site; after this, the site collection will be deleted permanently.

The following script shows how to delete a site, confirm that it is in the Recycle Bin, and then restore it and delete it permanently:

```
$siteUrl = 'https://mytest321.sharepoint.com/sites/testA1'

Remove-SPOSite $siteUrl -Confirm:$false

Get-SPODeletedSite

Url                                    Storage Quota Resource Quota Deletion
Time Days Remaining
---                                    ------------- -------------- -----------
-- --------------
https://mytest321..../sites/testA1         26214400                0
2/21/2017  4:58:48 AM 30

Restore-SPODeletedSite $siteUrl

Remove-SPOSite $siteUrl -Confirm:$false

Remove-SPODeletedSite $siteUrl -Confirm:$false
```

Scenario 4 - personal sites

Historically, personal sites (or My Sites) have been a management problem. When planning a deployment, you have to consider your user base, the turnover in your organization, the internal policy for content storage, and many other factors. In Office 365, some of these factors have been addressed, but broadly My Sites deployment (as well as any other large-scale site deployment) remains a usage problem.

With the introduction of quotas, you can cap both storage and resources allocated for a site. By default, My Sites gets 1 GB of space; unfortunately, the quotas cannot be set in the `Request-SPOPersonalSite` command, which is used to provision personal sites.

Another issue with personal sites is that it takes a few minutes to set them up. It is very common that an administrator will pre-provision personal sites for the organization. At the time of writing, OneDrive is implemented as personal sites, which means that the scripts we will review also apply for provisioning OneDrive. This is a very common task for migrations to the cloud:

```
Request-SPOPersonalSite -UserEmails <String[]> [-NoWait <SwitchParameter>]
```

The `Request-SPOPersonalSite` command has only two parameters, yet its usage is worth documenting due to some common issues.

When deploying for a small list of users, an inline array of strings will schedule the creation of the sites. It is worth noting that the command will not return errors if the users are not found or if the user count exceeds 200 items. In general, you will have to validate that the process is complete:

```
Request-SPOPersonalSite -UserEmails `
'test2@mytest321.onmicrosoft.com', `
'admin1@mytest321.onmicrosoft.com' -NoWait
```

It is very common that the list of users will be read from a file or a CSV input. In the following example, we parse a comma-separated list of emails using `Split`. Even though the documentation specifies an array of strings, this call will not work unless we transform the string array into an object array through the use of the `Where` command:

```
Request-SPOPersonalSite -UserEmails
('test2@mytest321.onmicrosoft.com,admin1@mytest321.onmicrosoft.com'.Split('
,')| `
 Where-Object {$true})
```

Another common scenario is to deploy personal sites for a list of users already in SharePoint Online. The following script will retrieve all users with a valid login (a login in the form of an email). Note the use of the `ExpandProperty` parameter to return just the `LoginName` property of the users:

```
$users = Get-SPOUser -Site https://mytest321.sharepoint.com |
 Where-Object { $_.IsGroup -ne $true -and $_.LoginName -like '*@*.*'} `
 | Select-Object -ExpandProperty LoginName;
```

If the list is small, we can iterate over the list of users or schedule the provisioning in one call. It is safe to schedule the personal site for a user that already has one (it will be silently skipped), but there will be no warning when submitting over 200 requests:

```
#indivudal request
$users | ForEach-Object {
 Request-SPOPersonalSite -UserEmails $_
}

#bulk
Request-SPOPersonalSite -UserEmails $users
```

When dealing with many users, we can create groups of 200 items and submit them in bulk instead:

```
# Group by requests of 200 emails ------------------------------------------
---------------------
$groups = $users | Group-Object {[int]($users.IndexOf($_)/200)}

# send requests in 200 batches, do no wait for a response
$groups | ForEach-Object {
 $logins = $_.Group;
 Write-Host 'Creating sites for: '$logins
 Request-SPOPersonalSite -NoWait -UserEmails $logins
}
```

It is up to the administrator to verify the successful completion of the request. By default the command will not show any messages if a user is not found.

To complete the scenario the following script will select and delete all personal sites:

```
$mySites = Get-SPOSite -IncludePersonalSite $true -Filter { Url -like `
'/personal/'}
$mySites | Remove-SPOSite -Confirm:$false
```

The last big topic concerning site collections is document migrations; we will cover these in depth in `Chapter 9`, PowerShell Core, since most content applies in both cases.

Scenario 5 - sharing and external access

Being able to collaborate with external partners has been a long-awaited feature. In SharePoint Online, you can easily share sites and files with guest accounts even in an anonymous scheme. This added flexibility comes with great responsibility to the users sharing the content. Ultimately, it is the administrators who are responsible for security policies that are aligned with the business needs.

Even though the feature is relatively new, the number of options for the external sharing feature can be daunting. The following screenshot tries to map security settings in the user interface with the corresponding PowerShell configuration setting:

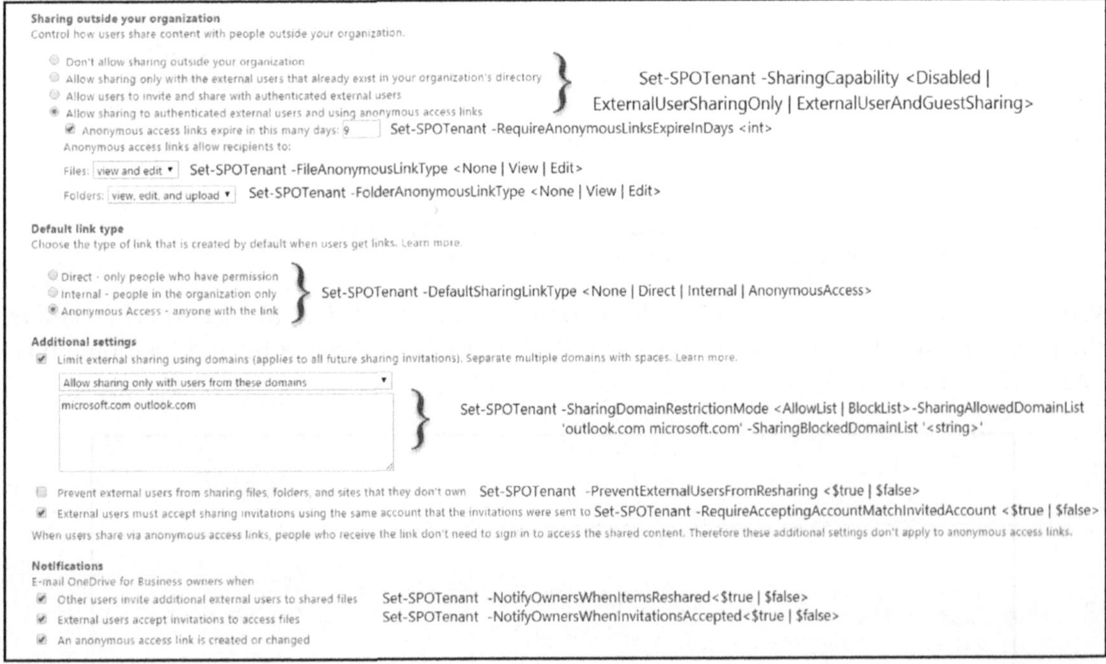

External sharing page in the SharePoint admin center: adminsiteurl/_layouts/15/online/ExternalSharing.aspx

The external sharing setting is set at the tenant level with the `Set-SPOTenant` command (however, some settings can also be set at the site-collection level).

Set the `SharingCapability` parameter to one of the following values:

- `Disabled`: External sharing is not allowed
- `ExistingExternalUserSharingOnly`: Sharing is allowed only with external accounts that have been added to your tenant
- `ExternalSharingOnly`: Sharing by email is enabled, but the guest link is disabled
- `ExternalUserAndGuestSharing`: Sharing by email and guest link is enabled

The `ExistingExternalUserSharingOnly` setting is useful if you have a set group of external accounts that need access. In this case, users will not be able to invite additional external accounts, neither will they be able to create guest links (anonymous access). You will have to add these accounts through Azure Active Directory.

For the other two settings where you allow invitations to external users, you have the option to limit access through either the inclusion or exclusion of a set of domains.

The following scripts limit invitations to accounts in the `outlook.com` and `microsoft.com` domains:

```
Set-SPOTenant -SharingDomainRestrictionMode AllowList `
-SharingAllowedDomainList 'outlook.com microsoft.com'
```

When trying to invite an account in a domain that is not whitelisted, the action is blocked in the people picker. The same result applies if you use the blocklist setting and the domain is in `SharingBlockedDomainList`:

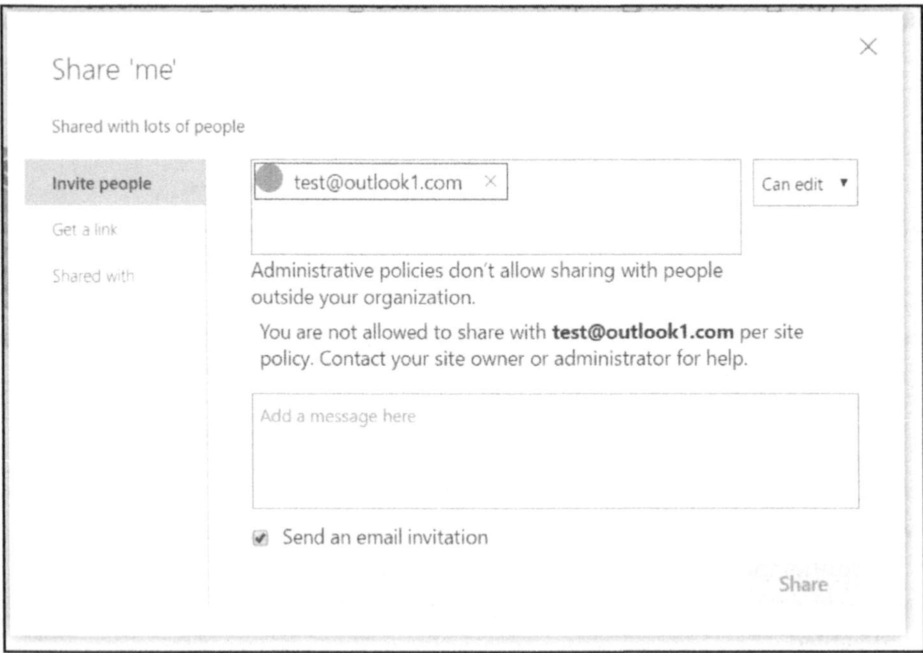

In this example, `test@outlook1.com` is not whitelisted; therefore, it is not allowed.

The invitation workflow can be locked down so that only the email invited can complete the invitation process. It is common, for example, that a user might receive the invitation to the intended email, but upon clicking on the link, the browser is opened with a personal account signed in. In this case, the workflow will be completed with the personal account, which might not be the desired outcome. To prevent this situation, we can use the `RequireAcceptingAccountMatchInvitedAccount` parameter:

```
Set-SPOTenant -RequireAcceptingAccountMatchInvitedAccount $true
```

To monitor the invitation workflow, you can be copied on invitation emails with `BccExternSharingInvitations`. You can also notify content owners when invitations are accepted and when items are re-shared:

```
Set-SPOTenant -BccExternalSharingInvitations $true `
-BccExternalSharingInvitationsList 'admin1@mytest321.onmicrosoft.com'
Set-SPOTenant -NotifyOwnersWhenItemsReshared $true `
-NotifyOwnersWhenInvitationsAccepted $true
```

Lastly, external users can be prevented from sharing files they do not own with `PreventExternalUsersFromResharing parameter`:

```
Set-SPOTenant -PreventExternalUsersFromResharing $true
```

Guest access

A user may generate a link to share a file. The link can be used by the recipient or shared with someone else:

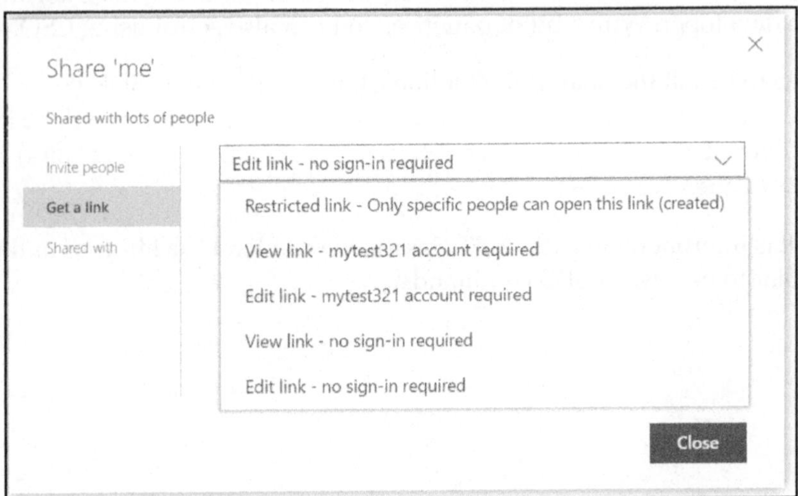

The links can require the user to be authenticated or not. For anonymous guest links, you can limit the permissions of the guest using the `FileAnonymousLinkType` and `FolderAnonymousLinkType` parameters:

```
Set-SPOTenant -FolderAnonymousLinkType <None|View|Edit> `
-FileAnonymousLinkType <None|View|Edit>
```

Additionally, you may want to limit the lifetime of guest links to a certain number of days:

```
Set-SPOTenant -RequireAnonymousLinksExpireInDays <int>
```

When using the **Get a link** feature, you can set the default type using the `DefaultSharingLinkType` parameter:

```
Set-SPOTenant -DefaultSharingLinkType
<None|Internal|Direct|AnonymousAccess>
```

Scenario 6 - CSOM scripting using PowerShell

At this point, we have covered the majority of SPO commands. As you can see, there is a significant number of tasks that are simply not covered by this API. The CSOM API is a set of .NET classes used by developers to configure and customize SharePoint and is needed in most scenarios not covered already.

Environment setup

At the minimum, you will be able to provide an environment that will be able to run scripts provided by a developer. With a bit of patience, you can also script using CSOM.

The first step is to install the SharePoint Online Client Components SDK (`https://www.microsoft.com/en-us/download/details.aspx?id=42038`). The libraries will be installed in this folder by default: `C:\Program Files\Common Files\Microsoft Shared\Web Server Extensions\16\ISAPI`.

As PowerShell is interoperable with .NET classes, we can load the libraries and use them in a manner similar to our use of SPO commands.

Connecting to SharePoint Online via CSOM

As a minimum, we will need to load modules via the `Add-Type` cmdlet:

```
Add-Type -Path "path to fileMicrosoft.SharePoint.Client.Runtime.dll"
Add-Type -Path "path to fileMicrosoft.SharePoint.Client.dll"
```

With the modules loaded, we need to establish a connection. The connection is managed by the `ClientContext` object. To create an instance of `ClientContext`, we need to pass a URL and user credentials. In contrast with the SPO command, `ClientContext` works with individual site collections. In this case, the URL should not be the admin URL but the URL of the site collection in question:

```
$siteUrl = "https://mytest321.sharepoint.com";
$user = "admin1@mytest321.onmicrosoft.com";
$password = Read-Host -Prompt "Input Password" -AsSecureString

$clientContext = New-Object
Microsoft.SharePoint.Client.ClientContext($siteUrl)
$credentials = New-Object
Microsoft.SharePoint.Client.SharePointOnlineCredentials($user, $password)
$clientContext.Credentials = $credentials
```

CSOM queries

Before proceeding with queries or updates, it is important to know that the CSOM API was built with performance in mind. In this case, the approach tries to minimize the calls to the server by caching operations until the `ExecuteQuery` command is run. What is more, values of objects such as the title of the web in the following example will not be available until the query is committed to the server through `ExecuteQuery`. It will take some time to get used to this disconnected paradigm. In the context of PowerShell scripting, we do not benefit much from it, and it is mostly a technical hurdle:

```
$web = $clientContext.Web;
$clientContext.Load($web);
$clientContext.ExecuteQuery();
$web.Title;

Team Site
```

In the following example, we iterate over the website lists and print basic metadata. Advanced CSOM is beyond the scope of this book, but we encourage you to go over to the GitHub repository for additional examples:

```
$lists = $web.Lists;
$clientContext.Load($lists);
$clientContext.ExecuteQuery();

$enumerator = $lists.GetEnumerator()

while( $enumerator.MoveNext()){
$list = $enumerator.Current;
 $list | Select Title, ItemCount, LastItemModifiedDate
}

Title                               ItemCount LastItemModifiedDate
-----                               --------- --------------------
Access Requests                             3 1/27/2017 2:41:50 AM
appdata                                     0 12/1/2016 6:19:16 AM
Composed Looks                             18 12/1/2016 6:19:16 AM
...
```

Scenario 7 - the REST API in PowerShell

The REST API appeals to developers and administrators because it is based on web standards. REST requests are HTTP requests that adhere to simple rules. In SharePoint, the REST API has been recently enhanced at a faster pace than the CSOM API.

To take advantage of the REST API through PowerShell, we are going to use an open source project from the Patterns and Practices team from Microsoft. We will cover this project in depths in the `Chapter 7`, *Patterns and Practices PowerShell*.

The *SharePointPnP.PowerShell Commands* project (`https://github.com/SharePoint/PnP-PowerShell`) contains a series of PowerShell commands that are implemented with CSOM. This is a good mix between CSOM functionality and the ease of use of PowerShell commands.

Before we get started, you can install the module using the following command:

```
Install-Module SharePointPnPPowerShellOnline -AllowClobber `
-Scope CurrentUser
```

The syntax is very similar to the SPOs but similarly to CSOM, we can target individual site collections. We establish a connection to a site collection through the `Connect-PnPOnline` command:

```
$siteUrl = 'https://mytest321.sharepoint.com'
Connect-PnPOnline $siteUrl
$ctx = (Get-PnPWeb).Context
```

To create a web request, we need to pass a valid cookie that we can obtain from the current context. With the credentials, we can establish a web request. The web request packages the credentials and settings that we will use to submit a request to SharePoint Online:

```
$creds = $ctx.Credentials
$cookies = $creds.GetAuthenticationCookie($siteUrl,$true)
$webSession = New-Object Microsoft.PowerShell.Commands.WebRequestSession
$webSession.Cookies.SetCookies($siteUrl, $cookies)
$webSession.Headers.Add('Accept', 'application/json;odata=verbose')
```

In the next script, we submit a GET request following the REST syntax to retrieve the title of the first item of the `Site Assets` list. The response is then parsed as a JSON object:

```
$restUrl =
"https://mytest321.sharepoint.com/_api/web/lists/getbytitle('Site
Assets')/items(1)?$select=Title"
$webRequest = Invoke-WebRequest -Uri $restUrl -Method Get -WebSession
$webSession
$webRequest.Content.Replace("ID", "_ID") | ConvertFrom-Json

odata.metadata : /_api/$metadata#SP.ListData.SiteAssetsItems/@Element
...
Created : 2016-12-01T06:19:40Z
AuthorId : 1073741823
Modified : 2016-12-01T06:19:40Z
EditorId : 1073741823
...
Title : Team Site Notebook
```

Hopefully, with this example, you see the potential of the REST API as well as the Patterns and Practices project and it has whetted your interest so that you will continue learning.

Summary

In this chapter, we introduced the SharePoint API landscape and showed how the SharePoint Online API complements existing APIs. We reviewed several scenarios and presented two cases to complement the SPO with the CSOM and REST APIs. Since SharePoint is such an important part of Office 365, we will work with it again in upcoming chapters.

In the next chapter, we will introduce concepts and techniques to streamline the automation of Office 365 scripting.

5
Managing Exchange Online Using PowerShell

In this chapter, we will introduce the basic concepts of Exchange. Most deployment and maintenance of Exchange revolve around users, contacts, groups, and mailboxes. You'll learn how to manage and monitor these.

We will cover the following topics:

- Connecting to Exchange Online
- Exploring the Exchange API
- Working with Exchange accounts
- User impersonation
- Role-based access control

Connecting to Exchange Online

The PowerShell Exchange API differs from others in its distribution form. To connect to Exchange Online, you will need to create and import a PowerShell session. The necessary modules are made available to you through the session. Exchange is the only case where a download is not needed.

If you need to connect using multi-factor authentication, you will need to download the Exchange Online remote PowerShell module for multi-factor authentication. Remember that at the time of writing this, multi-factor accounts cannot be used for unattended scripts.

The main advantage of this delivery method is that updates to modules are delivered whenever a new session is established. The publisher of the modules (Microsoft or the on-premises administrator) can easily update the modules and the scripting user is guaranteed to be running the latest version when establishing a new session.

We can speculate that a driving factor in choosing this approach is the critical importance of Exchange as a conduit for business communication and the quick turnaround needed to address security threats. However, the main reason for this approach is that the API's security is trimmed for the context of the user opening the session. At the end of the chapter, we will review how role-based access security impacts accessibility to commands and their parameters.

PowerShell sessions are a persistent connection to a computer, making a session a precious commodity in a shared environment such as Office 365. The disadvantage of this approach is that only a few sessions are allowed to be active concurrently. If you do not dispose of a session, it will remain active for a determined amount of time. The disconnected session can be re-established, but if you exceed the amount of allowed concurrent sessions, you will be unable to create a new connection through the API until the sessions are terminated from the server.

A common issue is not properly closing a session in the event of a failure during script execution. Orphaned sessions will eventually be closed, but this might take a significant amount of time. Be sure to close your sessions and plan for exception handling in your scripts.

In the following script, we call the `Get-Module` command before and after importing a session to show the implicit module added by the remoting session:

```
$creds= Get-Credential
$uri = 'https://outlook.office365.com/powershell-liveid/'

$Session = New-PSSession -ConfigurationName Microsoft.Exchange `
 -ConnectionUri $uri -Credential $creds -Authentication Basic `
 -AllowRedirection

Get-Module

ModuleType Version Name                                ExportedCommands
---------- ------- ----                                ----------------
Manifest   3.1.0.0 Microsoft.PowerShell.Management {Add-Computer, Add-
Content, Checkpoint-Computer...
Manifest   3.1.0.0 Microsoft.PowerShell.Utility    {Add-Member, Add-Type,
Clear-Variable, Compar...}
Script     1.2     PSReadline                          {Get-
PSReadlineKeyHandler, Remove-PS... }
```

```
Import-PSSession $Session
WARNING: The names of some imported commands from the module
'tmp_5hqgretu.crh' include unapproved verbs that might make them less
discoverable. To find the commands with unapproved verbs, run the Import-
Module command again with the Verbose parameter. For a list of approved
verbs, type Get-Verb.

Get-Module

ModuleType Version Name                                ExportedCommands
---------- ------- ----                                ----------------
Manifest   3.1.0.0 Microsoft.PowerShell.Management {Add-Computer, Add-
Content, Checkpoint-Computer...
Manifest   3.1.0.0 Microsoft.PowerShell.Utility    {Add-Member, Add-Type,
Clear-Variable...}
Script     1.2     PSReadline                          {Get-
PSReadlineKeyHandler...
Script     1.0     tmp_5hqgretu.crh                    {Add-
AvailabilityAddressSpace...

# Close the session when done
Remove-PSSession $Session
```

Exploring the API

At the time of writing this, there are 650 commands included in the Exchange module. The broad scope of the product makes it difficult to know and review all commands. Because the commands do not adhere to a naming convention, it is recommended that you target the module when searching for a command. Review previous chapters to see how to take advantage of the help features within PowerShell:

```
$exchangeModule = Get-Module -Name tmp_cozt5qry.a4u
$exchangeModule.ExportedCommands.Count

650

Get-Command -Module $exchangeModule -Name *User*

CommandType Name                               Version Source
----------- ----                               ------- ------
Function    Get-CsActiveUserReport             1.0 tmp_cozt5qry.a4u
Function    Get-CsUserActivitiesReport         1.0 tmp_cozt5qry.a4u
Function    Get-CsUsersBlockedReport           1.0 tmp_cozt5qry.a4u
Function    Get-DeviceComplianceUserInventory 1.0 tmp_cozt5qry.a4u
...
```

Because the module is used for both the online and on-premise versions of Exchange, you can easily run into errors when trying to use a command or parameter that does not apply to your version.

In the following example, we used `New-Mailbox` without specifying the necessary parameters for online execution. The command defaults to asking you for the on-premise parameter `UserPrincipalName` and consequently fails with a misleading error message:

```
New-Mailbox -Name test4 -Password $pass

cmdlet New-Mailbox at command pipeline position 1
Supply values for the following parameters:
UserPrincipalName: ForOnPremises@Only.net

The "UserPrincipalName" parameter can't be used on the "New-Mailbox" cmdlet
because it isn't present in the role definition for the current user. Check
the management roles assigned to you, and try again.
```

It is recommended that, before running any scripts in production, you first test your scripts in a development tenant. More importantly, review the documentation and parameter descriptions as they will indicate whether they can be used in the online version or not.

Working with Exchange accounts

Before we delve into scripting, we would like to review the different Exchange concepts we will be working with. All of these entities have the usual commands to create/update/delete them. As mentioned earlier, an exhaustive review of all the commands is impractical, but we will supply what we hope is a good review of the most common maintenance scenarios:

- **User**: An Active Directory account that can access Office 365 services but does not have Exchange access. These users cannot be recipients and are usually not accessible via Outlook.
- **Mailbox**: A mailbox is the most important entity within Exchange. In addition to emails, it contains scheduling, calendar, and all the Exchange features for a user account. Mailboxes are provisioned not only to users, but for also for shared, room, and other resources.
- **Mail user**: A mail user is an Active Directory account that can log in to the different services offered by Office 365. However, the account does not have a mailbox in the tenant's Exchange. The user can send an email to an external email address.

- **Contact**: A contact is available in Outlook and can receive email similarly to mail users. However, the contact does not have a username/password and, therefore, cannot access services. Contacts are usually used as email recipients and can also be included in distribution lists.
- **Group**: A group contains a list of members that can be sent emails or given access as a single entity.
- **Distribution list**: A distribution list is similar to groups in that it is a collection of recipients, but it cannot be given access to services via security assignments.

When creating new user accounts in Office 365, one of the steps is to create an Exchange mailbox for it. Regardless of whether you take this step or not, a user record will be created in Exchange. This record allows the user to be found by other users even if they do not have a mailbox. If a user is set up with an external email account, they may also receive emails. A user may also be part of a security group even if their mailbox is later removed.

User records are also created for other entities that you may not think of as a *user*, for example, meeting rooms, shared mailboxes, and equipment will get user accounts so that they can be included in meetings and other features. The user accounts for these entities are disabled (for most types) and cannot be used to log in (they also do not count in licensing equations). Even though Exchange management usually involves working with user mailboxes, it is important to know about users and mail users as they have different properties and you usually have to work with them in maintenance scenarios.

Mailbox users, as the name indicates, are users with an Exchange mailbox that will store their emails. Mail users are users with a valid email but without a local Exchange mailbox (an email account managed outside the tenant's Exchange). A record can change the type depending on the requirements. For example, if you delete a mailbox, its record will be demoted from `UserMailbox` to user and promoted back to `UserMailbox` if the mailbox is recreated.

We will begin with a query to show the existing user records. Note that the `RecipientType` parameter is set to `UserMailbox` for users with active mailboxes. The `Get-User` command will return `UserMailbox`, user, and `MailUser` records. The `Get-Mailbox` and `Get-MailUser` commands can be used to get `UserMailbox` and `MailUser` separately:

```
Get-User | Select Name, RecipientType, RecipientTypeDetails,
WindowsEmailAddress | Sort RecipientTypeDetails

Name                          RecipientType RecipientTypeDetails
WindowsEmailAddress
----                          ------------- -------------------- -------------
-----
```

```
DiscoverySearchMailbox... UserMailbox   DiscoveryMailbox
DiscoverySearchMailb...
Printer B                 UserMailbox   EquipmentMailbox
printerb@mytest321.o...
test4                     MailUser      MailUser
test4@gmail.com
Meeting Room A            UserMailbox   RoomMailbox
meetingrooma2@mytest...
Support                   UserMailbox   SharedMailbox
support@mytest321.on...
Accounting                UserMailbox   SharedMailbox
accounting@mytest321...
Test123                   User          User
test2                     User          User
chelsea                   UserMailbox   UserMailbox
chelsea@mytest321.on....
martin                    UserMailbox   UserMailbox
martin@mytest321.onm....
```

Creating new mailboxes

User records are not created directly through the Exchange API (since they are basically a reference to an Active Directory account). However, when creating a mailbox, you are implicitly creating a user account for it. In the following example, we pass a username and password to the `New-Mailbox` command. The result is a working account that can be used to log in to any Office 365 service and has an associated Exchange mailbox.

Scenario 1 - a new user mailbox

If you have an existing user without a mailbox, the account either does not have a license assigned, or the Exchange service option has been disabled. In either case, the setup is done through the Active Directory PowerShell API (refer to `Chapter 3`, *Azure AD and Licensing Management* for more information):

```
$pass = ConvertTo-SecureString -String 'password here' -AsPlainText -Force

New-Mailbox -Alias test3 -Name test3 -MicrosoftOnlineServicesID
test3@mytest321.onmicrosoft.com -Password $pass

WARNING: After you create a new mailbox, you must go to the Office 365
Admin Center and assign the mailbox a license, or it will be disabled after
the grace period.

Name  Alias ServerName     ProhibitSendQuota
```

```
---- ----- ----------    ------------------
test3 test3 cy1pr06mb1833 99 GB (106,300,440,576 bytes)
```

Scenario 2 - an unlicensed existing user

This scenario corresponds to an account initially created without a license. This can be done through the admin web site or through PowerShell.

The `Get-MsolUser` command has a useful filter parameter to get unlicensed users:

```
Get-MsolUser -UnlicensedUsersOnly

UserPrincipalName                    DisplayName isLicensed
-----------------                    ----------- ----------
test5@mytest321.onmicrosoft.com      test5       False
```

By assigning a license that has the Exchange service option, you will automatically provision their Exchange mailbox. The default licenses (a.k.a SKUs in PowerShell) will have the service enabled; however, you can also create your own SKUs, which might be useful if you have many user types. In any case, it is easy to check the service status of the license through PowerShell.

Let's review the available licenses and check whether the Exchange service is enabled for it:

```
Get-MsolAccountSku

AccountSkuId                        ActiveUnits WarningUnits ConsumedUnits
------------                        ----------- ------------ -------------
mytest321:ENTERPRISEPACK            5           0            5
mytest321:FLOW_FREE                 10000       0            0
mytest321:POWER_BI_STANDARD 1000000             0            1

$skus = Get-MsolAccountSku
$skus[0].ServiceStatus

ServicePlan           ProvisioningStatus
-----------           ------------------
FORMS_PLAN_E3         PendingProvisioning
...
SHAREPOINTENTERPRISE  Success
EXCHANGE_S_ENTERPRISE Success
```

Adding a license to a user is simple with the `Set-MsolUserLicense` command. After the license is assigned, a new mailbox will be attached to the user. In Exchange, the record will be switched from the user to `UserMailbox`.

```
Set-MsolUserLicense -UserPrincipalName test5@mytest321.onmicrosoft.net
 -AddLicenses mytest321:ENTERPRISEPACK
```

Scenario 3 - a licensed user without the Exchange service

If an account is created and assigned a license, the administrator can still disable individual services. The typical scenario where this is useful is giving access to a consultant who may need to access multiple services, while ensuring their email will be managed externally.

To remove Exchange from a license, we also rely on the `Set-MsolUserLicense` command using the `LicenseOptions` parameter (which takes a list of services to disable).

The `New-MsolLicenseOptions` command creates a `LicenseOptions` record that targets a particular license with a list of disabled services (in the `DisabledPlan` parameter). You then pass these options to the `Set-MsolUserLicense` command:

```
$opt = New-MsolLicenseOptions -AccountSkuId "mytest321:ENTERPRISEPACK"
 -DisabledPlans "EXCHANGE_S_ENTERPRISE"

Set-MsolUserLicense -UserPrincipalName test5@mytest321.onmicrosoft.com
 -LicenseOptions $opt
```

You can validate the effective services for the account by querying `ServiceStatus` of the user's `Licenses` property:

```
$user = Get-MsolUser -UserPrincipalName test5@mytest321.onmicrosoft.com
$user.Licenses.ServiceStatus

ServicePlan           ProvisioningStatus
-----------           ------------------
FORMS_PLAN_E3         PendingProvisioning
STREAM_O365_E3        PendingProvisioning
....
SHAREPOINTENTERPRISE  Success
EXCHANGE_S_ENTERPRISE Disabled
```

To enable the service (and trigger the creation of a mailbox), you simply pass a new `LicenseOption` record without a disable plan parameter:

```
$opt = New-MsolLicenseOptions -AccountSkuId "mytest321:ENTERPRISEPACK"
Set-MsolUserLicense -UserPrincipalName test5@mytest321.onmicrosoft.com
 -LicenseOptions $opt
```

The status of the service might be `PendingInput`, immediately following the execution of the command, as it takes a few minutes for the mailbox to be created.

Scenario 4 - MailUser

Although not technically a mailbox, mail users are typically used in the consultant scenario. Mail users can log into services and are available in the global catalog but do not have a mailbox. `MailUser` can receive emails to the email address set in the `-ExternlEmailAddress` parameter:

```
New-MailUser -name test6 -Password $pass -ExternalEmailAddress
"test6@test.com" -MicrosoftOnlineServicesID test6@mytest321.onmicrosoft.com

Name  RecipientType
----  -------------
test6 MailUser
```

The account can be found in Outlook and resolved in security form permission assignments. Note that the icon next to the account identifies it as an external user:

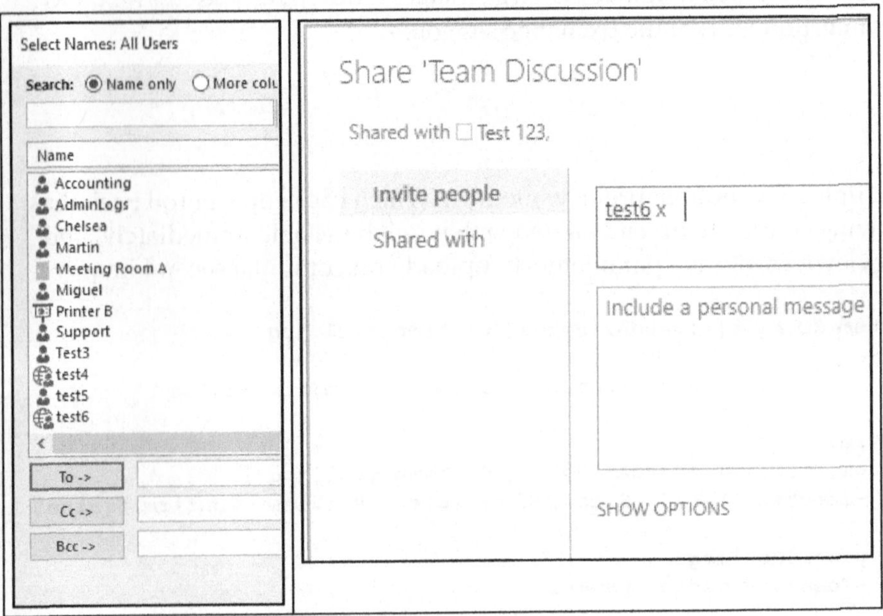

User photos

Mailbox photos can be managed with the `Get-UserPhoto`, `Set-UserPhoto`, and `Remove-UserPhoto` commands. At the time of writing this, it is not possible to set photos for MailUsers through PowerShell in Office 365 (the documentation points to the `Import-RecipientDataProperty` command, which is only available on premises). The photos are used in Outlook, Skype, Delve, and other services. Requirements for the image have changed over the years; previously, only JPEGs were allowed (PNGs work too now). It is recommended that you use small file sizes (minimum size is 48 pixels), and it is common for the command to hang for when trying to upload large files.

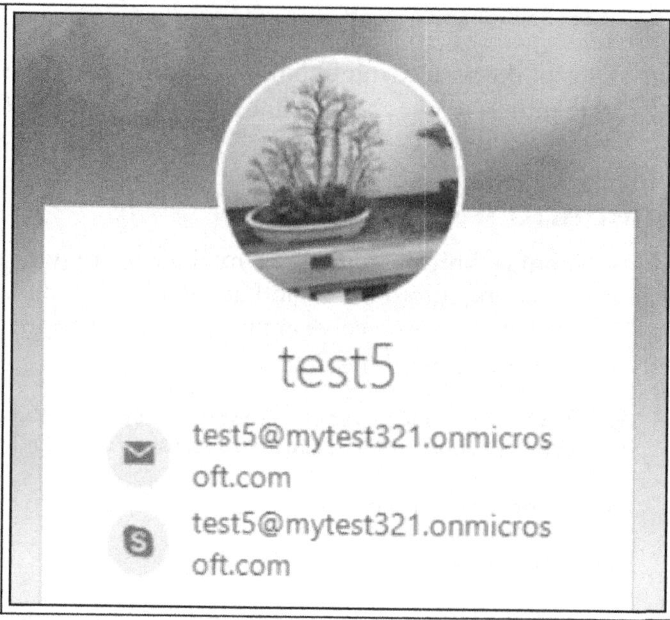

To avoid errors when uploading large images, add `?proxymethod=rps` to the connection URL of the Exchange session.

If required, you can upload a photo in preview mode, in which case you can roll back the upload. In the following script, we upload an image that will be visible immediately, and then we test the preview/cancel/save parameters to upload and commit a second image:

```
$pic1 = ([System.IO.File]::ReadAllBytes("C:\temp\pic1.jpg"))

Set-UserPhoto -Identity test5 -PictureData $pic1 -Confirm:$false

#Upload a preview
$pic2 = ([System.IO.File]::ReadAllBytes("C:\temp\pic2.jpg"))
Set-UserPhoto -Identity test5 -PictureData $pic2 -Preview -Confirm:$false

#roll back to previous image
Set-UserPhoto -Identity test5 -Cancel

# commit new image
```

```
Set-UserPhoto -Identity test5 -PictureData $pic2 -Preview -Confirm:$false
Set-UserPhoto -Identity test5 -Save
```

Images can be retrieved and removed with the `Get-UserPhoto` and `Remove-UserPhoto` commands. To make sure the image is valid, review the `IsValid` property of the `Get-UserPhoto` result:

```
Get-UserPhoto -Identity test5

RunspaceId : 1469e530-3fda-4249-ab61-7cb156761563
Identity : test5
PictureData : {255, 216, 255, 224...}
Thumbprint : 1382934473
IsValid : True
ObjectState : New

Remove-UserPhoto -Identity test5 -Confirm:$false
```

To finish our review of user photos, we will create a script to update records in bulk. First, we will create a CSV file with usernames and file paths for the accounts that we will be updating:

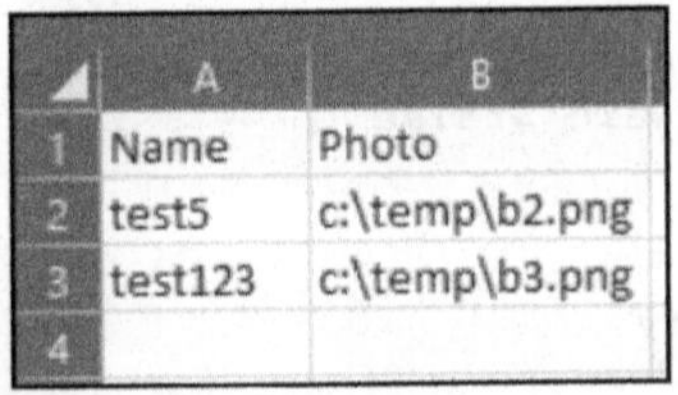

	A	B
1	Name	Photo
2	test5	c:\temp\b2.png
3	test123	c:\temp\b3.png
4		

The `Import-Csv` command makes it easy to process CSV rows. We then pass the rows to the `Set-UserPhoto` command:

```
$rows = Import-csv c:\temp\userphotos.csv

foreach($row in $rows){
 $photo = [System.IO.File]::ReadAllBytes($row.Photo)
 Set-UserPhoto -Identity $row.Name -PictureData $photo -Confirm:$false
}
```

Email forwarding

`MailUser` might be a convenience for consultants who get an account so they can access your system and use their existing email address. However, this might not be desirable if your organization needs to retain communication records. An alternative solution is to provide the consultant with a mailbox but configure it so that the incoming email is forwarded to the consultant's external email address.

In the following script, the `Set-Mailbox` command configures the `test5` account to forward the incoming email to an external email address (using `ForwardingSmtpAddress`). The `DeliverToMailboxAndForward` parameter set to true will keep the emails in the mailbox while forwarding a copy to the external address:

```
Set-Mailbox -Identity test5 -ForwardingSmtpAddress test5@hotmail.com
 -DeliverToMailboxAndForward $true
```

If you have a user that has left the organization or is temporarily unavailable, you can forward the email to another mailbox through the `ForwardingAddress` parameter. If there is no need to keep a copy of the emails in the original mailbox, you would set `DeliverToMailboxAndForward` to `$false`:

```
Set-Mailbox -Identity test5 -ForwardingAddress test6
 -DeliverToMailboxAndForward $false
```

Out-of-office reply

Although not technically challenging, setting out-of-office settings is worth reviewing since it is such a common activity. Interestingly, some of the settings available in PowerShell are not available through the user interface.

In this example, we schedule the out-of-office setting to be enabled within a start and end time. External and internal messages are used when replying to contacts outside and inside the organization:

```
$startTime = Get-Date
$endTime = (Get-Date).AddDays(10)
$externalMessage = "Please contact support@email for assistance"
$internalMessage = "I'm out of the office for 10 days"

Set-MailboxAutoReplyConfiguration -Identity test2 -AutoReplyState Scheduled
 -StartTime $startTime -EndTime $endTime -CreateOOFEvent $true
 -OOFEventSubject "Test2 Out"
```

The `-CreateOOFEvent` and `OOFEventSubject` parameters can be used to create an event in the account's calendar. The account will surface in the scheduling interface as unavailable during the out-of-office period:

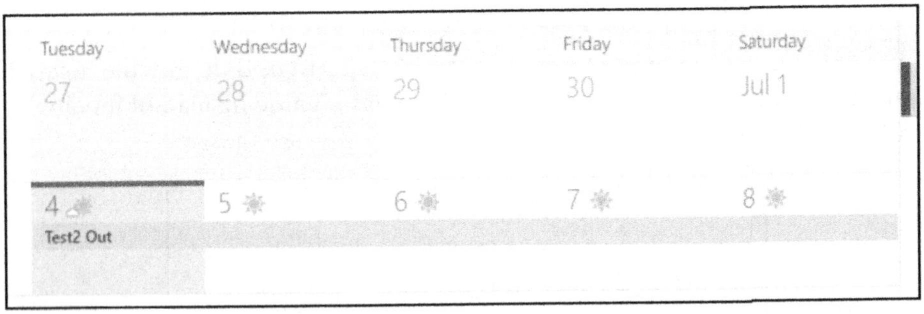

Additionally, you can set `ExternalAudience` (to known) so that the message will be sent to known external email addresses only. `DeclineEventsForScheduledOOF` (`true|false`) can be set to automatically decline events too.

Inbox rules

Inbox rules offer a wide array of activities that can be executed on an incoming message. They are an indispensable way to help users manage their email and are widely adopted. In addition to PowerShell, rules can be set up by the user both in Outlook and Outlook Web Access.

An example of where they can be useful could be pinning an important human resources message in the user inbox or in an emergency situation where you may want to send a text message across the organization.

The inbox-rules-related commands (`Disable-InboxRule`, `Enable-InboxRule`, `Get-InboxRule`, `New-InboxRule`, `Remove-InboxRule`, and `Set-InboxRule`) target individual accounts. If you need to roll out rules to the entire organization, you will need to write iterative scripts to update them one at a time.

In the following example, we set up a new rule to pin important messages for the `test2` account. We then use `Set-InboxRule` to set `StopProcessingRules` so no additional rules are run after this rule executes:

```
New-InboxRule -Name "Pin Important" -Mailbox test2 -WithImportance "High"
 -PinMessage $true

Name Enabled   Priority Rule Identity
```

```
---- -------   -------- ---- --------
Pin  Important True     1    11719621876991918081

Set-InboxRule -Mailbox test2 -StopProcessingRules $true -Identity
11719621876991918081
```

Note the use of the identity parameter in `Set-InboxRule` to update the rule; using the `-Name` parameter in this command would update the `Name` value instead of it being used to find the rule:

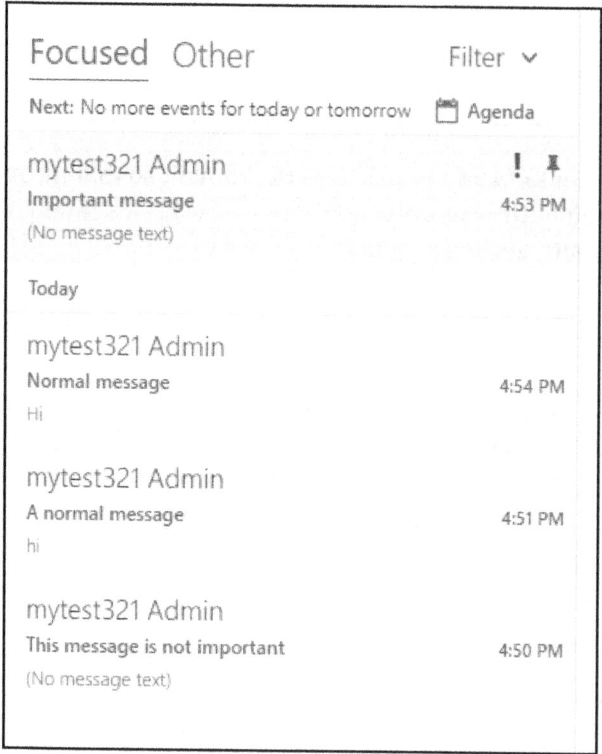

Commands have a long list of possible filters for actions (`BodyContainsWords`, `FlaggedForAction`, `From`, `FromAddressContainsWords`, `FromSubscription`, `HasAttachment`, `HasClassification`, `HeaderContainsWords`, and `MessageTypeMatches`, to name a few) and just as many actions.

In the following script, we set up a new rule to send a text message to the user if we get an email from a specific email address. Text messages can be a powerful delivery system for important information as long as they are not overused:

```
New-InboxRule -Name 'Emergency SMS' -Mailbox admin1 -StopProcessingRules
$true -From alerts@mytest321.onmicrosoft.com -SendTextMessageNotificationTo
'+3015555555'

Name          Enabled Priority RuleIdentity
----          ------- -------- ------------
Emergency SMS True    1        4639937978293026817

New-InboxRule -Name 'Emergency SMS' -Mailbox test2 -StopProcessingRules
$true -From alerts@mytest321.onmicrosoft.com -SendTextMessageNotificationTo
'+3015555555'

The operation on mailbox "test2" failed because it's out of the current
user's write scope. The object 'test2' must be within the read scope before
and after it's modified. Can't perform the save operation.
```

Note that the second command failed. This is due to a service account being used to run the command that does not have access to the text messaging settings of the target account. We will address permissions and this specific scenario later in the chapter. For the moment, we will say that text messaging settings cannot be set for another account through PowerShell.

In the next section, we will introduce **Exchange Web Services** (**EWS**), which will allow you to impersonate users and complete this and other scenarios.

User impersonation

As seen in the previous section, some activities can be executed only by the account being targeted. In the preceding example, not even a global administrator can create an inbox rule that uses text messaging (more on security on the next section). However, we have the option of user impersonation. At the time of writing this, user impersonation can be used only through EWS.

EWS pre-dates PowerShell and Office 365 and can be used for system integration and application development, hence its implementation of user impersonation. Fortunately, once we get familiar with the API, using EWS can be leveraged in our PowerShell scripts.

Installing Exchange Web Services

EWS can be downloaded from the Microsoft website (`https://www.microsoft.com/en-us/download/details.aspx?id=42951`); the project is open source and is available on GitHub (`https://github.com/OfficeDev/ews-managed-api`). The installation is straightforward and will copy the files to `Program Files\Microsoft\Exchange\Web Services` by default.

The Exchange 2013 101 Code Samples project is a comprehensive set of examples that will get you up-to-speed with the EWS API (`https://code.msdn.microsoft.com/exchange/Exchange-2013-101-Code-3c38582c`).

The API is a .NET DLL; we will load it and use it in PowerShell through `Import-Module`, as we have done earlier. In the following example, we use the API to establish a connection with Exchange Online through the `ExchangeService` object and use the `ImpersonatedUserId` property to execute commands as `test2`:

```
Import-Module -Name "path to dll\Microsoft.Exchange.WebServices.dll"

$exchWS = New-Object Microsoft.Exchange.WebServices.Data.ExchangeService

$exchWS.Credentials = $creds.GetNetworkCredential();
$exchWS.AutodiscoverUrl('admin1@mytest321.onmicrosoft.com', {$true})

$exchWS.ImpersonatedUserId = New-Object
Microsoft.Exchange.WebServices.Data.ImpersonatedUserId(
[Microsoft.Exchange.WebServices.Data.ConnectingIdType]::SmtpAddress,
"test2@mytest321.onmicrosoft.com")

$rule = New-Object Microsoft.Exchange.WebServices.Data.Rule

$mobilePhone = New-Object
Microsoft.Exchange.WebServices.Data.MobilePhone("test2","+3015555555")
$rule.Actions.SendSMSAlertToRecipients.Add($mobilePhone)

$rule.DisplayName = "SMS Alert 2"

$rule.Conditions.FromAddresses.Add("alerts@mytest321.onmicrosoft.com")

$createRequest = New-Object
Microsoft.Exchange.WebServices.Data.CreateRuleOperation($rule)
$operations = New-Object
Microsoft.Exchange.WebServices.Data.RuleOperation[] 1
$operations[0] = $createRequest
```

```
$exchWS.UpdateInboxRules($operations, $false)
```

Impersonating a user will work only if the account used to run the scripts is set up with access to do the operation. In the next section, we will do this as we introduce security and role-based access.

Role-based access control

Exchange has one of the most interesting security models within the Office 365 services. **Role-based access control** (**RBAC**) was introduced in Exchange 2010 and can be used to control access to individual PowerShell (including access to individual parameters). Not only can you limit what end users can do, but you can also security-trim the **Exchange admin center** (**EAC**) since it relies on the Exchange management API.

As part of this introduction to security, we will create a new admin role with a limited scope, which is the typical scenario for delegated administration.

With its level of granularity, the Exchange security model can be somewhat complex at first. As the name suggests, access to commands and features is managed through roles; in addition to roles, there are several other concepts that we will introduce in the following section.

Management roles

Management roles stand at the center of the RBAC model. Because every aspect of Exchange is secured through them, there is a long list of roles, which can be retrieved via `Get-ManagementRole`.

Roles are divided between end users and admin roles:

- **End user roles**: End user roles give access to individuals to manage features within their own mailbox. All commands have the `My` prefix.
- **Administrative roles**: Administrative roles are used to security-trim actions for organization-wide mailboxes and other administrative operations.

Roles themselves are a list of role entries. Role entries give access to a command while specifying access to individual parameters of the command.

As an example, let's review a list of role entries for the management role `Mailbox Search`:

```
Get-ManagementRoleEntry "Mailbox Search\*"

Name                    Role           Parameters
----                    ----           ----------
...
Write-AdminAuditLog     Mailbox Search {Comment, Confirm, ErrorAction,
ErrorVariable...}
Stop-MailboxSearch      Mailbox Search {Confirm, ErrorAction,
ErrorVariable, Identity...}
...
```

The command retrieves all entries associated with the `Mailbox Search` role. As you can see, each entry gives access to a PowerShell command and parameters for it. A management role is basically a list of entries that define the commands and parameters for which the users will have access.

Roles also determine the scope of execution for commands via their `Scope` properties. The `Scope` property is the allowed context in which the commands can be targeted.

Some examples of management scopes can be as follows:

- `Organization`: Execution will be allowed in all accounts
- `OU`: A specific organizational unit
- `Self`: Only the account of the current user

Read scopes cannot be modified; we will review how to modify write scopes later in this section.

The following example shows the use of the `Scope` property:

```
Get-ManagementRole -RoleType AddressList | Select *Scope | fl

ImplicitRecipientReadScope : Organization
ImplicitRecipientWriteScope : Organization
ImplicitConfigReadScope : OrganizationConfig
ImplicitConfigWriteScope : OrganizationConfig
```

Scopes types are:

- `RecipientReadScope`: This determines the scope when trying to read data from Active Directory. In this case, the user will be able to read address lists for all mailboxes in the organization.
- `RecipientWriteScope`: This determines whether the user will be allowed to save changes. In this case, the user will be allowed to update address lists in all mailboxes in the organization.
- `ConfigurationReadScope`: This determines whether the user will be allowed to retrieve configuration options.
- `ConfigurationWriteScope`: This determines whether the user will be allowed to update configuration options.

Note that in the preceding example, all the properties are `Implicit`. `Implicit` scopes are defined at the role level and cannot be modified even for inheriting roles. This means that an `Implicit` scope will determine the broadest scope for a role (you can override write scopes in role assignments, but the value can only be narrowed down).

Because you need to read an object before you write it, a write scope can only be as effective as the read scope. For example, if you have a `Self` read scope and an `Organization` write scope for a role, you will not be able to save changes because of the read scope.

We ran into this situation in the text messaging example. If you review the built-in management role's implicit scopes, you will see that the `MyTextMessaging` role is set to `Self` for both read and write scopes. This means that even an administrator cannot update someone else's text messaging settings:

Management role	Recipient read scope	Recipient write scope	Configuration read scope	Configuration write scope
`MyTextMessaging`	`Self`	`Self`	`OrganizationConfig`	`OrganizationConfig`

At the end of this section, we will create a role where we override the write scope to create a sub-administrator role.

Role groups

Because roles are so granular, managing access through them can be cumbersome. To simplify the assignment of roles, we can use role groups. As the name implies, they group a series of roles that can be assigned to users and security groups:

```
Get-RoleGroup | Select Name, Roles, Members | fl

Name : Organization Management
Roles : {Data Loss Prevention, Migration, Organization Configuration, Org
Custom Apps...}
Members : {TenantAdmins_85510073, admin1}

Name : Recipient Management
Roles : {Message Tracking, Distribution Groups, Team Mailboxes, Mail
Recipient Creation...}
Members : {admin1}
```

The management of role group properties is done through `Get-RoleGroup`, `New-RoleGroup`, `Set-RoleGroup`, and `Remove-RoleGroup`.

Managing members of a role group is done through the `Add-RoleGroupMember`, `Get-RoleGroupMember`, and `Remove-RoleGroupMember` commands.

Role assignments for roles (and users and security groups) are done through `New-ManagementRoleAssignment`, `Get-ManagementRoleAssignment`, `Remove-ManagementRoleAssignment`, and `Set-ManagementRoleAssignment`.

We will go through a real-world scenario at the end of this section.

Management role assignment

Role assignments allow you to assign roles to a user/security group with the option to override the write scope set at the role level. Role assignments can target role groups, users, policies, or security groups.

We will finish the text messaging example by giving permissions to the service account so that the EWS call can impersonate the user.

We initially try to call the EWS command that creates a new inbox rule; because the rule uses text messaging and impersonation has not been set up, the call with fail:

```
# trying to impersonate through EWS fails before role assignment
$exchWS.UpdateInboxRules($operations, $false)

Exception calling "UpdateInboxRules" with "2" argument(s): "The account
does not have permission to impersonate the requested user."

New-ManagementRoleAssignment -Name ImpersonateTest2 -Role
ApplicationImpersonation -User admin1 -Confirm:$false

Name             Role                      RoleAssigneeName RoleAssigneeType
AssignmentMethod
----             ----                      ---------------- ----------------
----------------
ImpersonateTest2 ApplicationImpersonation admin1           User
Direct

#reconnect so new assignment applies
Remove-PSSession $Session
$Session = New-PSSession -ConfigurationName Microsoft.Exchange -
ConnectionUri $uri -Credential $creds -Authentication Basic -
AllowRedirection
Import-PSSession $Session

# EWS impersonation should work now
$exchWS.UpdateInboxRules($operations, $false)
```

Note that in this example, the assignment was given to a user (`admin1`); in most scenarios, using a security group is a better practice. We also did not use a scoping mechanism to set the impersonation scope; using the scoping parameter is preferable as it is a good idea to limit the reach of the assignment as much as possible.

The scoping parameters of `New-ManagementRoleAssignment` are as follows:

- `CustomRecipientWriteScope`: Specifies a recipient-based management scope
- `ExclusiveRecipientWriteScope`: Specifies an exclusive recipient-based management scope
- `RecipientOrganizationalUnitScope`: Specifies an OU where the assignment will be effective

- `RecipientRelativeWriteScope`: Restricts the scope of the assignment to one of the following:
    - `None`
    - `Organization`
    - `MyGal`
    - `Self`
    - `MyDistributionGroups`

RBAC scenario - creating a custom administrator

To finish this section, we will go over a scenario that will allow us to apply the concepts that we have reviewed around security. In this scenario, we want to delegate the management of a group of users to a group of administrators. The administrators will only have access to change out-of-office settings for the user group.

First requirement - limiting access to PowerShell commands

As we reviewed in a previous section, out-of-office settings are managed by just two commands:

```
Get-Command *MailboxAutoReply* | select Name

Name
----
Get-MailboxAutoReplyConfiguration
Set-MailboxAutoReplyConfiguration
```

To limit access to just these commands, we need to identify a role that includes them as a starting point for our new role. To identify the role, we will search for role entries that include either of these commands. We rely on the `Get-ManagementRoleEntry` command with a wildcard to include all applicable entries. To keep the results simple, we used a unique filter, but we had to make sure both the `Get` and `Set` verbs are included.

```
Get-ManagementRoleEntry *\*MailboxAutoReplyConfiguration | Sort-Object
 -Property Role -Unique | Select

Name                              Role
----                              ----
Set-MailboxAutoReplyConfiguration Mail Recipients
```

```
Set-MailboxAutoReplyConfiguration MyBaseOptions
Set-MailboxAutoReplyConfiguration User Options
Get-MailboxAutoReplyConfiguration View-Only Recipients
```

Based on the results, we have four potential role candidates. Since we want to read and write, we immediately discard the `View-Only Recipients` role (which only has the `Get` verb). We also discard the `MyBaseOptions` role since the `My` prefix indicates that the scope is `Self` and therefore will not work in our administrator scenario.

To select between the two remaining roles, we will review their properties:

```
PS C:\> Get-ManagementRole | Where { $_.Name -in @("Mail Recipients","User
Options") } | Select Name, Description, RoleEntries | fl

Name : Mail Recipients

Description : This role enables administrators to manage existing
mailboxes, mail users, and mail contacts in an organization. This role
can't create these recipients. Use MailRecipientCreation roles to create
them.
 This role type doesn't enable you to manage mail-enabled public folders or
distribution groups. Use the MailEnabledPublicFolders and DistributionGroup
roles to manage these objects.
 If your organization has a split permissions model where recipient
creation and management are performed by different groups, assign the
MailRecipientCreation roles to the group that performs recipient
 creation and the MailRecipients roles to the group that performs recipient
management.

RoleEntries : {SetUserPhoto,
(Microsoft.Exchange.Management.Powershell.Support) Set-FocusedInbox -
FocusedInboxOn -Identity,
(Microsoft.Exchange.Management.Powershell.Support) Set-Clutter -
CleanUpClutter -Enable
 -ErrorAction -ErrorVariable -Identity -OutBuffer -OutVariable -
WarningAction -WarningVariable,
(Microsoft.Exchange.Management.Powershell.Support) Get-FocusedInbox -
Identity...}

Name : User Options

Description : This role enables administrators to view the Outlook Web App
options of a user in an organization. This role can be used to help
diagnose configuration problems.

RoleEntries : {(Microsoft.Exchange.Management.Powershell.Support) Set-
Clutter -CleanUpClutter -Enable -ErrorAction -ErrorVariable -Identity -
OutBuffer -OutVariable -WarningAction -WarningVariable,
```

```
(Microsoft.Exchange.Management.Powershell.Support) Get-Clutter -
ErrorAction -ErrorVariable -Identity -OutBuffer -OutVariable -WarningAction
-WarningVariable,
 (Microsoft.Exchange.Management.PowerShell.E2010) Write-AdminAuditLog -
Comment -Confirm -ErrorAction -ErrorVariable -OutBuffer -OutVariable -
WarningAction -WarningVariable -WhatIf,
 (Microsoft.Exchange.Management.PowerShell.E2010) Stop-UMPhoneSession -
Confirm -ErrorAction -ErrorVariable -Identity -OutBuffer -OutVariable -
WarningAction -WarningVariable -WhatIf...}
```

Either role would work in this case, but we will choose `Mail Recipients` since it has fewer role entries. The next step is to create a role that inherits from `Mail Recipients`, and then we will remove all the role entries that do not apply (leaving only entries for the two commands we want the administrators to have access to):

```
New-ManagementRole -Name "Out of the Office Admins" -EnabledCmdlets
 @("Set-MailboxAutoReplyConfiguration", "Get-
MailboxAutoReplyConfiguration") -Parent "Mail Recipients"

Name                     RoleType
----                     --------
Out of the Office Admins MailRecipients

Get-ManagementRoleEntry "Out of the Office Admins\*"

Name                           Role Parameters
----                           ---- ----------
Get-MailboxAutoReplyConfigu... Out of the Office Admins {ErrorAction,
ErrorVariable, Identity...
Set-MailboxAutoReplyConfigu... Out of the Office Admins
{AutoDeclineFutureRequestsWhenOOF, ...
```

Note that we made use of the`-EnabledCmdlets` parameter, which at the time of writing this, is not documented. Before this parameter was available, you would have to filter and remove role entries after the role was created.

To finish the role setup, we will remove the `-ExternalMessage` parameter from the `Set` command so that admins are not allowed to set the external message of the out-of-office settings:

```
Set-ManagementRoleEntry -Identity "Out of the Office Admins\Set-
MailboxAutoReplyConfiguration" -Parameters "ExternalMessage"
 -RemoveParameter

Get-ManagementRoleEntry "Out of the Office Admins\Set-
MailboxAutoReplyConfiguration" | Select -ExpandProperty Parameters
```

```
AutoDeclineFutureRequestsWhenOOF
...
EndTime
ErrorAction
ErrorVariable
EventsToDeleteIDs
ExternalAudience
Identity
...
```

Second requirement - limiting access to a group of users

The second requirement for our scenario is to limit the scope of the updates to a set group of users. We will begin by creating a security group to manage the administrator group.

To identify the users that the administrators can edit, we need to use a management scope. In the following example, the management scope will include all users in `Department B`. A management scope can also target a specific OU or user policy:

```
New-DistributionGroup -Type "Security" -Name 'OOTFAdmins'
 -MemberJoinRestriction ApprovalRequired

Name       DisplayName GroupType                          PrimarySmtpAddress
----       ----------- ---------                          ------------------
OOTFAdmins OOTFAdmins  Universal, SecurityEnabled
OOTFAdmins@mytest321.onmicrosoft.com

New-ManagementScope "DepartmentB" -RecipientRestrictionFilter { Department
-Eq "Department B" }

Name        ScopeRestrictionType Exclusive RecipientRoot RecipientFilter
----        -------------------- --------- ------------- ---------------
DepartmentB RecipientScope       False                   Department -eq
'Department B'
```

We need to decide how we will give access to our newly defined role (`Out Of the Office Admins`) to the `OOTFAdmins` security group. We have the option of creating a role assignment record that directly references the admin group. However, a more flexible alternative would be to create a new role group. This role group will only have the new role but gives us the option to add additional roles as well as additional security groups or users.

The following script creates a role group with the security group and role. In the next command, we set the `-CustomWriteScope` parameter to only allow updates on `DepartmentB`:

```
New-RoleGroup -Name "OOTF Admin" -Members OOTFAdmins -Roles "Out of the
Office Admins"

Name       AssignedRoles              RoleAssignments
ManagedBy
----       -------------              ---------------
---------
OOTF Admin {Out of the Office Admins} {mytest321...\Out of the Office
Admins-OOTF Admin} {Organizat...

Get-ManagementRoleAssignment -Role "Out Of the Office Admins" | Set-
ManagementRoleAssignment -CustomRecipientWriteScope "DepartmentB"
```

To be able to test the role, we will create an admin account (and add it to the `OOTFAdmins` group) and a user account in `Department B`:

```
New-Mailbox -Name admin2 -MicrosoftOnlineServicesID
admin2@mytest321.onmicrosoft.com -Password $pass
Add-DistributionGroupMember -Member admin2 -Identity OOTFAdmins

New-Mailbox -Name test4 -MicrosoftOnlineServicesID
test4@mytest321.onmicrosoft.com -Password $pass
Set-User -Identity test4 -Department "Department B"
```

We now log in as `admin2` and attempt to set the out-of-office settings for `test2` (which fails) and then for `test4` (which works as it has the correct department). In our last test, we attempt to update `ExternalMessage` on `test4`, which is also denied, as expected (due to the configuration of the role entry):

```
Set-MailboxAutoReplyConfiguration -InternalMessage "asd" -Identity test2

The operation on mailbox "test2" failed because it's out of the current
user's write scope. 'test2' isn't within your current write scopes. Can't
perform save operation.

# works
Set-MailboxAutoReplyConfiguration -InternalMessage "asd" -Identity test4

# fails as parameter was removed from role
Set-MailboxAutoReplyConfiguration -ExternalMessage "asd" -Identity test4

Recipient "test4" couldn't be read from domain controller
"DM5PR15A004DC04.NAMPR15A004.PROD.OUTLOOK.COM". This may be due to
```

```
replication delays. Switching out of Forest mode should allow this
operation to complete successfully.
```

The example shows how we can define custom access with up to one parameter level of granularity.

Summary

Exchange is a robust and mature communications product. We hope that this introduction has given you a good idea of how to manage it. We have skipped over a few entities that you will no doubt work with (groups, distribution lists, and contacts); however, you should not run into big surprises managing them since they are similar to the reviewed entities.

In the next chapter we learn how to automate script execution so that you can apply and automate all the maintenance tasks we have learned about until now

6
Script Automation

Up until this point, we have covered the different Office 365 APIs, and you should have a good foundation for scripting for the reviewed products. In this chapter, we will cover topics that help you develop a scripting infrastructure.

By the end of this chapter, you will have learned techniques to successfully implement, deploy, secure, and monitor automated scripts.

In this chapter, we will cover the following topics:

- PowerShell modules
- Certificates and code signing
- Credential management
- Tracing and script automation

PowerShell modules

In the previous chapters, we have used files to package scripts, functions to easily reuse our code, and the modules for each of the Office 365 APIs. As your code gets more complex, the logical progression is to implement your own modules.

Advantages of modules are as follows:

- Package functionality for distribution and reuse
- Provides documentation infrastructure
- Can have private and public functions

We will get started by reviewing the available commands to work with modules.

To showcase the advantages of modules, we will create an example. Our module will support a dashboard in SharePoint Online. The dashboard will display daily sales for each of the products in the database.

So that we do not deviate too much from the scope of this chapter, we will use the AdventureWorks schema (`http://msftdbprodsamples.codeplex.com/releases/view/55330`). This database contains a simple model of products, customers, and sales that we will use to calculate daily sales.

In this scenario, we calculate the product daily sales and update a SharePoint list with that information. Our module will contain functions to read from a SQL Server database and to connect to SharePoint Online and update a list:

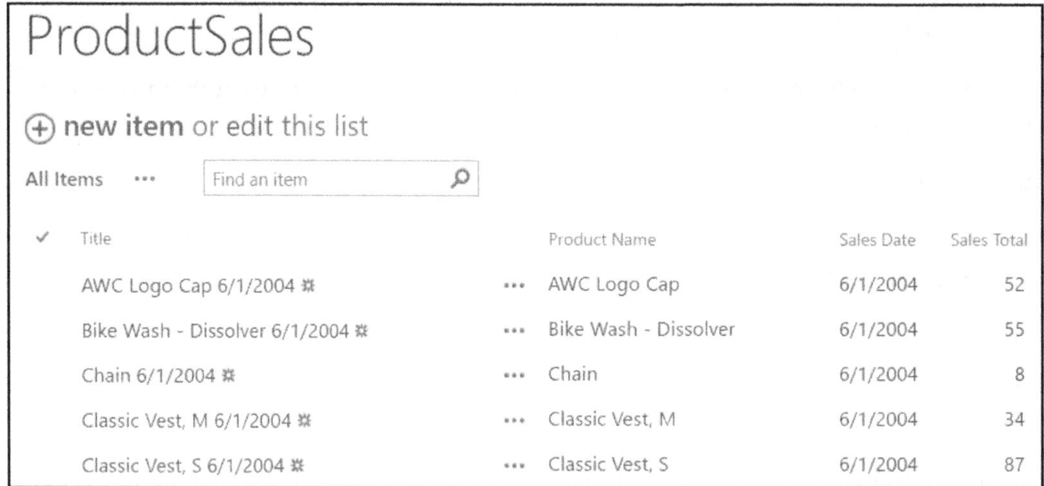

If you can expose your database publicly, this scenario could be better implemented with SharePoint **Business Connectivity Services** (**BCS**). BCS allows direct integration with SQL Server and other data sources.

Module manifest

A PowerShell module consists of at least a manifest file (the extension `.psd1`). It is common to at least have a main module file (the extension `.psm1`). A manifest file can reference additional modules, scripts, and supporting files as required.

The manifest file contains metadata of the script, including the name, dependencies, and version. The `New-ModuleManifest` command will generate the manifest file:

```
New-ModuleManifest -Path SalesDashboardModule.psd1 -Author Martin
 -CompanyName Packt -Copyright 2017
```

You can pass all of the parameters to the command, but it is usually easier to modify the manifest file directly after it's generated since it is a text file and will require constant updates during the development stage:

Use `Show-Command` to inspect a new command or one with many parameters.

The following screenshot shows the output for `Show-Command`. For the time being we will fill out the parameters used in the previous example. We will review the remaining parameters throughout the chapter:

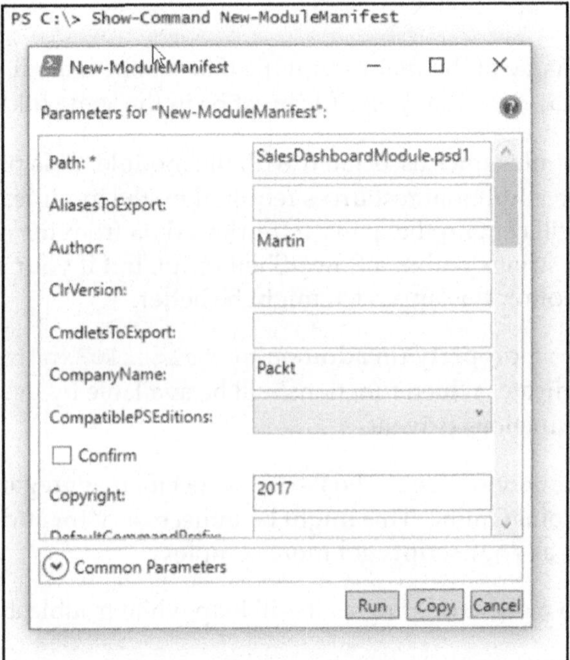

In the following manifest, we have modified the `RootModule`, `FileList`, `FunctionsToExport`, and `NestedModules` properties:

```
# Module manifest for module 'SalesDashboardModule'

@{ # Script module or binary module file associated with this manifest.
RootModule = 'SalesDashboardModule'

# Version number of this module.
ModuleVersion = '1.0.0.1'

# Functions to export from this module
FunctionsToExport = @('Get-DailyProductSalesQuery','Get-
DailyProductSalesTotals')

# List of all files packaged with this module
FileList = @("DailyProductSalesQuery.sql")

# Modules to import as nested modules of the module specified in RootModule
NestedModules = @('SqlFunctions.psm1', 'SPOFunctions.psm1')
...
}
```

`RootModule` is the filename of the main script file that will be loaded by the module. In this case, the `SalesDashboardModule.psm1` file must be in the same folder as the manifest file.

`FileList` is an array of filenames associated with the module. This property is public and can be used to reference additional resources required by the module. In this example, we added a SQL file that will contain the query to retrieve data from the sample database. It is common to have inline strings within a PowerShell script, but if your string is long or requires a specialized editor, this approach might be better.

The `FunctionsToExport` property (in addition to `CmdletsToExport` and `AliasesToExport`) indicates which functions will be available by users of your module. Use this array to keep functions private.

Lastly, we have two `NestedModules`. The two files specified aggregate functions related to SQL Server and SharePoint Online. This might be unnecessary for such a small example, but it is a good practice as your scripts get more complex.

`ModuleVersion` is also worth updating as it will help while troubleshooting.

In the following session, we load and inspect the module. Note the `ErrorAction` parameter in the `Remove-Module` command. This command will likely fail since the module should not be loaded at the beginning of the script. The `Ignore` setting will prevent the error message from being shown and continue execution:

```
PS C:> Remove-Module SalesDashboardModule -ErrorAction Ignore
PS C:> $module = Get-Module SalesDashboardModule
PS C:> if($module -eq $null) {
 Import-Module -Name C:\temp\SalesDashboardModule -Verbose
  $module = Get-Module SalesDashboardModule
}

VERBOSE: Loading module from path
'C:\temp\SalesDashboardModule\SalesDashboardModule.psd1'.
VERBOSE: Loading module from path
'C:\temp\SalesDashboardModule\SqlFunctions.psm1'.
VERBOSE: Loading module from path
'C:\temp\SalesDashboard\ModuleSPOFunctions.psm1'.
...
VERBOSE: Loading module from path
'C:\temp\SalesDashboard\ModuleSalesDashboardModule.psm1'.
VERBOSE: Exporting function 'Get-DailyProductSalesQuery'.
VERBOSE: Exporting function 'Get-DailyProductSalesTotals'.
...
VERBOSE: Exporting function 'Start-DbSync'.
VERBOSE: Importing function 'Get-DailyProductSalesQuery'.
VERBOSE: Importing function 'Get-DailyProductSalesTotals'.

PS C:> $module.Version
Major Minor Build Revision
----- ----- ----- --------
1     0     0     4

PS C:> $module.FileList
C:\temp\SalesDashboard\ModuleDailyProductSalesQuery.sql

PS C:> $module.ExportedFunctions.Keys
Get-DailyProductSalesQuery
Get-DailyProductSalesTotals
...
```

Removing the module at the beginning of the script is a good practice, particularly during development, when you will run the script repeatedly.

Script modules

In the SqlFunctions module, we have two functions. Get-DailyProductsSalesQuery will return the contents of the SQL file. Note that within the function, we get a reference to the module. We then use the FileList property to get the full path of the SQL file:

```
function Get-DailyProductSalesQuery{
 $module = Get-Module SalesDashboardModule;

 $filePath = $module.FileList | Where { $_ -like
'*DailyProductSalesQuery*'}

 $sql = [System.IO.File]::ReadAllText($filePath).Trim();

 Write-Debug "Sql: $($sql)";
 return $sql;
}
```

Before returning the SQL script, we use Write-Debug to show the message on the console. The output of this command will be visible only when running in debug mode.

Advanced functions can be called with the -Debug parameter. If you need to debug a function, you can set the $DebugPreference global variable.

The remaining function, Get-DailyProductSalesTotals, will retrieve the results of the query as rows. Using CmdletBinding, we enable a few additional features for the function (functions with this attribute are called **advanced functions**). First, we can make use of the -Verbose and -Debug parameters to configure the visibility of the Write-Verbose and Write-Debug statements within it:

```
function Get-DailyProductSalesTotals {
 [CmdletBinding()]
 param (
        [Parameter(
                Mandatory = $false,
                HelpMessage = 'Enter a date to start from e.g.:(Get-
Date("MM/DD/YYYY"))')]
        [Alias('StartDate','Date')]
        [DateTime]$dateFilter =
([System.Data.SqlTypes.SqlDateTime]::MinValue.Value)
 )

 Write-Debug "$($dateFilter)";
```

```
$sql = Get-DailyProductSalesQuery;
$sqlParams = "FILTERDATE=$($dateFilter.ToString('yyyy-MM-dd'))"

Write-Debug "$($sqlParams)";

return Invoke-Sqlcmd -Query $sql -ServerInstance "Sql17tests" -Variable
$sqlParams;
}
```

Parameters can also be defined with several attributes to help the user. The `StartDate` parameter is defined as an optional `Date` input. The parameter can be set as `StartDate` (or `Date` through the use of the `Alias` attribute) and has a default value. This parameter is used to filter all dates before its value from the results. When this parameter is not set, its default value is used, effectively including all rows (the `SqlDateTime.MinValue` value usually defaults to `1/1/1753`).

For the many other advantages of advanced functions, refer to `https://technet.microsoft.com/en-us/library/hh360993.aspx`.

In the following script, we call the function with the `-Debug` parameter and without a `StartDate` parameter:

```
PS C:> $rows = Get-DailyProductSalesTotals -Debug
DEBUG: 01/01/1753 00:00:00

DEBUG: Sql: USE [AdventureWorksLT2012]
 DECLARE @startDate as date;

 SET @startDate = cast('$(FILTERDATE)' as date);

 SELECT p.[Name] ProductName, sh.OrderDate ,SUM(OrderQty) Quantity
 FROM SalesLT.SalesOrderDetail sd
  JOIN SalesLT.SalesOrderHeader sh ON sd.SalesOrderID = sh.SalesOrderID
  JOIN SalesLT.Product p ON sd.ProductID = p.ProductID
 WHERE sh.OrderDate >= @startDate
 GROUP BY p.[Name], sh.OrderDate
 ORDER BY p.[Name]

DEBUG: FILTERDATE=1753-01-01

PS C:> $rows.Count
142

PS C:> $rows
```

```
ProductName          OrderDate                Quantity
-----------          ---------                --------
AWC Logo Cap         6/1/2004 12:00:00 AM     52
Bike Wash - Dissolver 6/1/2004 12:00:00 AM    55
Chain                6/1/2004 12:00:00 AM     8
...
```

`Invoke-Sqlcmd` will call the database with the SQL query and return the matching records. The `Variable` parameter takes an array of variables that will be replaced in the SQL query. The passed array accepts only those string values that will be replaced in the SQL query. Note that in the SQL query, we have the interpolation of the `FILTERDATE` variable. To minimize an opportunistic SQL injection attack, we set the value of the `FILTERDATE` variable into a SQL variable `@startDate` of type date. In addition, the input parameter in the PowerShell function is also `Date`, which minimizes the risk even further (in the case of a string filter, you could replace `Invoke-Sqlcmd` with the .NET `SqlCommand` class that allows the use of SQL parameters, adding an additional layer of parameter validation and supporting additional data types).

To access SharePoint Online, we will need to store user credentials (application access tokens are a better approach but are beyond the scope of this book). The `Get-SalesDashboardCreds` function will prompt for credentials and save them as a serialized string on the filesystem. By default, `PSCredentials` stores the password as `SecureString`. The credentials are encrypted and can only be used by the account that created it (within the machine where it was created):

```
# get credentials from a file or prompt the user
function Get-SalesDashboardCreds(){
 $credPaths = 'C:\temp\pass1.txt'
 if (Test-Path -Path $credPaths){ #file exists
 Write-Host "Loading credentials from file: $credPaths" -BackgroundColor
Yellow -ForegroundColor Black

 $rawCreds = Get-Content $credPaths

 # load from file
 $creds =
[System.Management.Automation.PSSerializer]::Deserialize($rawCreds )
 }else{
  $creds = Get-Credential # prompt user for credentials
  [System.Management.Automation.PSSerializer]::Serialize($creds) |
   Out-File $credPaths # Save to file
 }
 return $creds;
}
```

The `Get-SalesDashboardContext` function simply uses the credentials to create `ClientContext`. The context will be used to read and write to the SharePoint list:

```
function Get-SalesDashboardContext ($siteUrl){
 $creds = Get-SalesDashboardCreds;
 Write-Debug "$($siteUrl) $($user)"

 $clientContext = New-Object
Microsoft.SharePoint.Client.ClientContext($siteUrl);

 $credentials = New-Object
Microsoft.SharePoint.Client.SharePointOnlineCredentials($creds.UserName,
$creds.Password);
 $clientContext.Credentials = $credentials;
 return $clientContext;
}
```

Cmdlets

Cmdlets were the original way of extending PowerShell. Cmdlets have basically the same functionality as functions (PowerShell cmdlets are comparable with advanced functions), but they are implemented in C# and packaged in .NET assemblies.

It is more common to implement scripts as functions in PowerShell files as they can be edited easily. Still, cmdlets might be useful in a few scenarios:

- There is a significant investment in C# as a scripting language
- The code needs to be protected (.NET assemblies can be obfuscated)

In the following example, we define the `GetListCommand` cmdlet. It inherits from the `Cmdlet` class from the `System.Management.Automation` namespace.

To consume SharePoint, the `Cmdlet` class accepts a `ClientContext` parameter that will let us check whether the list exists and create it and the custom fields required to hold the data for the dashboard.

The `ClientContext` parameter is as follows:

- It is required as the `Mandatory` attribute will cause an exception if a value is not set
- It can accept values from the pipeline through the `ValueFromPipeline` attribute
- It will check whether the value is null and prevent execution if needed

Following is the `GetListCommand` Cmdlet:

```
[Cmdlet(VerbsCommon.Get, "DashboardList")]
public class GetListCommand : Cmdlet
{
  [Parameter(Mandatory = true, ValueFromPipeline = true)]
  [ValidateNotNullOrEmpty]
  public ClientContext ClientContext { get; set; }

  protected override void ProcessRecord()
  {
    var list = EnsureList(ClientContext);
    WriteObject(list);
  }

  List EnsureList(ClientContext ctx) {
    var lists = ctx.Web.Lists;
    var listTitle = "ProductSales";
    ctx.Load(lists, ls => ls.Where(i => i.Title == listTitle));
    ctx.ExecuteQuery();

   List list = lists.FirstOrDefault();
   if (lists.Count == 0) {
     var listInfo = new ListCreationInformation() {
       TemplateType = (int)ListTemplateType.GenericList,
       Title = listTitle
     };

     list = ctx.Web.Lists.Add(listInfo);
     var fields = new List<string>()
     {
       "<Field Type='Text' Name='ProductName'
         DisplayName='Product Name'/>",
       "<Field Type='DateTime' Name='SalesDate'
         DisplayName='Sales Date' Format='DateOnly' />",
       "<Field Type='Number' Name='SalesTotal'
         DisplayName='Sales Total'/>"
     };
     foreach (var field in fields)
     {
       list.Fields.AddFieldAsXml(field, true,
       AddFieldOptions.AddFieldInternalNameHint);
     }
   }

   ctx.Load(list);
   ctx.ExecuteQuery();
```

```
        return list;
      }
    }
```

The `ProcessRecord` method implements the functionality of `Cmdlet` by calling the `EnsureList` method and returning the result (a SharePoint list) to the pipeline through the `WriteObject` method.

The `EnsureList` method first checks whether the list exists by searching for it by name. If it is not found, a new list is created. When adding the fields, it is worth noting that the `AddFieldInternalNameHint` parameter is used to make that `Name` attribute pass and is used as the field's internal name (by default, the display name is used).

Parameters passing from PowerShell to .NET cmdlets can be riddled with conversion issues if the assemblies used by PowerShell and the `Cmdlet` class do not match.

Next, we will review the only function in the main module. The `Start-DashboardSync` function (defined in the main module) ties it all together by inserting or updating records in SharePoint with the data retrieved from SQL Server:

```
function Start-DashboardSync{

  Write-Debug 'Starting DB to SharePoint Online Sync'
  $ctx = Get-SalesDashboardContext 'https//test.sharepoint.com';
  $list = Get-DashboardList -ClientContext $ctx

  $items =  $list.GetItems([Microsoft.SharePoint.Client.CamlQuery]::
    CreateAllItemsQuery());
  $ctx.Load($items);
  $ctx.ExecuteQuery();

  $salesRows = Get-DailyProductSalesTotals;
  "Sales Records: $($salesRows.Count)"

  ForEach ($dbRow in $salesRows) {
    $spRecord = $items | Where { $_["SalesDate"].Date -eq
     $dbRow.OrderDate.Date -and     $dbRow.ProductName -eq
     $_["ProductName"]};

    if ($spRecord -eq $null){
      Write-Information "New record for $($dbRow.ProductName)
       $($dbRow.OrderDate.Date)"
      $newItemInfo = New-Object
       Microsoft.SharePoint.Client.ListItemCreationInformation
```

```
          $spRecord = $list.AddItem($newItemInfo);
          $spRecord["Title"] = "$($dbRow.ProductName)
          $($dbRow.OrderDate.Date.ToShortDateString())";
          $spRecord["SalesDate"] = $dbRow.OrderDate;
          $spRecord["ProductName"] = $dbRow.ProductName;
        }
        $spRecord["SalesTotal"] = $dbRow.Quantity;
        $spRecord.Update();
      }
      $ctx.ExecuteQuery();
    }
```

Lastly, we will review the script that will run on a schedule. To make sure we can review its results even when running in unattended mode, we will make use of the `Start-Transcript` command. When using `Start-Transcript`, all the commands and their outputs are included in the specified log file:

```
Start-Transcript -Path c:\scripts\SyncLog.txt -Append -
IncludeInvocationHeader

Remove-Module SalesDashboardModule -ErrorAction Ignore
$module = Get-Module SalesDashboardModule

if($module -eq $null){
 Import-Module -Name C:\temp\SalesDashboardModule

 $module = Get-Module SalesDashboardModule
}
$module.Version

Start-DashboardSync

Stop-Transcript
```

The `Append` parameter will create or append contents to the file in the `Path` parameter. The `IncludeInvocationHeader` parameter adds useful information to logs:

```
**********************
Windows PowerShell transcript start
Start time: 20170326190703
Username: devpshell
RunAs User: devpshell
Machine: app22 (Microsoft Windows NT 10.0.14393.0)
Host Application:
C:\Windows\System32\WindowsPowerShellv1.0\powershell_ise.exe
C:\temp\SalesDashboardModule\RunSalesSync.ps1
Process ID: 7348
```

```
PSVersion: 5.1.14393.953
PSEdition: Desktop
PSCompatibleVersions: 1.0, 2.0, 3.0, 4.0, 5.0, 5.1.14393.953
BuildVersion: 10.0.14393.953
CLRVersion: 4.0.30319.42000
WSManStackVersion: 3.0
PSRemotingProtocolVersion: 2.3
SerializationVersion: 1.1.0.1
**********************
INFO: SalesDashboardModule.Init

Major Minor Build Revision
----- ----- ----- --------
1     0     0     6
Loading credentials from file: C:\temp\pass1.txt
Loaded list: ProductSales
Sales Records: 1
**********************
Windows PowerShell transcript end
End time: 20170326190707
**********************
```

With this, we conclude the implementation of the module. The full project can be downloaded from the GitHub repository: `https://github.com/xsolon/powershellOffice365`.

Visual Studio's PowerShell project template simplifies the authoring of PowerShell modules. The module manifest and supporting files are automatically created in addition to source control and debugging capabilities.

Scheduled execution

Before we begin the setup, let's review the requirements to complete our scenario:

- Execution needs to happen without a user session
- The account's minimum privileges include access to a local database
- The account's password should not expire
- Script results need to be available for review in the event of an error

So that we do not use password credentials in clear text (for the database connection), we will use a domain account to run the script. When creating the account, make sure you check the **Password never expires** setting:

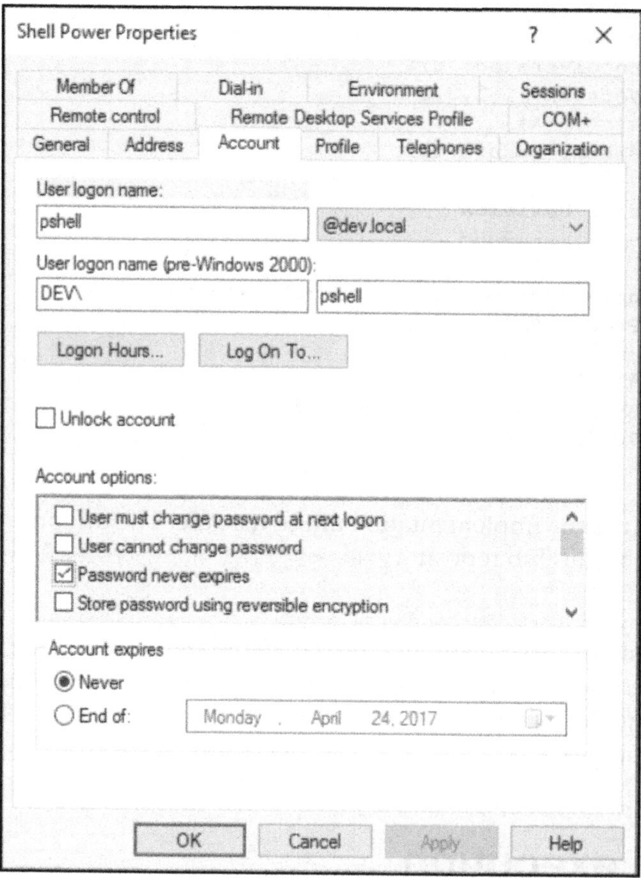

In SQL Server, we give the account **Select** access only to the tables we are using. A better approach would be to set up a view and give access to it instead:

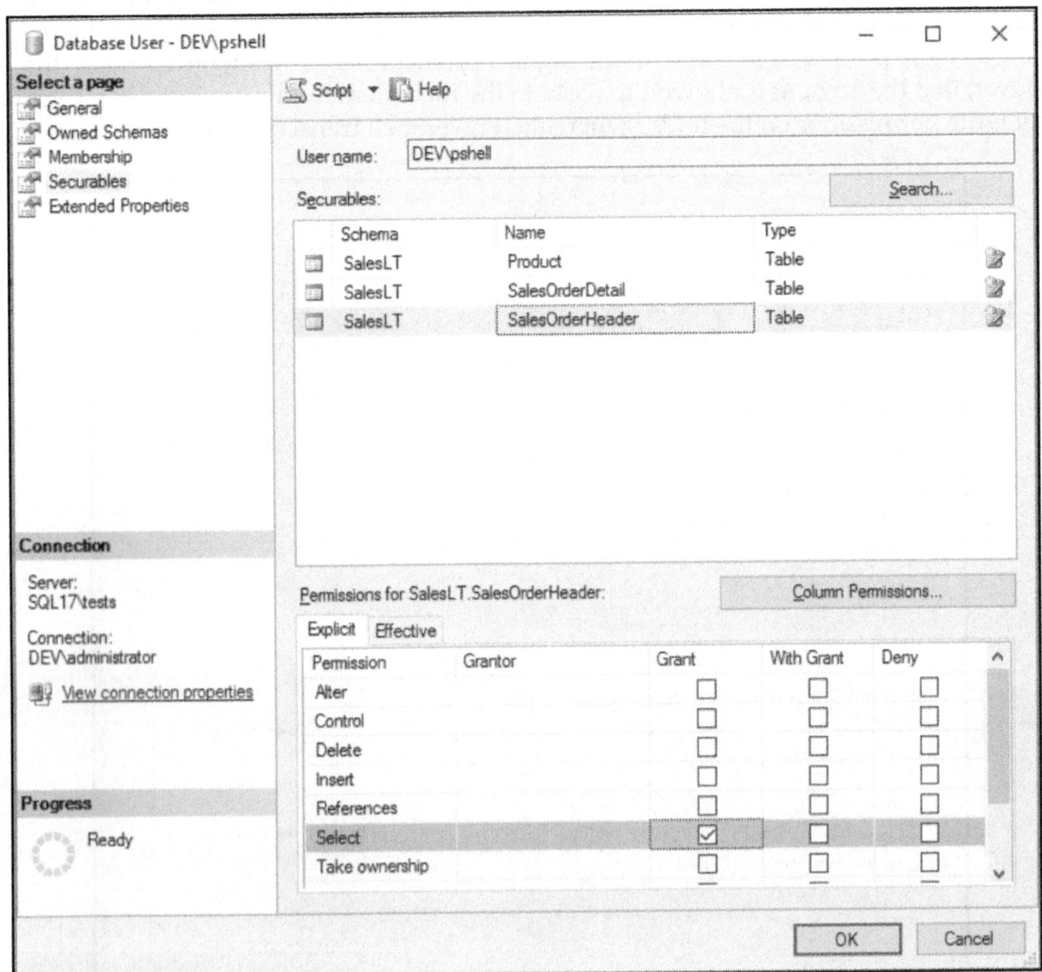

The task account will also need access to write logs to a directory and the **Log on as a service** permission on the machine to run the task unattended. We can set permissions on the log folder using the explorer and the permission will be assigned automatically through the Windows **Task Scheduler**.

The Windows **Task Scheduler** is a reliable platform for script automation. You can create and manage multiple tasks that can run in many scenarios. We will set up a daily task using the **Create Task** option. In the **Security options** panel, configure the task to run with the dedicated account credentials. In this case, we are accessing a database and SharePoint Online so there is no need to run with the highest privileges. You will have to make sure, however, that the account is allowed to write to the filesystem in this case (use File Explorer to set write permissions on the folder where the PowerShell transcript will be saved):

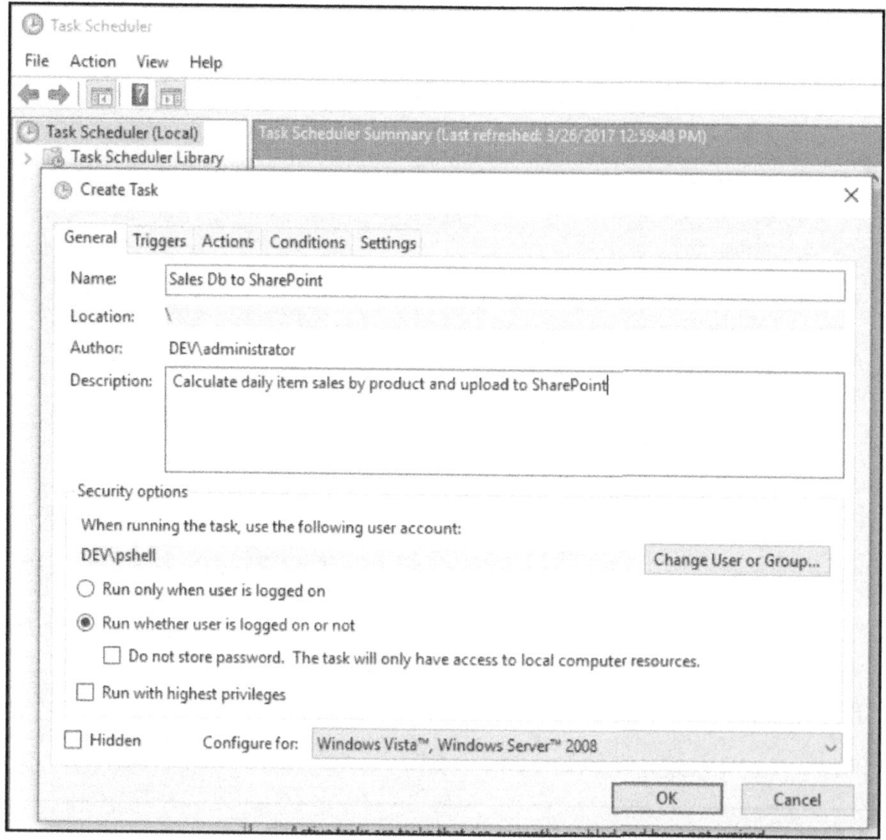

Configure the schedule for the task in the **Triggers** tab. In the **Actions** tab, we will run PowerShell with the script as an argument. The **Start in** parameter is useful if you reference files (or set up transcripts) with relative paths. The path of execution will be set to `C:\scripts`, which is the location in which the scripts are located and where the transcripts will be saved:

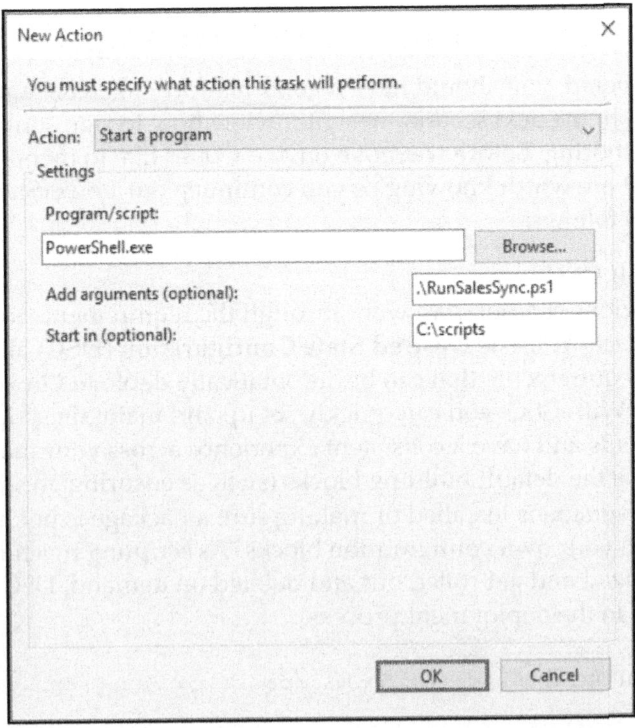

When you are done configuring the task, you will be prompted for the credentials for the account. The following message indicates that **Log on as a batch job** right needs to be assigned. This permission can be assigned to the user through the **Local Security Policy** manager:

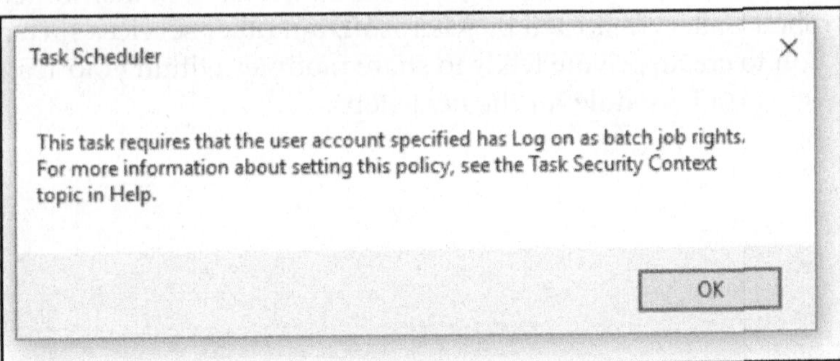

Scripting instrumentation - the next steps

With the material covered, you should have a good platform to create and maintain modules and scripts. In the next section, we will review how to sign scripts, which is an important part of authoring. Before we move on, we would like to mention other topics that we will not cover but are worth knowing as you continue your PowerShell scripting journey. These are as follows:

- **PowerShell DSC**:
  In the previous chapters, we went through the requirements to get samples to work for each API. The **Desired State Configuration** (**DSC**) allows you define a group of requirements that can be automatically deployed in your scripting machines. With DSC, you can quickly set up and maintain scripting environments and have a consistent experience across your machines. Not only can you use the default building blocks (such as ensuring an `.msi` file of a particular version is installed or making sure a package is not installed), you can also design your own configuration blocks. As scripting machines become commoditized and get rolled out and deleted on demand, DSC can save you some time in the deployment process.

Learn more at `https://msdn.microsoft.com/en-us/powershell/dsc/overview`.

- **Module repositories**:
  You can author and publish modules to public or private online repositories. This makes it easy to share and update your modules even in distributed scenarios. PowerShell Gallery is hosted by Microsoft, but other services such as MyGet allow you to create private feeds to share modules within your team. Review the `PowerShellGet` module for the next steps.

Code signing

PowerShell's execution policy adds another layer of security to administrators. The default setting prevents executing scripts in order to be able to support automation, modules, or complex scripts. There are two other settings, that allow us to run scripts as long as they are signed.

Prevention of code execution is not the ultimate goal of these execution policy settings. A malicious agent may simply copy the remote script and execute it by copying and pasting the code in a PowerShell Terminal. The signed script's goal is to guarantee that the source of it is known and trusted and that the contents of the script code have not been tampered with.

Being able to validate the signature of a script allows some flexibility, such as being able to download scripts from a file share or web location. As long as the private key used to sign the scripts is kept safe by the author and the public key of the certificate is valid and remains trusted, the consumer can validate that the contents of the scripts are from the author and they have not been modified after being signed.

An Office 365 administrator will either author scripts or manage scripts created by developers or third-parties. In either case, the task is to establish a secure means of storing and executing scripts.

Setting up a signing infrastructure

Certificates are issued by a **certification authority** (**CA**). A CA can be internal or from a third-party. In either case, a certificate is issued by the CA following a request. The request specifies the requestor's information, purpose, lifetime, a friendly name, and other characteristics of the certificate.

Once approved, the certificate is signed and issued by the CA's certificate. This new certificate will be trusted as long as the CA's certificate is trusted by the consumer.

Third-party CAs such as Verisign and others have the trust of most consumers; therefore, a certificate issued by them is automatically trusted worldwide. In practice, this is implemented by packaging the CA's public signature in operating systems, browsers, and other products and devices. You can imagine that this bundling requires lots of coordination and effort. Therefore, the inherent value of a certificate lies in it being issued by a trusted CA.

A globally trusted CA is important when you have an unmanaged consumer base, public websites being the most common case. If you are an ISV that is distributing software to the general public, a globally trusted certificate might be required as well. When authoring scripts for Office 365, you will probably have a small audience for your scripts. In this case, you can simply distribute the keys directly to your users and avoid third-party costs. We will also review how to take advantage of Active Directory Certificate Services when working within a domain.

Of course, there is more to the CA infrastructure. Being able to centrally manage requests, certificates, security, and policies makes for a compelling story in large deployments.

We will review how to work with a CA or issue self-signed certificates (a self-signed certificate is a special case where the CA is the certificate itself).

The PKI module

The PowerShell PKI module is a relatively new API for certificate management. If you have any experience with MakeCert or OpenSSL (the most documented tools for certificate generation), you will notice that some tasks seem quite involved in comparison. Indeed, it is a new API and will continue to evolve. Our recommendation if you are just learning to work with certificates is that you also look at these tools. MakeCert has been recently deprecated and is being replaced by the PKI module; however, the many samples online are still helpful.

Certificate specifications have not changed. The differences in the examples (specially between MakeCert and PKI) lie mostly in syntax.

Granted that you have proper access to the CA and the infrastructure setup (more on this later), you should be able to work with certificates directly from PowerShell.

The following examples were run in PowerShell 5.

Self-signed certificates

Self-signed certificates are convenient during development and can also be used in production scenarios as long as the author and the consumer can agree to trust the certificate. The main advantage of self-signed certificates is that you can quickly generate certificates without having to go through a process involving others.

The drawback is that you have to specify all the details of the certificates and that involves more code than in a CA scenario where you can, for example, use templates.

In the following scripts, we will set up a self-signed CA and use it to create signing certificates for our PowerShell scripts.

Creating a CA certificate

The `New-SelfSignedCertificate` command packages a lot of functionality. In the following sample, we are creating a self-signed certificate authority certificate:

```
$enforceLevels = $true
$levelOfSubCertsAllowed = 0;
$isCa = $true;
$isCritical = $true;

$caConstraint = New-Object
System.Security.Cryptography.X509Certificates.X509BasicConstraintsExtension
`
 -ArgumentList @($isCa, $enforceLevels, $levelOfSubCertsAllowed,
$isCritical)

$caCert = New-SelfSignedCertificate -CertStoreLocation
'Cert:\CurrentUser\MY' -Subject "My Certificate Authority" -Extension
@($caConstraint) -NotAfter (Get-Date).AddYears(20) -KeyLength 4096
 -KeyAlgorithm RSA -FriendlyName 'MyCA' -Type Custom -KeyUsage
DigitalSignature, CRLSign, CertSign
```

Let's review each parameter of the command:

- `CertStoreLocation`: You can specify the certificate store where the certificate will be saved. You can select the current user or local machine store. We used the current user store because the local machine store requires administrator permissions.
- `Subject`: The name or identifier of what is being secured by the certificate. In the context of a web certificate, this is usually a URL. In the case of a CA, we specify its name.
- `Extension`: Before the `New-SelfSignedCertificate` command, we defined a `X509BasicConstraintsExtension` class that is passed to the `Extension` parameter.
  Extensions can be used to define additional properties of the certificate. In this case, the `BasicConstraints` extension was introduced with version 3 of the PKI (`https://tools.ietf.org/html/rfc3280.html`), and it is used to set additional properties of a CA certificate.
  In this case, we are creating an instance of the extension with the following constructor (`https://msdn.microsoft.com/en-us/library/dae4893s(v=vs.110).aspx`):

```
public X509BasicConstraintsExtension(
  bool certificateAuthority,
  bool hasPathLengthConstraint,
  int pathLengthConstraint,
  bool critical
)
```

  Let's review each parameter:

  - `CertificateAuthority`: If `true`, the certificate will act as a CA
  - `HasPathLengthConstraint`: If `true`, it will allow only a certain number of sub-CAs (otherwise know as **intermediate CAs**)
  - `PathLengthConstraint`: The number of levels of intermediate CAs to be allowed
  - `Critical`: Identifies whether the certificate is critical (true for CAs)

In this case, we do not allow intermediate CAs, but in production deployments it is a good idea to issue intermediate CAs for different activities (for example, SSL certs and code signing certs can be issued and managed by different teams) so that these tasks can be delegated, at the same time limiting access to the root CA.

- `NotAfter`: Sets the expiration date of the certificate. Note that the lifetime of certificates issued by this certificate will not exceed this date.
- `KeyLength` and `KeyAlgorithm`: The key length and algorithm define the complexity of the certificate asymmetric keys. Both the parameters affect encryption, signature performance, and compatibility.
- `FriendlyName`: This parameter can be used as an identifier when filtering certificates from a store. We will use it in other examples.
- `Type`: Sets the type of certificate being created. Depending on the value, additional properties will be added to the certificate. In the case of a CA, the `Custom` value is necessary. Available values are as follows:
    - `CodeSigningCert`
    - `Custom`
    - `DocumentEncryptionCert`
    - `DocumentEncryptionCertLegacyCsp`
    - `SSLServerAuthentication` (default)
- `KeyUsage`: If specified, the `KeyUsage` extension will be added to the certificate. The extension lists the scenarios that the certificate will support. In the case of a CA, these are required: `DigitalSignature`, `CRLSign`, and `CertSign`. Available values are as follows:
    - `CertSign`
    - `CRLSign`
    - `DataEncipherment`
    - `DecipherOnly`
    - `DigitalSiganture`
    - `EncipherOnly`
    - `KeyAgreement`
    - `KeyEncipherment`
    - `None` (default)
    - `NonRepudiation`

There are some additional parameters too.

We have barely scratched the surface of this command and will delve into it further in the following examples.

For the sake of keeping the example as simple as possible, we have omitted some parameters that might be important. `KeyExportPolicy` and `KeyProtection` play an important role in securing a certificate. Also, several parameters' default values will allow the certificate to inherit the values from an underlying **cryptographic service provider** (**CSP**) or **key storage provider** (**KSP**). Moreover, parameters may not be necessary for some situations. For example, when issuing a root CA, the basic constraint extension is not required; however, an intermediate CA may not function properly without it.

We encourage you to review the certificate specifications and experiment further with the PKI module:

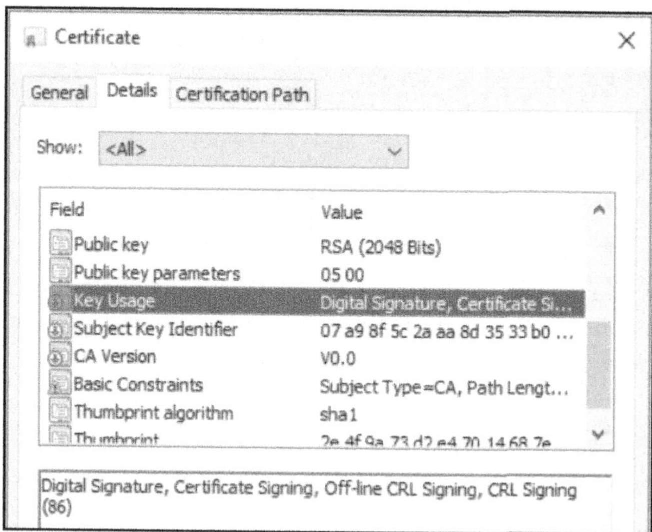

Because the options are so vast, we recommend that you review an existing certificate configuration and compare the certificate created by the command.

Compare the properties of the generated certificates with existing certificates to validate their completeness.

Querying certificate stores

In the preceding sample, we saved the generated certificate in a variable. This is a very convenient when creating a new certificate, but usually you will be loading certificates from a store or the filesystem.

A certificate's thumbprint is used as the directory where it is stored and is usually used to retrieve it. However, you can use other identifiers such as `FriendlyName` and `Subject` using PowerShell's filtering features:

```
$caCert.Thumbprint
2A0290A44F5052EB5E4F26C55858324B4870EFD6

Get-ChildItem -Path
Cert:\CurrentUser\My\2A0290A44F5052EB5E4F26C55858324B4870EFD6

Thumbprint                                  Subject
----------                                  -------
2A0290A44F5052EB5E4F26C55858324B4870EFD6    CN=My Certificate Authority

$caCert = Get-ChildItem -Path Cert:CurrentUsermy | Where { $_.Subject -eq
'CN=My Certificate Authority'}

$caCert = Get-ChildItem -Path Cert:\CurrentUser\my | Where {
$_.FriendlyName -eq 'MyCA'}
```

Exporting, importing, and publishing certificates

At this point, you should be able to create certificates and sign scripts with them. However, the underlying PKI infrastructure will not trust a certificate unless its issuer is a trusted authority. Public CAs are already included in the Trusted Root Certification Authorities store as well as private CAs in an Active Directory environment:

```
$exportType =
[System.Security.Cryptography.X509Certificates.X509ContentType]::Cert

$rawCert =
$caCert.Export($exportType) [System.IO.File]::WriteAllBytes('c:\temp\ca.cer'
,$rawCert)
```

In the preceding sample, we use the cert content type to export the public key of the certificate (all that is required for the PKI to trust a certificate). The `X509ContentType` enumeration has several values for multiple scenarios. Most likely, you will use the `.pfx` value to export the private key to be used in another system.

Alternatively, the `Export-Certificate` and `Export-PfxCertificate` commands can accomplish the same task:

```
$caCert = Get-ChildItem -Path
Cert:\CurrentUser\My\2A0290A44F5052EB5E4F26C55858324B4870EFD6

$password = ConvertTo-SecureString -String "password here" -Force
 -AsPlainText

$caCert | Export-Certificate -FilePath C:\myCa.cer #public key

$caCert | Export-PfxCertificate -FilePath C:\myCapfx.pfx -Password
$password
```

Private keys should be kept safe and are only for internal use. Consumers should have access only to the public key of your certificates.

Now let's import the public key of the CA to the store so that the certificate and any certificates issued by it will be trusted through the `Import-Certificate` command:

```
Import-Certificate -FilePath 'c:\myCa.cer' -CertStoreLocation
'Cert:\CurrentUser\Root'
```

Upon running this command, you will be asked whether you actually want to trust the certificate. Since it is self-signed, there is no authority to validate with:

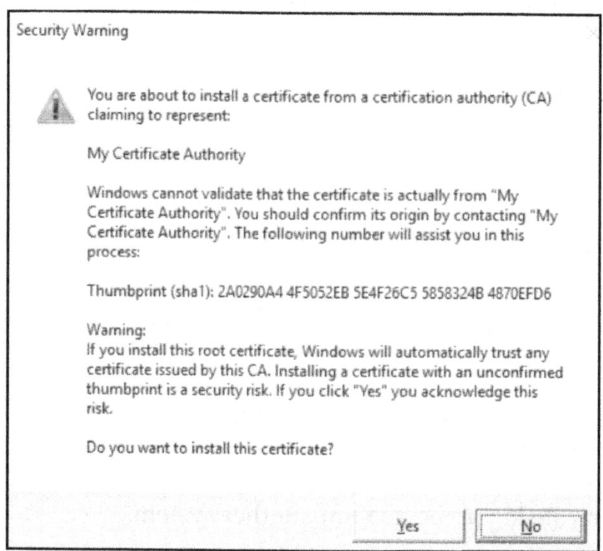

Once imported, you should be able to see the certificate in the Trusted Root Certification Authorities store. Going forward, the certificate and any certificates issued by it will be trusted as long as the certificate is valid:

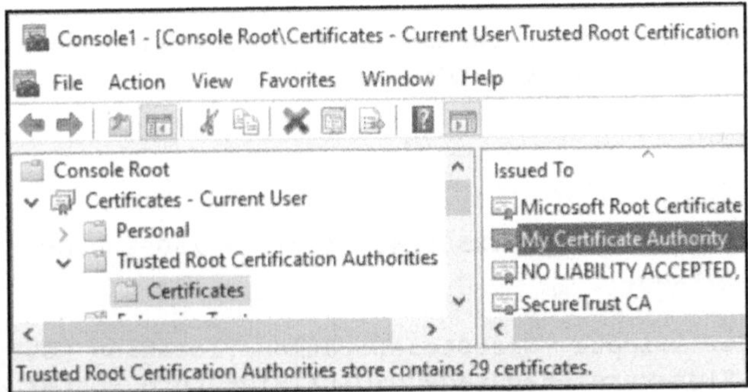

Issuing certificates with a self-signed CA

With reference to our CA certificate, we can issue certificates as required. Before we do that, we need to review the characteristics required for a self-signed certificate.

Certificate policy extensions define the scenarios that the certificate will support. **Object Identifiers (OIDs)** are used to identify the policies that will apply when using a certificate. In the case of a code-signing certificate, the corresponding OID is `1.3.6.1.5.5.7.3.3`:

```
[System.Security.Cryptography.Oid]::FromFriendlyName("Code
Signing",[System.Security.Cryptography.OidGroup]::All)

Value              FriendlyName
-----              ------------
1.3.6.1.5.5.7.3.3  Code Signing
```

In the case of a root CA, the policy extensions are not required. Self-signed CAs automatically pass any policy validation. By attaching the policy extension, you have granular control over the capabilities of the certificate. For example, you may delegate the issuing of code signing certificates by creating an intermediate CA (policy or issuing CA in this context) with only this OID. The intermediate CA administrator would only have access to issue code signing certificates and would not have access to the root or any other certificates up the certificate chain.

A collection of OIDs can be passed (in `X509EnhancedKeyUsageExtension`) to the `New-SelfSignedCertificate` command through the `Extension` parameter:

```
$oidCol = [System.Security.Cryptography.OidCollection]::new()

$oid = [System.Security.Cryptography.Oid]::FromFriendlyName("Code Signing",
System.Security.Cryptography.OidGroup]::All)

$oidCol.Add($oid)

$usage =
[System.Security.Cryptography.X509Certificates.X509EnhancedKeyUsageExtensio
n]::new($oidCol,$true)

New-SelfSignedCertificate -CertStoreLocation $location -Subject "My Signing
Cert" -KeySpec Signature -KeyUsage DigitalSignature -NotAfter (Get-
Date).AddYears(20) -FriendlyName 'MySigningCert' -Extension $usage -Type
CodeSigningCert -Signer $caCert
```

You should be able to generate the certificate as long as you have access to the targeted store and to the private key of the signing certificate:

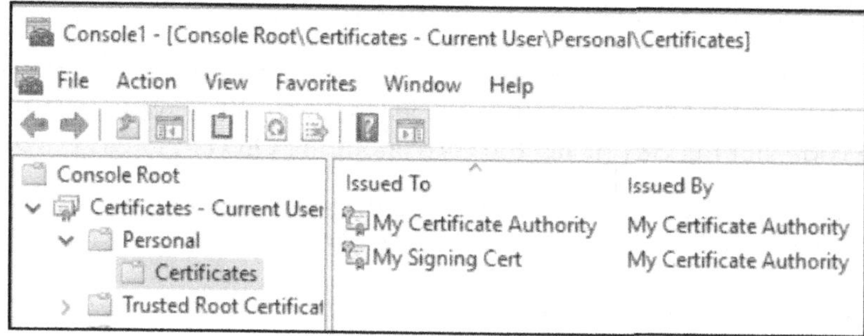

The key in the icon indicates that the private key is available in the store.

When using the signing certificate, you do not need access to the private key of certificates up the certificate chain (other than the CA that is issuing the cert). It is important to limit access to the private keys in order to prevent security issues.

Active Directory Certificate Services

Even though self-signed certificates are very practical, when working within an organization, it is very common to take advantage of an internal CA. As a script author, you will have to go through a request approval process before you can obtain a signing certificate.

Prerequisites

In **Active Directory Certificate Services** (**AD CS**), certificates can be issued and managed through certificate templates. Templates define the purpose, extensions, private key access, security, and many other features for issued certificates. By default, the code signing certificate template is not available in the template list:

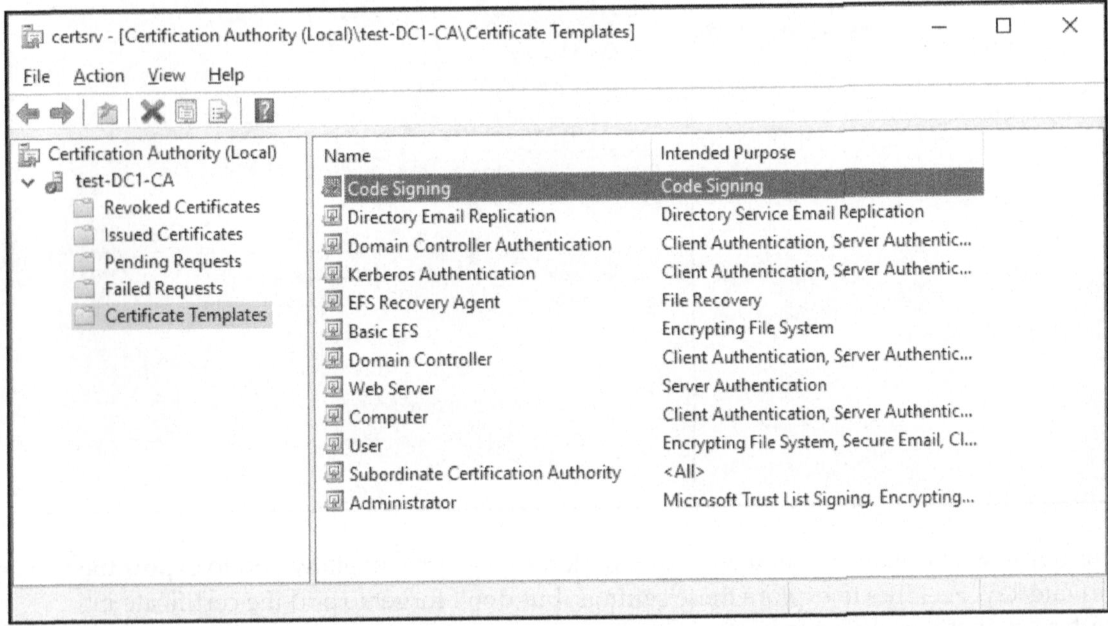

Manage available templates through the CA console (certsrv). You will have to add the code signing template as it is not listed by default.

The `Certificate Templates` node in the **certsrv** console is simply a list of available templates. You can add and remove templates, but their properties are managed in the `Certificate Templates` snap-in of the Microsoft Management Console (`mmc.exe`).

Some of the properties of the **Code Signing** template might require configuration. For example, this type of certificate is set to expire yearly; private keys cannot be exported and the certificate can only be issued to a user (the certificate's subject is set to `user`). Instead of customizing the built-in template, it is usually preferable to create a new template using the **Duplicate Template** context option:

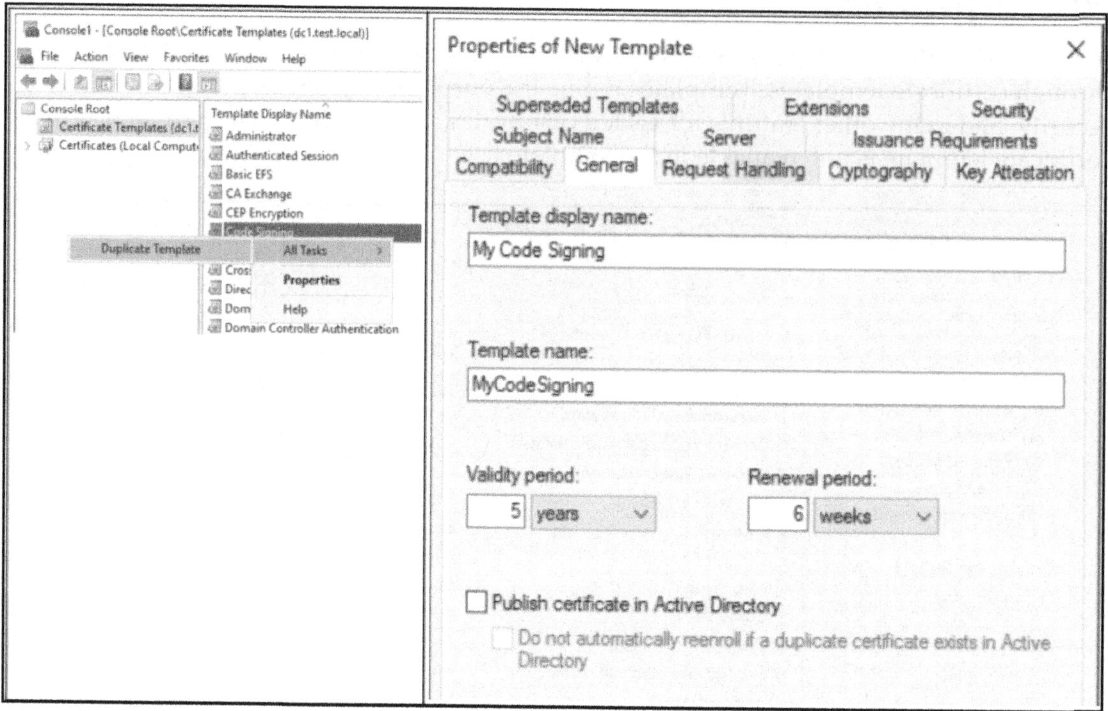

For our new template, we set the validity period to `5` years and allow you to export the private key. Feel free to explore these settings, but don't forget to add the certificate in **certsrv** so that it is available in your CA.

By default, only Domain and Enterprise Admins have access to issue certificates. For the following examples, we will give our scripting account **Read** and **Enroll** permissions for our template.

Certificate template updates may take several minutes to propagate across the domain. Run a `gpupdate` command on the machine submitting requests to make sure the local certificate template cache is up-to-date.

Requesting and issuing certificates in AD CS

Certificates are requested with the `Get-Certificate` command. Depending on multiple factors (such as security, key usage, and issuance requirements), a certificate may be issued immediately or the request will be submitted and set as pending until an administrator's approval.

If the request does not need to go through approval, the certificate will be placed in the local store and returned as a result of the command:

```
Get-Certificate -Template MyCodeSigning -CertStoreLocation
'Cert:\CurrentUser\My' -Url ldap:

Status     Certificate Request
------     -------------------
Pending    [Subject]...
```

If approval is needed, the request will be returned by the command and the pending request will be added in the local store `Certificate Enrollment Requests` as well as in the CA's `Pending Requests` storage. At this time, the administrator must issue the certificate from the CA console:

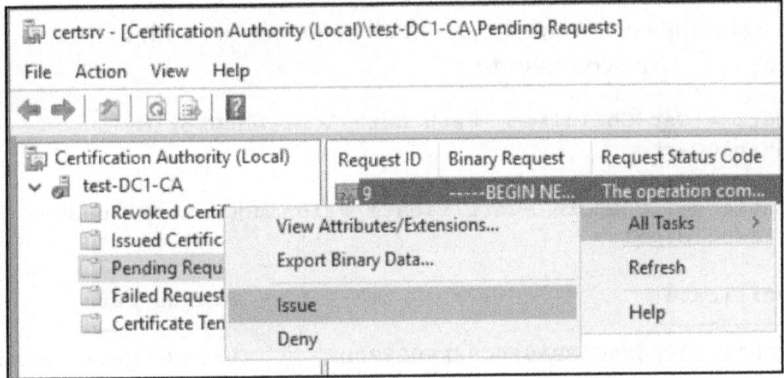

Then, the issuer can complete the submission by retrieving the request from the store and calling the `Get-Certificate` command with it. The certificate will then be available at the location specified in the request (the current user personal store in this case):

```
$request = Get-ChildItem Cert:\CurrentUser\REQUEST
Get-Certificate -Request $request

Status Certificate
------ -----------
Issued [Subject]...
```

The following screenshot shows the location specified in the request:

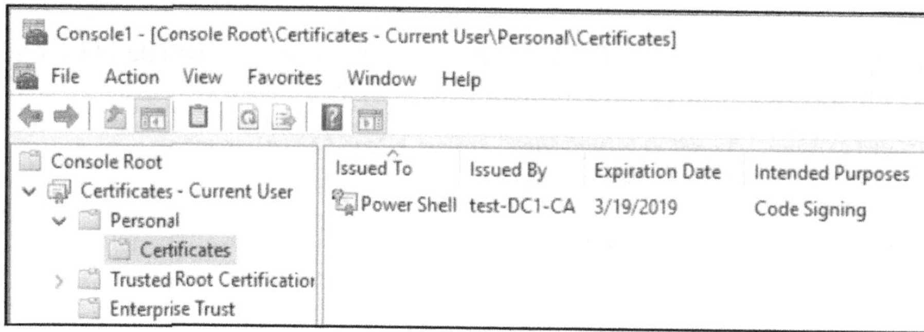

The subject name corresponds to the account requesting the certificate (as specified in the code signing certificate template).

Signing PowerShell scripts

With access to a signing certificate, we can finally sign scripts with the `Set-AuthenticodeSignature` command:

```
$signingCert = Get-ChildItem -Path Cert:\CurrentUser\My
 -CodeSigninigCert

Set-AuthenticodeSignature -Certificate $signingCert -FilePath
C:tempHelloWorld.ps1

SignerCertificate                            Status Path
-----------------                            ------ ----
62092339EDBA1C50E86B4C6BBA960C98FF02820D     Valid  HelloWorld.ps1
```

A signature section will be appended to the script. If you make any changes, you will have to sign the script again before the script can run again (as long as the applicable execution policy requires certificates to be signed):

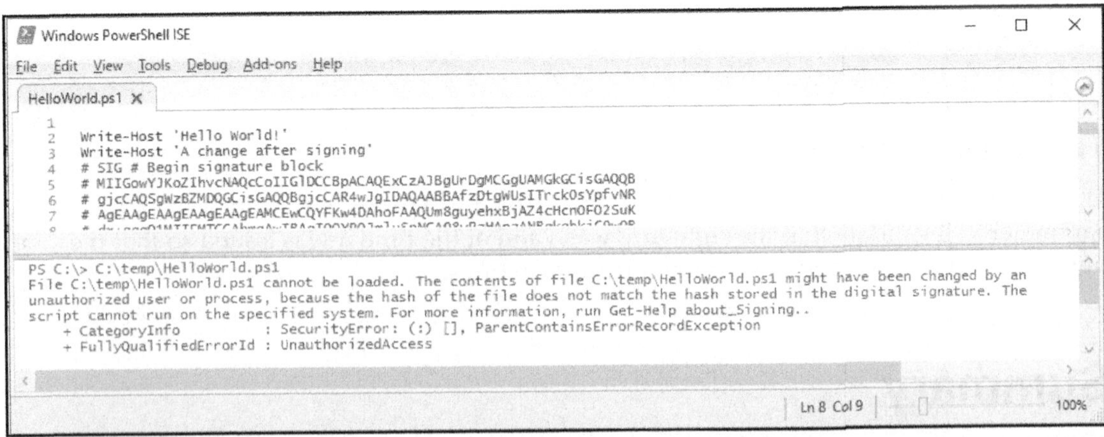

If you have multiple signing certificates, you can filter them by their properties:

```
$signingCert = Get-ChildItem -Path Cert:\CurrentUser\My | Where {
$_.Subject -eq 'CN=My Signing Cert'};
```

If your certificate is stored as a file, you can use it through the `Get-PfxCertificate` command:

```
$signingCert = Get-PfxCertificate -FilePath c:tempmycert.pfx
```

The `Set-AuthenticodeSignature` command is simple, but two parameters deserve comments.

IncludeChain

This parameter will include the public keys of intermediate CAs and the root CA (if using `All`). The inclusion of the intermediate certificates will speed up the chain validation process but will contribute to the file size. It is worth noting that including the root certificate is not very useful since, in order to be valid, it needs to be installed on the certificate store.

Values are as follows:

- `All`
- `NotRoot`
- `Signer`

TimestampServer

By default, a signature becomes invalid if the certificate expires. A `TimestampServer` parameter will validate that the signature was valid at the time it was issued so that the signature will still be valid even if the certificate expires.

Summary

Script automation is a powerful tool for administrators. As your team grows or the complexity of your system increases, doing script automation in a secure and supportable approach becomes increasingly important. In this chapter we introduce the concept of modules that allow you to scale your scripting solutions and the concept of script signing and execution policies that allow you to secure your scripts. In the `Chapter 9`, *PowerShell Core,* we will also review PowerShell remoting which will let you run and monitor scripts remotely and will be a good addition to your automation tool belt.

7

Patterns and Practices PowerShell

SharePoint **Patterns and Practices** (**PnP**) is an open source initiative coordinated by the PnP core team, which consists of Microsoft's internal folks and external **Microsoft Most Valuable Professionals** (**MVP**) and provides guidance, samples, reusable components, and documentation for the community `https://dev.office.com/patterns-and-practices`. PnP contains a library of PowerShell commands (PnP PowerShell) that allows you to perform complex provisioning and artifact management actions for SharePoint. The commands use the **client-side object model** (**CSOM**) and can work against both SharePoint Online as well as SharePoint on-premise. In this chapter, we will cover PnP PowerShell cmdlets for SharePoint Online.

Specifically, we will cover the following topics:

- Why do we need to learn Office 365 PnP PowerShell?
- Installing and working with the Office 365 PnP PowerShell
- Creating your first SharePoint Online site using PnP Provisioning Engine

Why do we need to learn PnP PowerShell?

In this ever-changing technology landscape, we should always ask this question while learning something new. Why do I need to learn this? Is it worth investing time and effort in this topic?

Microsoft has already provided cmdlets to manage SharePoint Online for administrative tasks in Office 365, for example, to create a site collection, to delete/remove site collections, adding users, creating groups, and so on. The PnP PowerShell cmdlets are complementary to the SharePoint Online cmdlets. I think the PnP PowerShell cmdlets are developer-focused and provide the means to manage artifacts in SharePoint, such as lists, views, fields, content types, upload files, and so on.

Right now with the June 2017 release, there are more than 150 cmdlets available and the team is working to constantly add new cmdlets. Some cmdlets are duplicated, such as creating site collections and deleting site collections. We have covered PnP PowerShell briefly in `Chapter 5`, *Managing Exchange Online using PowerShell* on SharePoint Online.

Now you may be wondering why an administrator needs to learn PnP PowerShell cmdlets if they are developer-focused. The reasons are as follows:

- Office 365 PnP cmdlets provide an easy and secure way to manage credentials using Windows Credential Manager, and we don't need to hardcode user IDs and passwords in the scripts.
- When we need to work with the artifacts of SharePoint Online using CSOM, we are effectively using C# code. With PnP PowerShell, we don't need to know C#, and it offers a more *PowerShell-like* approach to working with SharePoint Online artifacts.
- We can script the governance logic and provisioning logic without writing C# code.
- While executing the scripts, we don't need to load the runtime **dynamic-link libraries (dlls)**, for example, `Microsoft.SharePoint.Client.dll` and `Microsoft.SharePoint.Client.Runtime.dll.`
- Office 365 is used by thousands of organizations irrespective of size, ranging from a few users to thousands of users. Depending on the size of the organization, sometimes an Office 365 administrator needs to perform tasks that require few developer skills. A good example will be uploading multiple files into a document library to create a new site collection with a predefined template for the publishing/team site.

- If you have the hybrid deployment of SharePoint, it means you are using SharePoint Online as well as SharePoint on-premises, and PnP PowerShell is available for SharePoint 2013 and SharePoint 2016 on-premises as well. The key difference between the native SharePoint 2013 and SharePoint 2016 PowerShell cmdlets is they are not built for remote management. This means you need direct access to the SharePoint servers to execute these commands. On the other hand, PnP PowerShell cmdlets are built for remote management. Hence, you will use remote management for both SharePoint Online as well as SharePoint on-premises 2013 and 2016.
- A lot of organizations have blurred lines in terms of responsibilities for administrators and developers. Also, having additional skill helps.
- Also, in some organizations, because of governance, developers do not have the required access to execute certain PowerShell cmdlets and they rely on administrators to execute them. If you are familiar with the cmdlets, then as an administrator you will feel more comfortable executing scripts provided by the developers.
- Even though some cmdlets are duplicates, such as creating site collections and deleting site collections since PnP is a community-driven initiative, more and more cmdlets get added almost every month. Right now, there are more than 150 cmdlets in the June 2017 release and by the time you are reading this book, many more new cmdlets will have been added.

If you have a full-fledged development team or your organization/tenant does not use SharePoint Online much, then you can skip this chapter.

By now, if you are convinced that you would like to learn to use PnP PowerShell cmdlets, then let's continue to the next section.

Installing and working with PnP PowerShell cmdlets

There are three ways to install the PnP: PowerShell cmdlets in the PowerShell Gallery, setup files, and installation scripts. PowerShell Gallery (`https://www.powershellgallery.com/`) is the approach recommended by the PnP team. There are three different versions of PnP PowerShell cmdlets: SharePoint Online, SharePoint on-premises 2013, SharePoint on-premises 2016. The reason they have separate modules for SharePoint on-premises 2013, 2016 and SharePoint Online is that they have different versions of CSOM libraries/SDKs for SharePoint Online and SharePoint on-premises 2013 and 2016.

PowerShell Gallery

If you are using Windows 10 or if you have PowerShellGet (`https://github.com/powershell/powershellget`) installed, you can use the following commands to install the PnP PowerShell cmdlets for different versions of SharePoint:

- For SharePoint on-premises 2013:

```
Install-Module SharePointPnPPowerShell2013
```

- For SharePoint on-premises 2016:

```
Install-Module SharePointPnPPowerShell2016
```

- For SharePoint Online:

```
Install-Module SharePointPnPPowerShellOnline
```

The output for the preceding command is shown in the following screenshot:

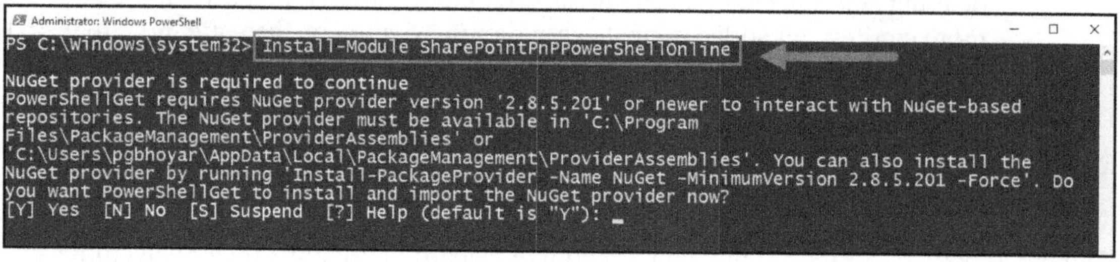

```
Administrator: Windows PowerShell
PS C:\Windows\system32> Install-Module SharePointPnPPowerShellOnline

NuGet provider is required to continue
PowerShellGet requires NuGet provider version '2.8.5.201' or newer to interact with NuGet-based
repositories. The NuGet provider must be available in 'C:\Program
Files\PackageManagement\ProviderAssemblies' or
'C:\Users\pgbhoyar\AppData\Local\PackageManagement\ProviderAssemblies'. You can also install the
NuGet provider by running 'Install-PackageProvider -Name NuGet -MinimumVersion 2.8.5.201 -Force'. Do
you want PowerShellGet to install and import the NuGet provider now?
[Y] Yes  [N] No  [S] Suspend  [?] Help (default is "Y"):
```

If the machine you are using does not have the NuGet provider, you will need to install that first by typing `Y` or `Yes` and then hitting the *Enter* key. The NuGet provider will get installed in the background.

You may get the prompt for `Untrusted repository`. PnP PowerShell is an open source initiative, and Microsoft is currently working on making PnP PowerShell a trusted repository. To continue with the installation, type `Yes` or `Yes to All` and then hit the *Enter* key:

```
Select Administrator: Windows PowerShell
PS C:\Windows\system32> Install-Module SharePointPnPPowerShellOnline

NuGet provider is required to continue
PowerShellGet requires NuGet provider version '2.8.5.201' or newer to interact with NuGet-based
repositories. The NuGet provider must be available in 'C:\Program
Files\PackageManagement\ProviderAssemblies' or
'C:\Users\pgbhoyar\AppData\Local\PackageManagement\ProviderAssemblies'. You can also install the
NuGet provider by running 'Install-PackageProvider -Name NuGet -MinimumVersion 2.8.5.201 -Force'. Do
you want PowerShellGet to install and import the NuGet provider now?
[Y] Yes  [N] No  [S] Suspend  [?] Help (default is "Y"): Yes

Untrusted repository
You are installing the modules from an untrusted repository. If you trust this repository, change its
 InstallationPolicy value by running the Set-PSRepository cmdlet. Are you sure you want to install
the modules from 'PSGallery'?
[Y] Yes  [A] Yes to All  [N] No  [L] No to All  [S] Suspend  [?] Help (default is "N"):
```

The PnP PowerShell module for SharePoint Online will get downloaded and installed in the background. If the installation is successful, you will not get any error message:

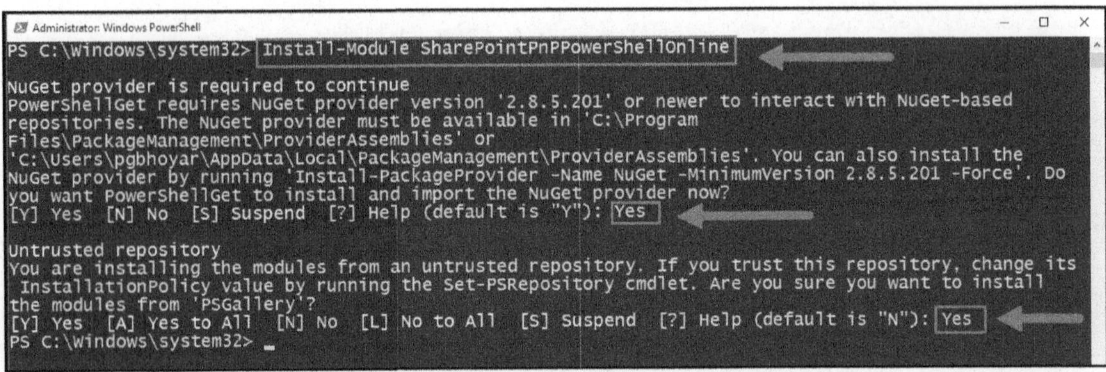

Can we install all three modules (SharePoint Online, SharePoint on-premises 2013, and SharePoint on-premises 2016) on a single machine? The answer is yes, but as of the June 2017 release, this requires a little bit of work as the default paths are set for each module and it is beyond the scope of this book. All the examples in this chapter are created with the installation of the SharePoint Online module only.

Using Setup files/binaries

We can use following steps to install the PnP PowerShell Cmdlets using Setup files/binary files:

1. You can download the binary installer (the `.msi` files) from `https://github.com/SharePoint/PnP-PowerShell/releases`:

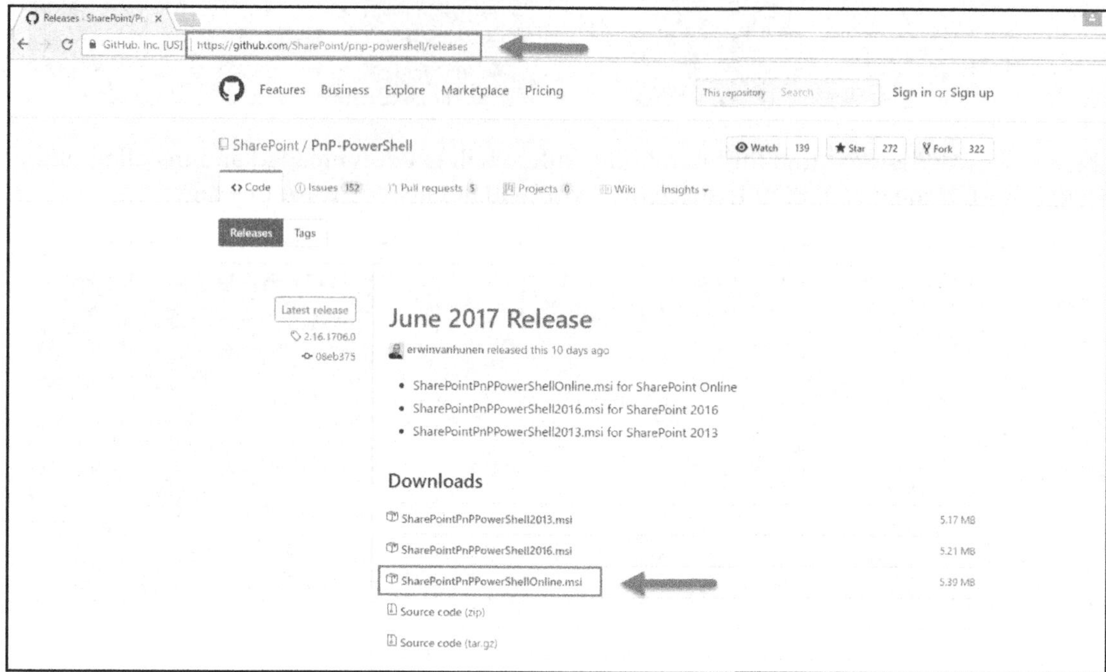

2. Run the binary installer and accept the terms of the License Agreement and then click on **Install**:

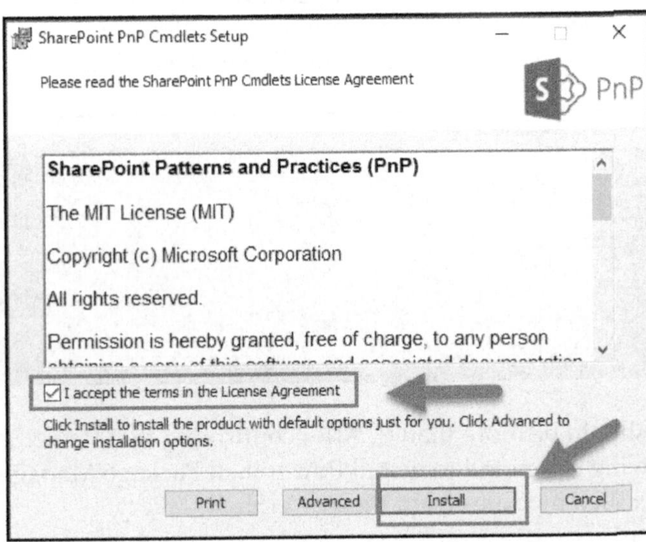

3. If the installation is successful, you will get the following message notifying you that the installation is complete:

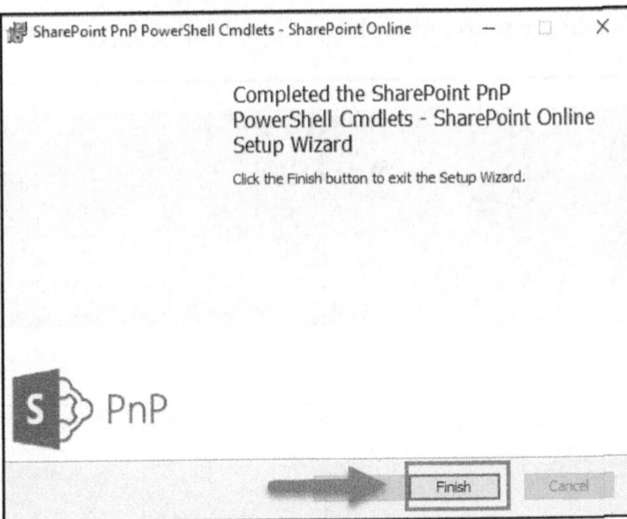

Installation script

If your machine has at least PowerShell v3 installed, we can use this alternative for installation. To find the version of PowerShell on the machine, type the `$PSVersionTable.PSVersion` command in the PowerShell window:

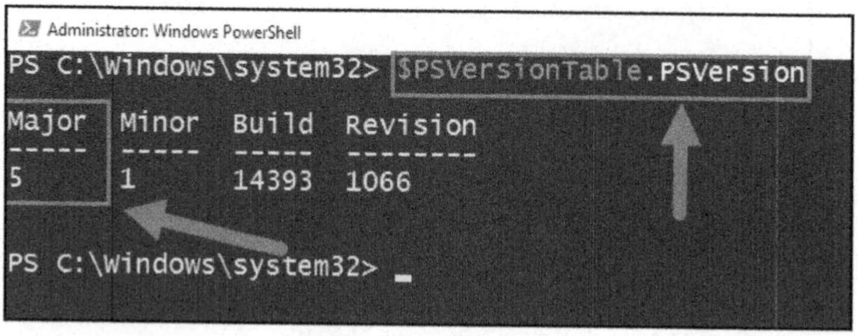

The value of `Major` should be more than `3`. After confirming that PowerShell v3 is installed, we can use the following command to install PowerShell Package Management and then install the PnP PowerShell modules from the PowerShell Gallery:

```
Invoke-Expression (New-Object
Net.WebClient).DownloadString('https://raw.githubusercontent.com/OfficeDev/
PnP-PowerShell/master/Samples/Modules.Install/Install-
SharePointPnPPowerShell.ps1')
```

The output of the preceding command is shown in the following screenshot:

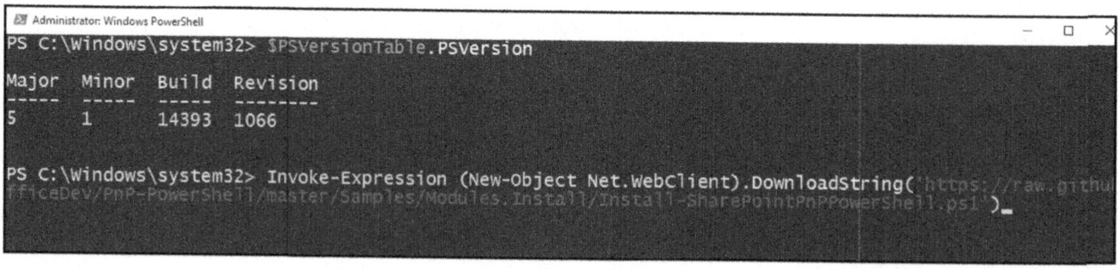

You will need to confirm the version of the PnP PowerShell module. In our case, it is *SharePoint Online*. Since `0` is the default, hit the *Enter* key. Once the installation is successful, you will get the following message:

```
PS C:\Windows\system32> $PSVersionTable.PSVersion

Major  Minor  Build  Revision
-----  -----  -----  --------
5      1      14393  1066


PS C:\Windows\system32> Invoke-Expression (New-Object Net.WebClient).DownloadString('https://raw.githu
fficeDev/PnP-PowerShell/master/Samples/Modules.Install/Install-SharePointPnPPowerShell.ps1')
PowerShellPackageManagement now installed we will now run the next command in 10 Seconds

Confirm
Which version of the Modules do you want to install?
[O] SharePoint Online  [6] SharePoint 2016  [3] SharePoint 2013  [?] Help (default is "O"):
The modules for SharePoint Online have been installed and can now be used
On the next release you can just run Update-Module -force to update this and other installed modules
PS C:\Windows\system32> _
```

If you have the PowerShell session open, close the session after the installation and open it again to use the PnP PowerShell cmdlets.

The PnP team releases a new version of PnP PowerShell cmdlets every time the core PnP library gets updated, which is is every month right now. To update the PnP PowerShell modules, we can use the setup files method mentioned earlier, or we can use the following PowerShell command:

```
Update-Module SharePointPnPPowerShell*
```

The following screenshot shows the output of the preceding command:

```
PS C:\Windows\system32> Update-Module SharePointPnPPowerShell*
PS C:\Windows\system32> _
```

I always get this question, especially for open source projects/initiatives: How can we update the modules/installation files? I recommend that you use the latest build in the test environment first, test the scripts/cmdlets that you normally use and verify that they are not broken, and then roll out the latest build in production machines.

Verifying the installation of the PnP PowerShell module for SharePoint Online

To verify the installation, we can use the following PowerShell command. You can also use this command if you are new to the machine and would like to find out whether the PnP PowerShell module is already installed or not:

```
Get-Module SharePointPnPPowerShell* -ListAvailable | Select-Object
Name,Version | Sort-Object Version -Descending
```

The following screenshot shows the output of the preceding command:

```
Administrator: Windows PowerShell
PS C:\Windows\system32> Get-Module SharePointPnPPowerShell* -ListAvailable | Select-Object Name,Versio
rsion -Descending

Name                          Version
----                          -------
SharePointPnPPowerShellOnline 2.16.1706.0
```

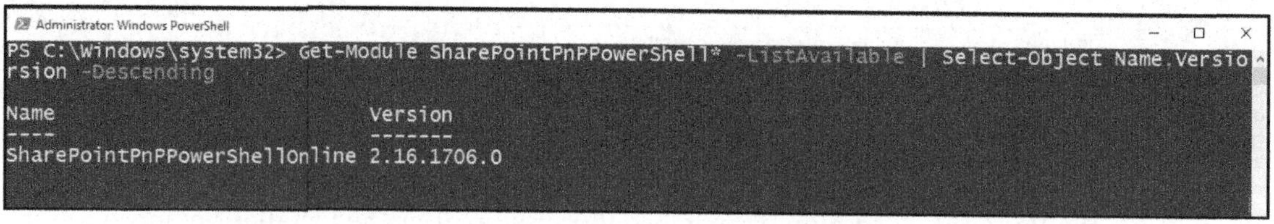

Once you've verified that the PnP PowerShell module for SharePoint Online is installed, we can then get started with executing the cmdlets. Since Office 365 is hosted by Microsoft, we don't have direct access to the servers SharePoint is installed on and running from. We need to use remote management.

To use the PnP PowerShell module, we need to first connect to our SharePoint Online tenant/SharePoint Online site using the following command:

```
Connect-PnPOnline -Url https://yoursite.sharepoint.com -Credentials (Get-
Credential)
```

The following screenshot shows the output of the preceding command:

```
Administrator: Windows PowerShell
PS C:\Windows\system32> Connect-PnPOnline -Url https://          .sharepoint.com/sites/
et-Credential)

cmdlet Get-Credential at command pipeline position 1
Supply values for the following parameters:
Credential
PS C:\Windows\system32> _
```

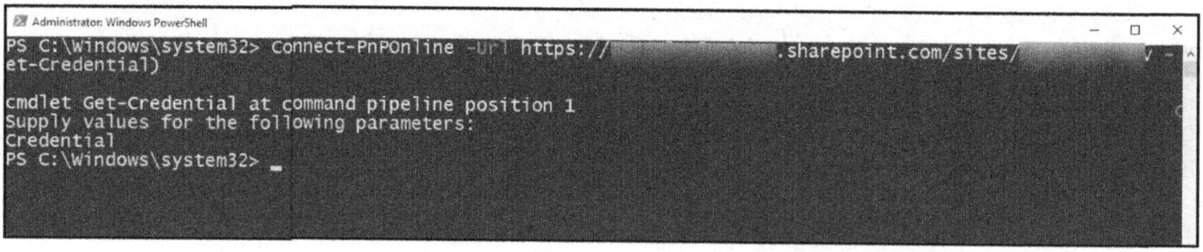

If your credentials are correct and the connection is successful, you will not get any error message. To get another visual confirmation, you can execute the following command:

```
Get-PnPSite
```

The following screenshot shows the output of the preceding command:

```
Administrator: Windows PowerShell
PS C:\Windows\system32> Connect-PnPOnline -Url https://          .sharepoint.com/sites/
et-Credential)

cmdlet Get-Credential at command pipeline position 1
Supply values for the following parameters:
Credential
PS C:\Windows\system32> Get-PnPSite

Url                                                CompatibilityLevel
---                                                ------------------
https://          .sharepoint.com/sites/        .. 15


PS C:\Windows\system32> _
```

PnP PowerShell cmdlets use this pattern: <Verb>-PnP<Noun>, where PnP is Pattern and Practices. The cmdlets with *SPO* are deprecated in the June 2017 release, and you should use *PnP* instead, for example, Get-PnPSite, New-PnPTenantSite.
To view all cmdlets, we can use Get-Command -Module *PnP*. Or, go to the page https://msdn.microsoft.com/en-us/pnp_powershell/pnp-powershell-overview. To get help on a particular cmdlet, the command is Get-Help New-PnPList -Detailed.

Using Windows Credential Manager with PnP PowerShell

If you are managing multiple site collections in single Office 365 tenant or multiple Office 365 tenants, then getting a prompt for credentials every time you would like to connect to SharePoint Online is a bit annoying and also slows down you a bit. If you are using the script, you could hardcode the credentials in your PowerShell script. However, this is not secure and is not the recommended way.

The PnP PowerShell module supports Windows Credential Manager, which helps you securely manage and use the credentials in scripts and PowerShell sessions.

To use the Windows Credential Manager, use the following steps:

1. Open **Control Panel**.
2. Select **Credential Manager**:

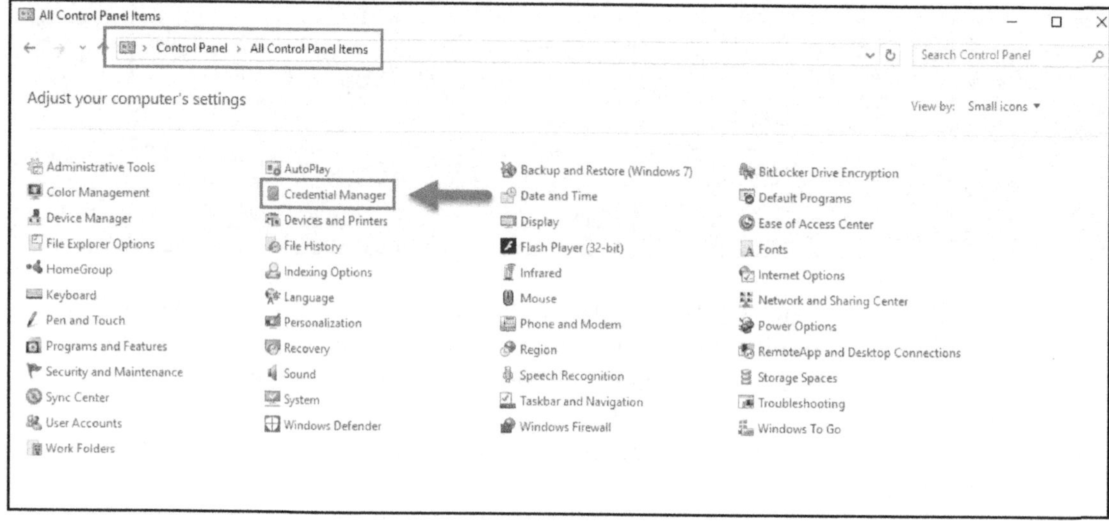

3. Select **Add a generic credential**:

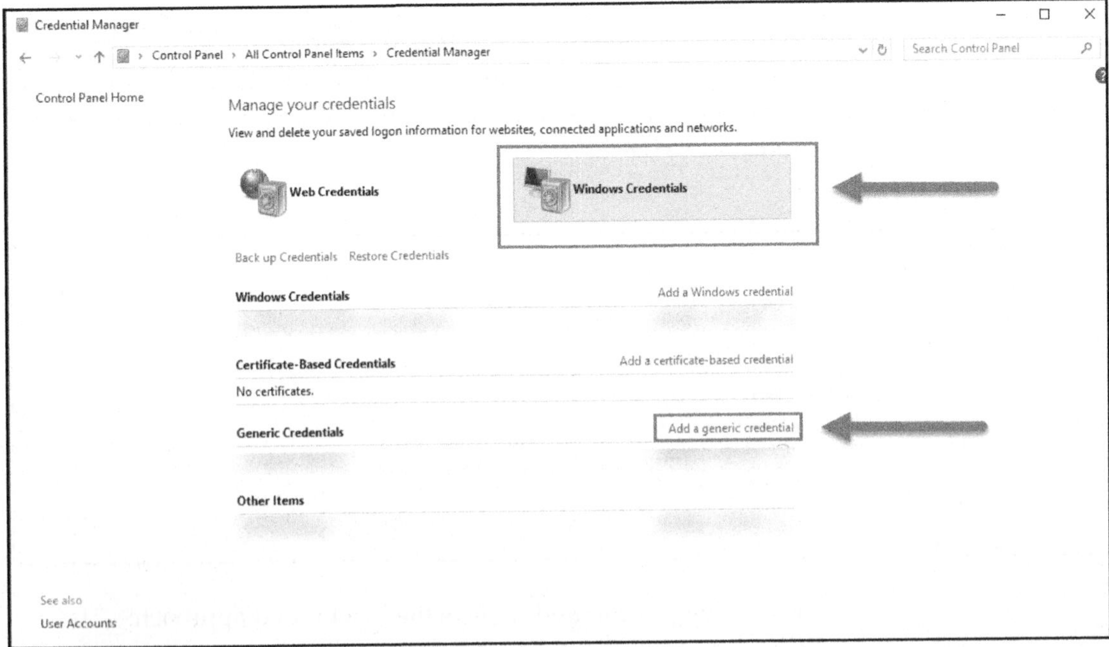

4. There are two approaches available:
    - URL-based approach: **Internet or network address**—enter the URL of the site you would like to set up the credentials for. Enter the username and password in the **User name** and **Password** fields:

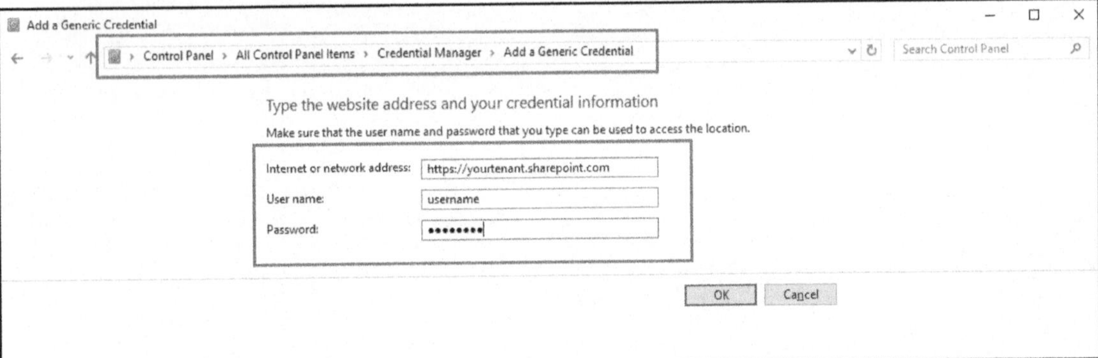

The following command depicts the URL-based approach:

```
Connect-PnPOnline -Url `
https://yourtenant.sharepoint.com
```

- Label-based approach: **Internet or network address**—unique label for the credential. Enter the username and password in the **User name** and **Password** fields:

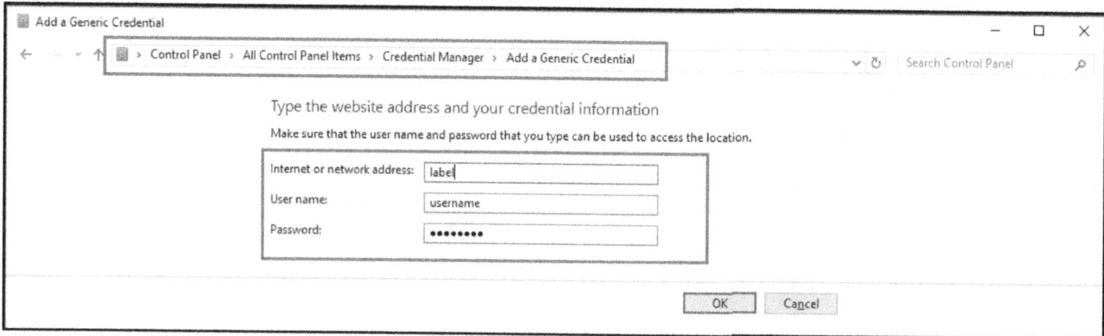

The following command depicts the label-based approach:

```
Connect-PnPOnline
-Url https://yourtenant.sharepoint.com
-Credentials YourLabel
```

If you are managing multiple site collections, using labels is convenient.

An example of provisioning site collection using a standard template

The PnP PowerShell module is a very powerful tool to implement governance in your SharePoint Online tenant. We can automate the creation of SharePoint Online site collections using PnP cmdlets. A common ask for SharePoint Online administrators is to create new site collections. Some organizations have strict governance policies, and they would like to have specific assets (content types, list, libraries, pages, branding, and so on) in all new site collections. Normally, you need a developer to automate the site provisioning and provision the required assets. Using PnP PowerShell cmdlets, we can automate this process even without a developer.

PnP PowerShell cmdlets help extract/export most site settings, assets/contents, into the XML-formatted template file and later on import them to a new site collection.

This is a five-step process:

1. Connect to the source site collection using the following command:

   ```
   Connect-PnPOnline -Url https://yoursite.sharepoint.com
    -Credentials (Get-Credential)
   ```

2. Export/extract the site settings and assets into the XML-formatted template file using the following command:

   ```
   Get-PnPProvisioningTemplate -Out pnpdemo.pnp
   ```

   The preceding cmdlet will extract the template of the site specified in the `Connect-PnPOnline` cmdlet in the form of XML. The template has information about all the supported artifacts, such as site columns, content types, lists, libraries, images, and so on. Later on, we can use this template to create a new site collection with artifacts such as lists, libraries, and so on.

   This cmdlet uses PnP Provisioning Engine behind the scenes. This is the recommended way for the **Save as site template** option we get in SharePoint 2013 and 2016 on-premises.

   If you would like to debug the provisioning process, you can use the following cmdlet to store the information in the form of XML:

   ```
   Get-PnPProvisioningTemplate -Out pnpdemo.xml
   ```

3. Create a new site collection. If the new site collection is already created, you can skip this step:

```
New-PnPTenantSite -Title 'Title of the site"
-Url "https://yoursite.sharepoint.com/sites/siteUniqueUrl"
-Owner "username@tenantname.onmicrosoft.com" -TimeZone "4"
-Template STS#01
```

4. To apply this template to another site, we will need to connect to it first and then use the following cmdlet:

```
Connect-PnPOnline
-Url https://yoursite.sharepoint.com/sites/siteUniqueUrl
-Credentials (Get-Credential)
```

5. To apply the exported template, use the following command:

```
Apply-PnPProvisioningTemplate  -Path .\pnpdemo.pnp
```

Similarly, there are a lot of other admin tasks we can accomplish using PnP PowerShell, for example, setting the default email address for access request emails, setting the default page of a site, bulk-uploading of documents, bulk-deleting list items, and so on.

Summary

In this chapter, we covered PnP PowerShell cmdlets for SharePoint Online, followed with the steps we need to take to set up PnP PowerShell. You also learned the steps that we need to take in order to connect to SharePoint Online using the PnP PowerShell module. Finally, we covered the provisioning of the new site collection using PnP Provisioning Engine.

In the next chapter, we will learn about OneDrive which is another key component for the digital workplace and go over common provisioning and management scenarios.

8
OneDrive for Business

In the early days, SharePoint was positioned as a great replacement for file shares. SharePoint addressed some important weaknesses of file shares: versioning, the recycle bin, check in/check out, history/auditing, the web interface, and custom metadata features, to name a few.

Fast forward to the present, SharePoint and other content management system products have effectively replaced file shares in the collaboration space. Yet, file shares still remain very relevant to personal storage, although you would hardly qualify OneDrive for Business as only a file share (at least not one from 10 years ago). Officially defined as file-hosting products, OneDrive and OneDrive for Business still offer the convenience of operating system integration of file shares while adopting important features from the CMS world.

Recently, Microsoft has also rolled out OneDrive for Office 365 groups, making the case for small group collaboration through OneDrive.

Why start with SharePoint in the chapter on OneDrive, you ask? I am glad you did. At the time of writing, there are a few differences between OneDrive and SharePoint. All the OneDrive administration commands are included within the SPO API. OneDrive's web interface is a trimmed down SharePoint site, and you can use the same SharePoint CSOM/REST APIs to work with OneDrive.

From an administrator's perspective, OneDrive can be thought of as a synchronization client (in charge of keeping data consistent between local copies and online storage) and a web interface (a branded and customized SharePoint site).

Will this be the case in the long run? At the moment, we are going through a transition period. From the writer's point of view, SharePoint will continue to provide infrastructure for OneDrive and other services. However, Microsoft is making an ongoing effort to provide one API for all its online services. Also, as the platform matures, the lines between OneDrive, SharePoint, Exchange and other services seem to blur more and more. In the long run, it is quite possible that these products will merge or change in ways we have not thought of. With the maturity of the Microsoft Graph API (the promised API to access all your services), the internal implementation of the services will be less important for developers and administrators.

In the Graph API, both OneDrive and SharePoint document libraries are referred to as **drives** and files or list items within them as **driveItems**. This is an indication that, even though change is certain, both feature sets will remain similar.

In this chapter, we will cover OneDrive administration, which can be divided into three different areas:

- Feature configuration
- Personal site management
- Data migration

Feature configuration

As OneDrive has a limited interface (its primary interface is integrated in the file system), there are few options for the user experience. OneDrive maintenance revolves around quotas and file sharing. All of these settings are part of the tenant configuration.

The following are properties of the `Set-SPOTenant` command that can be used to configure the OneDrive user experience:

- `OneDriveStorageQuota`: By default, OneDrive's storage quota is set to 1 TB. The policy value can be changed through the `Set-SPOTenant` command, and existing site quotas can be changed through the `Set-SPOSite` command. This value is set in megabytes (1048576 for 1 TB) and will be capped by the user's assigned license.

In the following example, we change the quota policy to 6 TB, but the value is effectively set at 5 TB as it is the highest value allowed for standard licenses:

```
$quota = 6TB / 1024 / 1024

Set-SPOTenant -OneDriveStorageQuota $quota

Get-SPOTenant | Select OneDriveStorageQuota

OneDriveStorageQuota
--------------------
     5242880
```

Individual site quotas can be reviewed and updated using the `Get-SPOSite` and `Set-SPOSite` commands. In the following sample, note that, after updating the quotas for the individual sites, we have to use `Get-SPOSite` to see the updated values (changes to sites will not be updated in local variables):

```
$mySites = Get-SPOSite -IncludePersonalSite $true
 -Filter { Url -like '/personal/'}
$mySites | Select StorageQuota,
 StorageUsageCurrent

StorageQuota  StorageUsageCurrent
------------  -------------------
1048576                         6
1048576                         1
5242880                        15

$quota = 3TB / 1024 / 1024

foreach ($site in $mySites) {
  Set-SPOSite -Identity $site -StorageQuota $quota
}

$mySites = Get-SPOSite -IncludePersonalSite $true
 -Filter { Url -like '/personal/'}
$mySites | Select StorageQuota

StorageQuota
------------
  31457286
  31457286
  31457286
```

- `NotifyOwnersWhenInvitationsAccepted`: When set to `true`, the OneDrive owner will be notified when an external user accepts an invitation to access a file or folder.
- `NotifyOwnersWhenItemsReshared` : When set to `true`, the OneDrive owner will be notified when a file or folder is shared by another user.
- `OrphanedPersonalSitesRetentionPeriod`: When a user is deleted, the OneDrive will be retained for a default of 30 days; after the threshold the site will be deleted (value in days from 30 to 3650).
- `ProvisionSharedWithEveryoneFolder`: If set to `true`, a public folder will be set up when a OneDrive site is set up. The `Shared with Everyone` folder is not accessible through the OneDrive client, but it can be used through the browser and is accessible by all users.
- `SpecialCharactersStateInFileFolderNames`: Allows the use of special characters in files and folders (applies to both SharePoint and OneDrive). Currently, the only special characters that can be allowed are `#` and `%`. Microsoft has announced that support for additional special characters will be rolled out soon.

Please review `Chapter 4`, *Managing SharePoint Online Using PowerShell* for additional settings that apply to SharePoint as well as OneDrive.

Personal site management

Historically, personal sites (or My Sites) have been a management problem. When planning a deployment, you have to consider your user base, the turnover in your organization, the internal policy for content storage, and many other factors. In Office 365, some of these factors have been addressed, but largely the My Sites deployment (as well as any other large-scale site deployment) remains a usage problem.

With the introduction of quotas, you can cap both storage and resources allocated for a site. By default, My Sites get 1 TB of space; unfortunately, the quotas cannot be set in the `Request-SPOPersonalSite` command, which is used for the provisioning of personal sites.

Another issue with personal sites is that it takes a few minutes to set them up. It is very common that an administrator will pre-provision personal sites for the organization. At the time of writing, OneDrive is implemented as personal sites, which means that the scripts we will review also apply to provisioning OneDrive. This is a very common task for migrations to the cloud:

```
Request-SPOPersonalSite -UserEmails <String[]> [-NoWait <SwitchParameter>]
```

The `Request-SPOPersonalSite` command has only two parameters, yet its usage is worth documenting due to some common issues.

If you are deploying for a small list of users, an inline array of strings will schedule the creation of the sites. It is worth noting that the command will not return errors if the users are not found or if the user count exceeds 200 items. In general, you will have to validate that the process has completed:

```
Request-SPOPersonalSite -UserEmails 'test2@mytest321.onmicrosoft.com',
'admin1@mytest321.onmicrosoft.com' -NoWait $true
```

It is very common that the list of users will be read from a file or a CSV input. In the following example, we parse a comma-separated list of emails using `Split`. Even though the documentation specifies an array of strings, this call will not work unless we transform the string array into an object array through the use of the `Where` command:

```
Request-SPOPersonalSite -UserEmails
('test2@mytest321.onmicrosoft.com,admin1@mytest321.onmicrosoft.com'.Split('
,')|
 Where-Object {$true})
```

Another common scenario is deploying personal sites for a list of users already in SharePoint Online. The following script will retrieve all users with a valid login (a login in the form of an email). Note the use of the `ExpandProperty` parameter to return just the `LoginName` property of the users:

```
$users = Get-SPOUser -Site https://mytest321.sharepoint.com |
Where-Object { $_.IsGroup -ne $true -and $_.LoginName -like '*@*.*'} |
Select-Object -ExpandProperty LoginName;
```

If the list is small, we can iterate over the list of users or schedule provisioning in one call. It is safe to schedule the personal site for a user that already has one (it will be silently skipped), but there will be no warning when submitting over 200 requests:

```
#indivudal request
$users | ForEach-Object {
 Request-SPOPersonalSite -UserEmails $_
}
```

```
#bulk
Request-SPOPersonalSite -UserEmails $users
```

If you are dealing with many users, you can create groups of 200 items instead and submit them in bulk:

```
# Group by requests of 200 emails ------------------------------------------
--------------------
$groups = $users | Group-Object {[int]($users.IndexOf($_)/200)}

# send requests in 200 batches, do no wait for a response
$groups | ForEach-Object {
 $logins = $_.Group;
 Write-Host 'Creating sites for: '$logins
 Request-SPOPersonalSite -NoWait -UserEmails $logins
}
```

It is up to the administrator to verify the completion of the request or whether any of the users were not found.

To complete the scenario, the following script will select and delete all personal sites:

```
$mySites = Get-SPOSite -IncludePersonalSite $true -Filter { Url -like
'/personal/'}
$mySites | Remove-SPOSite -Confirm:$false
```

To be able to access and manage OneDrive, administrators need to be site collection administrators of OneDrive (remember that it is a SharePoint site). The SharePoint tenant administration site has an option to add a secondary administrator when sites are provisioned, but this setting will not apply to sites that are already created. In the following script, we add an additional site collection administrator to all existing OneDrives:

```
$mySites = Get-SPOSite -IncludePersonalSite $true -Filter { Url -like
'/personal/'}

foreach ($site in $mySites) {
 Set-SPOUser -Site $site -LoginName admin@mytest321.onmicrosoft.com
 -IsSiteCollectionAdmin $true
}
```

Data migration

The last topic concerning site collections is document migrations. All the content covered in this chapter also applies to SharePoint sites.

There are three alternative methods to upload data in Office 365:

- The CSOM API
- The SPO API
- Office 365 Import service

Let's look at each one in detail.

The CSOM API

Initially, the CSOM API was the only method available to upload documents to SharePoint Online. CSOM is a comprehensive API that is used for application development and administration. It is a great tool for a myriad scenarios, but it is not specialized for content migrations. When used for this purpose, we can go over the API throttling limits (Microsoft has purposely not put a specific number to this as it depends on multiple factors). Your scripts might get temporarily blocked (requests will get a **429 Too Many Requests** HTTP error), and if the misuse continues for an extended period of time, your tenant might get blocked altogether (**503 Service Unavailable**). The tenant administrator would have to take action in this case.

API throttling is put in place to guarantee platform health. The Patterns and Practices throttling project shows how to work around this limitation for legitimate scenarios at `https://github.com/SharePoint/PnP/tree/dev/Samples/Core.Throttling`.

Moreover, the bandwidth allocated for the CSOM API will allow you to upload approximately 1 GB/hour only (depending on multiple factors such as the file size, the number of files, networking, and concurrent API usage), which makes it impractical for large content migrations.

In the next sections, you will explore faster and easier approaches to bulk migrations, yet the CSOM API remains relevant in this scenario. This is because at the time of writing, it is the only method that allows metadata modification. It is also worth mentioning that CSOM changes are reflected immediately, whereas updates through the other methods will take some time to be effective due to the architecture of the process.

In our experience doing content migrations, most tasks are done with the SPO API, yet CSOM is better suited for last minute changes or ad hoc requests.

The following sample shows how to upload a file and set its metadata. Refer to `Chapter 4`, *Managing SharePoint Online Using PowerShell* for additional information on CSOM scripting. This method will be used for small migrations or to set the file metadata:

```
$siteUrl = "https://mytest321.sharepoint.com/personal/admin1";

$clientContext = New-Object
Microsoft.SharePoint.Client.ClientContext($siteUrl)
$credentials = New-Object
Microsoft.SharePoint.Client.SharePointOnlineCredentials($spoCreds.UserName,
$spoCreds.Password)
$clientContext.Credentials = $credentials

$stream = [System.IO.File]::OpenRead('c:tempfileToMigrate.xml')
$overwrite = $true

$fileUrl = '/personal/admin1/Documents/file.xml'

[Microsoft.SharePoint.Client.File]::SaveBinaryDirect($clientContext,
$fileUrl, $stream, $overwrite)

$listItem =
$clientContext.Web.GetFileByServerRelativeUrl($fileUrl).ListItemAllFields
$listItem["Title"] = 'Updated via script'
$listItem.Update()

$clientContext.ExecuteQuery()
```

The SPO Migration API

The SPO API has a handful of commands to support the migration of content to SharePoint or OneDrive sites. The main advantage in this case is that the migration package is first uploaded to the Azure Blob storage. The contents are encrypted while in the temporary storage and can be processed in parallel. Being able to take advantage of the enhanced bandwidth and parallel processing makes this approach necessary when dealing with hundreds of gigabytes or many different destinations (typically the case when migrating OneDrive content). The costs of transfer and storage of your data are minimal when you consider that the upload speed increases ten-fold in comparison to the CSOM approach. With this approach, you can submit multiple packages and execute them in parallel. When first released, the platform allowed up to 16 concurrent migrations; however, this number has increased lately. As an administrator, you will have to monitor the state and results of each migration package.
Let's look at a few commands that will help us in achieving this:

- `New-SPOMigrationPackage`:

```
New-SPOMigrationPackage -OutputPackagePath  <String>
 -SourceFilesPath <String> [-IgnoreHidden <SwitchParameter>]
 [-IncludeFileSharePermissions <SwitchParameter>]
 [-NoAzureADLookup <SwitchParameter>]
 [-NoLogFile <SwitchParameter>]
 [-ReplaceInvalidCharacters <SwitchParameter>]
 [-TargetDocumentLibraryPath <String>]
 [-TargetDocumentLibrarySubFolderPath <String>]
 [-TargetWebUrl <String>]
```

We begin by creating a migration package using `New-SPOMigrationPackage`. The command will create a package with the contents of a folder and include options to match accounts by name, include file permissions, and upload to a specific subfolder of a library:

```
$sourceFolder = 'C:\mydocs'
$packageFolder = 'C:\temppackage1'

$targetWeb =
 'https://mytest321-my.sharepoint.com/personal/admin1'
$targetLib = 'Documents'

New-SPOMigrationPackage -SourceFilesPath $sourceFolder
 -OutputPackagePath $packageFolder ` -NoAzureADLookup `
```

- `ConvertTo-SPOMigrationTargetedPackage`:
  The `ConvertTo-SPOMigrationTargetPackage` command allows you to set the target website URL, library, and folder for the migration. In the following sample, we use the `ParallelImport` and `PartitionSizeInBytes` parameters to break up the migration into multiple packages. Breaking up the upload into multiple packages can significantly reduce the overall migration time:

```
$packages = ConvertTo-SPOMigrationTargetedPackage
 -ParallelImport -SourceFilesPath `
$sourceFolder -SourcePackagePath $packageFolder
 -OutputPackagePath $finalPackage `
 -TargetWebUrl $targetWeb -TargetDocumentLibraryPath
  $targetLib `
 -TargetDocumentLibrarySubFolderPath 'migration3' `
 -Credentials $spoCreds -PartitionSizeInBytes 500MB

$packages

PackageDirectory FilesDirectory
---------------- --------------
  1                 C:mydocs
  2                 C:mydocs
```

- `Invoke-SPOMigrationEncryptUploadSubmit`:
  The next step is to upload the packages. `Invoke-SPOMigrationEncryptUploadSubmit` will upload the contents of the package into Azure Blob storage and create a migration job:

```
$jobs = $packages | % {
  Invoke-SPOMigrationEncryptUploadSubmit `
 -SourceFilesPath $_.FilesDirectory.FullName
 -SourcePackagePath $_.PackageDirectory.FullName `
 -Credentials $spoCreds -TargetWebUrl $targetWeb }

Creating package for folder:
  C:mydocs
Converting package for office 365:
  c:tempfinalPackage

$jobs

JobId                                ReportingQueueUri
-----                                -----------------
f2b3e45c-e96d-4a9d-8148-dd563d4c9e1d
https://sposn1ch1m016pr.queue.core.windows.net/...
78c40a16-c2de-4c29-b320-b81a38788c90
```

```
https://sposn1ch1m001pr.queue.core.windows.net/...
```

- `Get-SPOMigrationJobStatus`:
  `Get-SPOMigrationJobStatus` will return the status of the active jobs. This command can be used to monitor the status and wait until all the submitted jobs are completed:

```
# retrieve job status individually
foreach( $job in $jobs){
  Get-SPOMigrationJobStatus -TargetWebUrl $targetWeb
   -Credentials $spoCreds -JobId $job.JobId
}

None
Processing
```

In a real-world scenario, you can use the command without the `JobId` parameter to get an array of the job status and wait until all are complete. Running jobs will have the `Processing` state, and completed jobs have the `None` status. Completed jobs are removed automatically so that the job status array is not guaranteed to have the same length on each call and will eventually be zero.
In the following example, we wait until the active number of jobs is `15` or fewer before continuing with the script:

```
$jobs = Get-SPOMigrationJobStatus -TargetWebUrl $targetWeb
while ($jobs.Count -ge 15)
{
  $active = $jobs | Where { $_.JobState -eq 'Processing'}
  Write-Host 'Too many jobs: ' $jobs.Count
  ' active: ' $active.Length ',
   pausing...';

  Start-Sleep 60
  $jobs = Get-SPOMigrationJobStatus -TargetWebUrl $targetWeb
}
```

- `Get-SPOMigrationJobProgress`:
  The `Get-SPOMigrationJobProgress` command will return the result of each job; by default, a log file is placed in the folder specified in `SourcePackagePath`. By default, the command will wait for the job to complete unless the `DontWaitForEndJob` parameter is used:

```
foreach( $job in $jobs){
  Get-SPOMigrationJobProgress -AzureQueueUri
  $job.ReportingQueueUri.AbsoluteUri `
```

```
    -Credentials $spoCreds -TargetWebUrl $targetWeb
    -JobIds $job.JobId -EncryptionParameters `
    $job.Encryption -DontWaitForEndJob
}

Total Job(s) Completed = 1, with Errors = 0, with Warnings = 1
Total Job(s) Completed = 1, with Errors = 0, with Warnings = 0
```

- `Remove-SPOMigrationJob`:
  If needed, you can manually remove jobs with the `Remove-SPOMigrationJob` command:

```
$jobStatus = Get-SPOMigrationJobStatus -TargetWebUrl
  $targetWeb -Credentials $spoCreds -JobId $job.JobId

if ($jobStatus -eq 'None'){
  Write-Host 'Job completed:' $job.JobId
  Remove-SPOMigrationJob -JobId $job.JobId -TargetWebUrl
  $targetWeb -Credentials $spoCreds
}
```

Office 365 Import service

The Office 365 Import service was the first method to migrate content into Office 365 in order to take advantage of Blob storage. It is available in the data import section of the tenant administration website. It lets you create the Blob storage and associated parameters to be used for the uploads and monitor the progress and result of each upload package.

Being able to take advantage of an existing Blob storage might be necessary in scenarios where the content and destinations are in different locations (you can select the region where the Blob storage will be set up). You can access the logs and monitor job status either through the tenant administration website or through the Azure Blob storage explorer.

A disadvantage of this method is that the content is not encrypted while in Blob storage. The documentation on the administrator website shows you how to create upload containers and how to access them through their **shared access signature** (**SAS**) URL. These are generated through the data import wizard and are private, so encryption of the content might not be a problem unless it is for very sensitive information.
The main issue with this approach is that you need to generate the SAS URLs and containers for each package individually, making it suitable for a handful of destinations but not for a large-scale migration where full automation is needed.

You can find detailed instructions on how to create and submit migration packages through the Import service at `https://support.office.com/en-us/article/Use-network-upload-to-import-SharePoint-data-to-Office-365-ed4a43b7-c4e3-45c8-94c8-998153407b8a?ui=en-US&rs=en-US&ad=US`.

As the focus of this book is on achieving tasks through scripting, we will review an alternative approach that leverages the Office 365 Import service through the SPO API. The main difference is that, instead of generating SAS URLs for each file container through the website wizard, we will use the Azure Blob storage account instead as well as the key that will let us create the containers through PowerShell.

Creating an Azure Blob storage account

Let's create an Azure Blob storage account:

1. Go to `https://manage.windowsazure.com`.
2. Navigate to **NEW** | **DATA SERVICES** | **STORAGE**.
3. Enter the **URL**, **LOCATION**, and **REPLICATION** type for the new Blob storage:

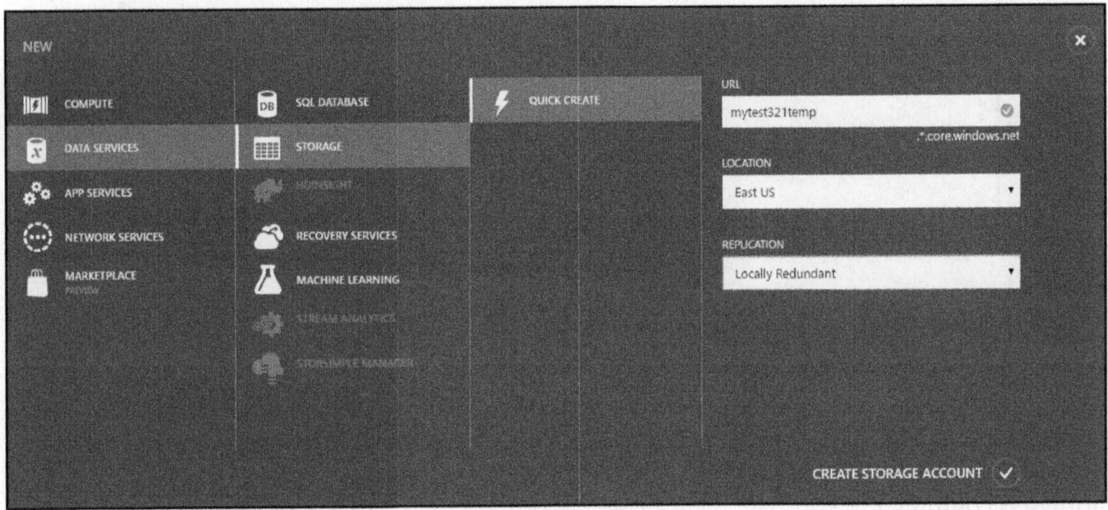

4. When the deployment completes, you will have access to the **Manage Access Keys** dialog, where you can copy the account name and access key. These values are used for storage through the SPO API:

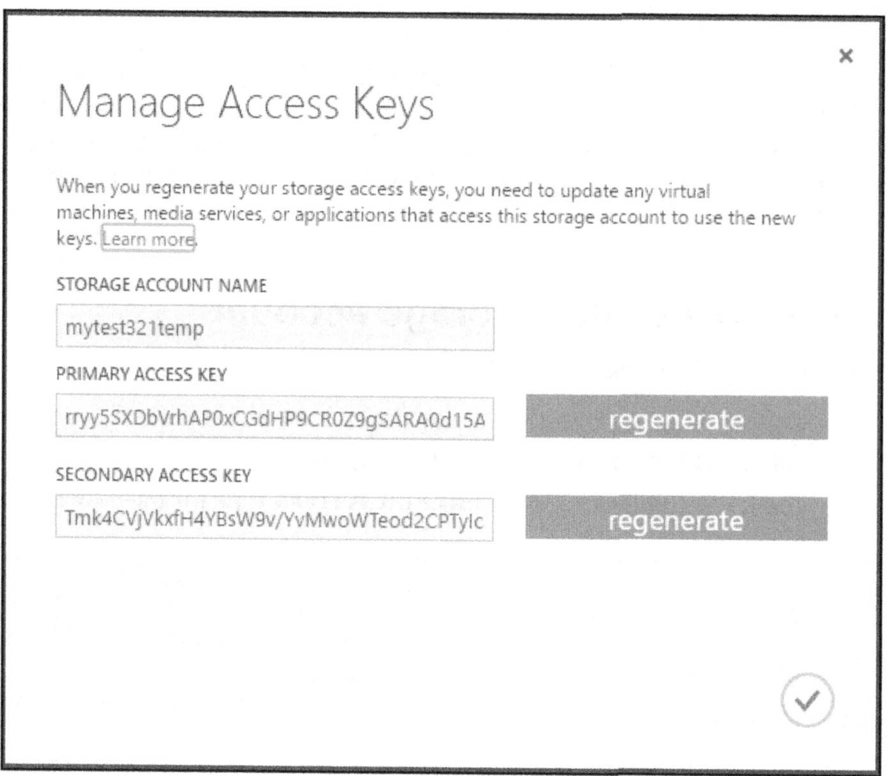

Migrating data using Azure Blob storage

By having access to the account name and access key, we can create storage containers via scripting using the `Set-SPOMigrationPackageAzureSource` command. Using this command, you can fully script migrations of multiple packages. In the following sample, we have a complete script to migrate data to OneDrive using a dedicated Azure Blob storage account.

The script is very similar to the preceding script, but in this case we are replacing the use of the `Invoke-SPOMigrationEncryptUploadSubmit` command with `Set-SPOMigrationPackageAzureSource` to create the blob containers, and `Submit-SPOMigrationJob` to upload the migration packages.

The first block of the script will also clear temporary folders in the filesystem, which is typically needed when creating multiple packages:

```
$sourceFolder = 'C:mydocs'
$packageFolder = 'C:tempsourcepackage'
$finalPackage = 'c:tempfinalPackage'

$targetWeb = 'https://mytest321-my.sharepoint.com/personal/admin1'
$targetLib = 'Documents'

$packageFolder, $finalPackage | ForEach {
 if (Test-Path $_) {
  # get confirmation from the user
  Remove-Item -Recurse -Path $_ -Confirm:$true
  if (Test-Path $_){ # if folder still exists
   Write-Warning "Script cancelled"
   # user did not accept, cancel script
   exit
  }

 }
}

# create the temporary folder
New-Item -ItemType directory -Path $packageFolder | Out-Null

echo 'Creating package for folder: ' $sourceFolder
New-SPOMigrationPackage -SourceFilesPath $sourceFolder -OutputPackagePath
$packageFolder  -NoAzureADLookup

echo 'Converting package for office 365: ' $finalPackage
$packages = ConvertTo-SPOMigrationTargetedPackage -ParallelImport
 -SourceFilesPath `
 $sourceFolder -SourcePackagePath $packageFolder -OutputPackagePath
$finalPackage `
 -TargetWebUrl $targetWeb -TargetDocumentLibraryPath $targetLib `
 -TargetDocumentLibrarySubFolderPath 'migration4' -ErrorAction Stop `
 -Credentials $spoCreds

$storageAccount = 'mytest321temp';
$storageKey = 'rryy5SXDbVrhAP0xCGdHP9CR0Z9gSARA0d15ApC3rscB...';

$azurelocations = Set-SPOMigrationPackageAzureSource -SourceFilesPath
$sourceFolder -SourcePackagePath $packageFolder `
 -AccountName $storageAccount -AccountKey $storageKey -FileContainerName
'filecontainer1' `
 -PackageContainerName 'packagecontainer1'
```

```
$jobs = Submit-SPOMigrationJob -TargetWebUrl $targetWeb
 -MigrationPackageAzureLocations $azurelocations -Credentials $spoCreds;

$jobStatus = Get-SPOMigrationJobStatus -TargetWebUrl $targetWeb
 -Credentials $spoCreds -JobId $jobs[0].Guid
```

You can review Blob storage and access packages logs through **Microsoft Azure Storage Explorer**. After the migration is done, you will have to delete the storage containers as they will remain in your storage account otherwise:

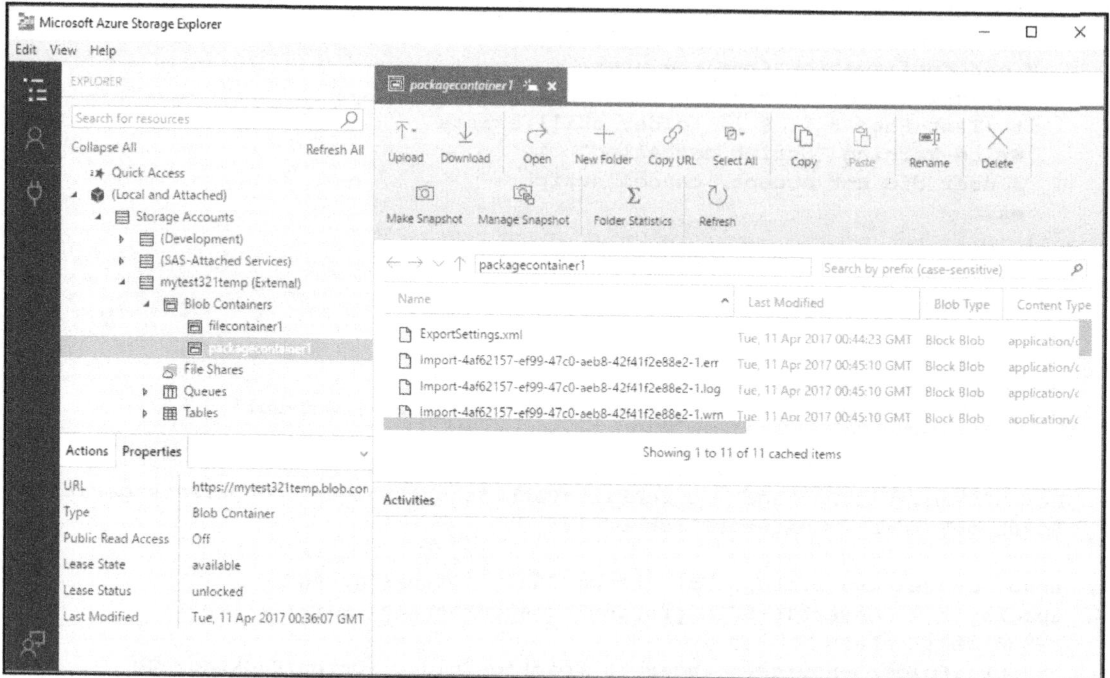

Keep in mind that this method is preferable only to using `Invoke-SPOMigrationEncryptUploadSubmit` in a few scenarios, such as reusing packages to deploy the same content to multiple destinations or when a specific location for the storage is needed (due to bandwidth or scheduling constraints).

We finish this chapter by mentioning that there is an alternative way of deploying content through BitLocker encrypted drives. This method will apply only to scenarios where the amount of data would take more time to be uploaded through the network than by being shipped through snail mail. If you run into this situation, you will also have to consider the time that it takes for the drives to ship and be processed by the Azure engineers

For more information, refer to `https://support.office.com/en-us/article/Use-drive-shipping-to-import-SharePoint-data-to-Office-365-4eef85f1-3dd1-4b44-bd55-9aea1eb47e50?ui=en-US&rs=en-US&ad=US`.

Summary

OneDrive offers a compelling service for storing files on multiple devices and operating systems. OneDrive continues to evolve to target individuals and small collaboration groups. As an administrator, you can help your organization quickly migrate to this service and manage its use through the different scripting methodologies we reviewed.

9

PowerShell Core

In this chapter, we will preview the next version of PowerShell. You might be surprised to know that there are no major updates in terms of syntax or functionality. Instead, Microsoft has focused on making sure that the upcoming version of PowerShell (*Core*) is:

- Free
- Open source
- Cross-platform

The previous version of PowerShell will continue to be supported and patched, but no future enhancements are expected. PowerShell Core is the new cross platform implementation and its first version will be PowerShell 6.

PowerShell has become the cornerstone for scripting and instrumentation in the Microsoft stack. Many partners and competitors have also embraced it for their APIs (for example, VMWare). Having cemented PowerShell as the scripting platform of choice for their own products, Microsoft is now going for what is left of the market. The promise is that PowerShell will run in any environment and provide administrators with a standard language and patterns for management. The change in paradigm is significant for PowerShell, yet we should not be very surprised. Microsoft has been open sourcing strategic projects for several years.

There are many challenges for the vision to materialize (we are currently on beta 4). PowerShell Core is limited when it comes to managing Office 365. Indeed, the changes are many and therefore we will have to be patient and follow (and possibly contribute to) the maturity of the product.

For PowerShell to be cross-platform, its implementation has moved to Microsoft .NET Core. .NET Core is also cross-platform and open source and is also maturing slowly. Some of the limitations (and workarounds) that we will review are due to the fact that the .NET Core platform is still lacking features. This affects the PowerShell Core development but also puts limitations on the use of the Office 365 API, which currently still runs on the Microsoft .NET platform.

We will look through the following topics:

- Installing PowerShell Core
- Managing Exchange from PowerShell Core
- Connecting to SharePoint Online from PowerShell Core

Installing PowerShell Core

Installing PowerShell Core is very straightforward. However, it differs slightly depending on the environment. Since we are still in beta, the best place to download the bits is the GitHub repository `https://github.com/PowerShell/PowerShell/releases`.

In Windows, simply installing the `.msi` package is sufficient. In the case of Linux, you have the option of downloading the binaries or subscribing to the repository for your distribution of choice.

Linux repositories simplify package maintenance. Microsoft actively maintains repositories for several distributions (`https://docs.microsoft.com/en-us/windows-server/administration/linux-package-repository-for-microsoft-software`):

```
sudo rpm -Uvh
http://packages.microsoft.com/config/rhel/7/packages-microsoft-prod.rpm
sudo yum install powershell
```

Downloading the binaries directly from the release link is also possible using `curl` or `wget` or simply by passing the URL of the binary to `yum`:

```
sudo yum install
https://github.com/PowerShell/.../powershell-6.0.0_beta.4-1.el7.x86_64.rpm
```

Once installed, simply typing `powershell` in the console will open a PowerShell session. Keep in mind that, even though PowerShell is not case-sensitive, Unix-based systems are. In the following example, we use some of the commands available from PowerShell to work with the Linux filesystem:

```
[psuser@centos7B ~]$ powershell
PowerShell v6.0.0-beta.4
Copyright (C) Microsoft Corporation. All rights reserved.

PS /home/psuser> mkdir test123
PS /home/psuser> New-Item file1.txt
Directory: /home/psuser

Mode        LastWriteTime Length Name
----        ------------- ------ ----
------ 7/16/17 12:23 AM        0 file1.txt

PS /home/psuser> dir

 Directory: /home/psuser

Mode        LastWriteTime Length Name
----        ------------- ------ ----
d----- 7/16/17 12:21 AM          test123
------ 7/16/17 12:23 AM        0 file1.txt

PS /home/psuser> del ./test123/
```

Being able to maintain machines with different operating systems with the same syntax eases the learning curve for administrators and developers.

Remoting on PowerShell Core

The cross-platform aspect of PowerShell Core will empower administrators to manage diverse operating systems. Being able to manage servers remotely has always been a focus of the product and this is still the case in PowerShell Core. The Windows platform has a robust offering for remote management (WMI, RPC, and WS-Management). However, remote management through PowerShell Core is still in the early stages.

PowerShell Core does support **Windows Remote Management** (**WinRm**) through NLTM and Kerberos connectivity in most scenarios. In scenarios involing macOS, only basic authentication is supported. Most Linux/Windows scenarios are supported through two alternative protocols: **Simple and Protected Negotiate** (**SPNEGO**) authentication, which is implemented in the PowerShell Remoting Protocol (`https://github.com/powershell/psl-omi-provider`), and remoting over SSH (`https://github.com/PowerShell/PowerShell/blob/master/demos/SSHRemoting/`). If you're interested, you should go through the installation of these components; at the time of writing, both approaches are in the early stages.

We will instead configure our server to accept basic authentication in the scenarios that require it (Linux/macOS versus Windows), with the warning that this is an unsecured method and should be replaced with a better model once it is available. When using basic authentication, you will not be able to use domain accounts; instead, make sure the credentials passed are of local administrators for the targeted server.

WinRM remote management

To be able to remotely manage a Windows Server, we need to enable the `WinRM` service and make sure that traffic is allowed through the firewall. The `Enable-PSRemoting` command takes care of both requirements. `Get-Service` (and related commands) can be used to monitor the service status. We also use quick config (`winrm qc`) to set the `LocalAccountTokenFilterPolicy` (there is an open bug for `Enable-PSRemoting`, as this should also be done by the command):

```
# On works on PowerShell 5
Enable-PSRemoting -Confirm:$false

winrm qc
WinRM service is already running on this machine.
WinRM is not set up to allow remote access to this machine for management.
The following changes must be made:

Configure LocalAccountTokenFilterPolicy to grant administrative rights
remotely to local users.
Make these changes [y/n]? y
WinRM has been updated for remote management.

Get-Service WinRM

Status  Name   DisplayName
------  ----   -----------
Running winrm  Windows Remote Management (WS-Manag...
```

As `Enable-Remoting` does not currently work on PowerShell Core you will have to run a script (included in the installation folder) to enable remoting for PowerShell Core. When connecting to the server (using `New-PSSession` or `Enter-PSSession`) you will also have to identify the endpoint by name using the `ConfigurationName` parameter:

```
C:\Program Files\PowerShell\6.0.0-beta.4\Install-PowerShellRemoting.ps1
 -PowerShellHome "C:\Program Files\PowerShell\6.0.0-beta.4\"
 -PowerShellVersion "6.0.0-alpha.9"
```

If the client is also running Windows Server but is not part of the domain of the server, you will also have to white-list the server (using `winrm` in this example). In the following script, we add our server name to the `TrustedHosts` setting and then we establish a connection. The `ComputerName` variable set in this setting needs to be resolved by the client's DNS. Depending on your settings, you may have to use the server's fully qualified name or manually map the IP to the name in the `hosts` file of the client:

```
winrm s winrm/config/client '@{TrustedHosts="testb"}'
Client
    NetworkDelayms = 5000
    URLPrefix = wsman
    AllowUnencrypted = false
    Auth
        Basic = true
        Digest = true
        Kerberos = true
        Negotiate = true
        Certificate = true
        CredSSP = false
    DefaultPorts
        HTTP = 5985
        HTTPS = 5986
    TrustedHosts = testb

New-PSSession -ComputerName testb -Credential $creds

Id Name     ComputerName ComputerType  State
 -- ----    ------------ ------------  -----
 11 WinRM11 testb        RemoteMachine Opened
```

If using basic authentication from Linux, you will also need to configure the Windows Server to allow basic authentication and unencrypted traffic (remember, this is not secure):

```
Set-Item -Path WSMan:\localhost\Service\Auth\Basic -Value $true
Set-Item -Path WSMan:\localhost\Service\AllowUnencrypted -Value $true
Restart-Service -Name WinRM
```

We should now be able to connect remotely from a macOS/Linux client. Notice in the following example that we do not qualify the administrator account with either a domain (not supported with basic authentication) or the name of the computer (for example, `testb\Administrator` will not work):

```
PS /home/psuser> $creds = Get-Credential Administrator
Windows PowerShell credential request Enter your credentials.
Password for user Administrator: ****************

PS /home/psuser> New-PSSession -ComputerName testb -Credential $creds
 -Authentication Basic
Id Name    ComputerName ComputerType  State
-- ----    ------------ ------------  -----
21 WinRM21 testb        RemoteMachine Opened
```

SSH Remote management

Secure Shell (**SSH**) is a network protocol used connecting to remote computers securely. It is the standard connection mechanism in Unix systems. The PowerShell Core team is actively working on PowerShell remoting over SSH (including a Win32 port of OpenSSH) to support secure connections for both Unix and Windows systems.

As our last remoting example, we will configure a Windows Server to accept PowerShell session over SSH and remotely manage it from a Linux machine.

We will begin by downloading and installing Win32-OpenSSH (`https://github.com/PowerShell/Win32-OpenSSH/releases`) and copying the files to `C:\openssh`.

As an administrator execute the PowerShell script `install-sshd.ps1` included in the folder to install the SSH services. We then generate and secure the SSH host keys for the services:

```
.\install-sshd.ps1
.\ssh-keygen.exe -A
.\FixHostFilePermissions.ps1 -Confirm:$false
```

SSH connections commonly use port `22` so you will have to configure your firewall to allow traffic through this port:

```
New-NetFirewallRule -Protocol TCP -LocalPort 22 -Direction Inbound
 -Action Allow -DisplayName SSH
```

On the OpenSSH folder we will add the following lines to the configuration file sshd_config to allow connections using passwords and install the PowerShell subsystem (the PowerShell executable that will receive the connections):

```
Subsystem powershell C:/Program Files/PowerShell/6.0.0-
beta.4/powershell.exe -sshs -NoLogo -NoProfile
PasswordAuthentication yes
```

On the client machine we can now establish the connection using the SSHTransport parameter on the New-PSSession command:

```
PS /root> powershell
PowerShell v6.0.0-beta.4
Copyright (C) Microsoft Corporation. All rights reserved.

PS /root> New-PSSession -HostName testb -UserName admin1 -SSHTransport
admin1@testb's password:

Id Name ComputerName ComputerType  State  ConfigurationName Availability
-- ---- ------------ ------------  -----  ----------------- ------------
1 SSH1  testb        RemoteMachine Opened DefaultShell      Available

PS /root> Get-PSSession | Enter-PSSession
[testb]: PS C:\Users\admin1\Documents>
```

These are the most basic scenarios and should enable you to continue experimenting with PowerShell Core. However, there are other scenarios worth exploring. Due to the beta state of the products, it would be very difficult to cover all of these (with all their nuances); we recommend that you review the documentation and follow the progress of the project in GitHub.

In the following examples, we will focus on using the Office 365 API from PowerShell Core.

Managing SharePoint with PowerShell Core

Since Exchange is managed through a remote session, the commands are simply issued from the PowerShell Core instance but executed on the remote machine (the Office 365 remote connection that we set up with New-PSSession).

The following script is very similar to the connection script in `Chapter 5`, *Managing Exchange Online Using PowerShell*. To showcase how we can combine Unix and PowerShell commands, we pipe the results of the `Get-User` command to a file and then use the `cat` command to show the contents of the `result.txt` file on the screen:

```
Last login: Sat Jul 15 16:34:48 2017 from martinp7.localdomain
[psuser@centos7B ~]$ powershell

PowerShell v6.0.0-beta.4
Copyright (C) Microsoft Corporation. All rights reserved.

PS /home/psuser> $creds = Get-Credential # prompt user for credentials
Windows PowerShell credential request
Enter your credentials.
User: admin1@mytest321.onmicrosoft.com
Password for user admin1@mytest321.onmicrosoft.com: ****************

PS /home/psuser> $uri =
'https://outlook.office365.com/powershell-liveid/?proxymethod=rps'
PS /home/psuser> $Session = New-PSSession -ConfigurationName
Microsoft.Exchange -ConnectionUri $uri -Credential $creds -Authentication
Basic -AllowRedirection
PS /home/psuser> Import-PSSession $Session
WARNING: The names of some imported commands from the module
'tmp_vnlud1wj.ujr' include unapproved verbs that might make them less
discoverable. To find the commands with unapproved
verbs, run the Import-Module command again with the Verbose parameter. For
a list of approved verbs, type Get-Verb.

ModuleType Version Name              ExportedCommands
---------- ------- ----              ----------------
Script     1.0     tmp_vnlud1wj.ujr {Add-AvailabilityAddressSpace...}

PS /home/psuser> Get-User > result.txt
PS /home/psuser> ls
result.txt
PS /home/psuser> cat ./result.txt

Name     RecipientType
----     -------------
test1    User
admin1   UserMailbox
test2    UserMailbox
test4    UserMailbox
admin2   UserMailbox
...
PS /home/psuser> Remove-PSSession $Session
```

Managing SharePoint Online from PowerShell Core

As the SharePoint Online API needs to be installed on the scripting machine, running it outside of Windows is not as straightforward as with Exchange. The libraries of the module are compiled for the .NET Framework, and PowerShell Core uses .NET Framework Core, so we have an incompatibility problem. Once .NET Framework Core matures, the Office 365 API should be offered compiled for this new platform.

However, we can still use the SharePoint Online API from PowerShell Core through remoting. For the sake of an example, we will implement a client/server approach, similar to the way Exchange works. We will connect from a Linux machine running PowerShell Core to a server running PowerShell and with the SharePoint Online API also installed.

The example would be the same as the previous one, if not for the problem of passing credentials across the sessions. To open a connection with SharePoint Online, we need to pass credentials to the `Connect-SPOService` command. The problem is that the passing credentials across the sessions is not supported.

```
$spAdmin = Get-Credential admin1@mytest321.onmicrosoft.com

Windows PowerShell Credential Request...

Enter your credentials.
Password for user admin1@mytest321.onmicrosoft.com: ****************

Unable to load DLL 'api-ms-win-security-cryptoapi-l1-1-0.dll': The
specified module or one of its dependencies could not be found.
 (Exception from HRESULT: 0x8007007E)
 + CategoryInfo : ResourceUnavailable: (:) [],
ParentContainsErrorRecordException
 + FullyQualifiedErrorId :
System.Management.Automation.Remoting.PSRemotingDataStructureException
```

As a workaround, you can create new credentials by passing a secure string. This method is not ideal as your credentials will be in clear text, but consider that this is just a workaround until this bug is resolved:

```
Invoke-Command -Session $session -ScriptBlock { `
 $password = ConvertTo-SecureString "password here" -AsPlainText -Force
 $user = "admin1@mytest321.onmicrosoft.com"
 $creds = New-Object PSCredential -ArgumentList  $user , $password
 $uri = 'https://mytest321-admin.sharepoint.com'
 Connect-SPOService -Url $uri -Credential $creds
}
```

A better approach is reusing the credential-serialization function we used in `Chapter 6`, *Script Automation*. This function serialized and encrypted the password on a file. We will load the credentials through a remote session so that all the serialization and decryption occurs on the server. To make sure this occurs on the server, we use `Invoke-Command`:

```
Invoke-Command -Session $session -ScriptBlock { `
  $credPaths = 'C:\temp\mytest321_admin.txt'
  $rawCreds = Get-Content $credPaths

  $creds =
[System.Management.Automation.PSSerializer]::Deserialize($rawCreds )
  $uri = 'https://mytest321-admin.sharepoint.com'
  Connect-SPOService -Url $uri -Credential $creds
}
```

Once the connection to SharePoint Online is established, we can import the session as done in previous chapters and manage SharePoint from a Linux console. Here is the full example:

```
$localServerCreds = Get-Credential admin1

Windows PowerShell credential request
Enter your credentials.
Password for user admin1: **************

$session = New-PSSession -ComputerName pc11.dev.local -Credential `
$localServerCreds -Authentication Basic

Invoke-Command -Session $session -ScriptBlock {
 $credPaths = 'C:\temp\mytest321_admin.txt'
 $rawCreds = Get-Content $credPaths

 $creds =
[System.Management.Automation.PSSerializer]::Deserialize($rawCreds)

 $uri = 'https://mytest321-admin.sharepoint.com'
```

```
 Connect-SPOService -Url $uri -Credential $creds
}

Import-PSSession $session

Get-SPOSite | Select Url

Url
---
https://mytest321-my.sharepoint.com/
https://mytest321.sharepoint.com/portals/hub
```

Even though this type of remoting will not be necessary for Office 365 products in the long run, it is very possible that some on-premise products will not have assemblies compatible with .NET Core. As PowerShell is replaced with PowerShell Core, this scenario will become more relevant for using legacy APIs.

Summary

Keeping in mind that the product is still in beta, it is too early to rely on PowerShell Core for production scenarios. The prospects of its adoption across the industry however are truly exciting. Microsoft has taken the first step into positioning PowerShell as the de facto standard for cross-platform management.

As .NET Core matures and becomes mainstream, Office 365 and other products will be undoubtedly supported in PowerShell Core. Soon, we should be able to fully manage Office 365 through scripting in any platform.

Index

E

F

I

J

K

L

M

O

P

R

S

T

U

W

X

Made in the USA
Middletown, DE
08 October 2021